KARL BARTH
AN INTRODUCTION TO HIS
EARLY THEOLOGY
1910–1931

To the memory of
HUGH ROSS MACKINTOSH
who first introduced me to the
theology of Karl Barth

KARL BARTH

AN INTRODUCTION TO HIS
EARLY THEOLOGY
1910–1931

THOMAS F. TORRANCE

T&T CLARK
EDINBURGH

T&T CLARK LTD
59 GEORGE STREET
EDINBURGH EH2 2LQ
SCOTLAND
www.tandtclark.co.uk

First published 1962 by SCM Press
First published in paperback 2000 by T&T Clark Ltd

ISBN 0 567 08762 X

British Library Cataloguing-in-Publication Data
A catalogue record for this book is available from the British Library

Printed and bound in Great Britain by MPG Books, Bodmin

CONTENTS

PREFACE

T HIS work is not a compendium of Barth's early teaching, for I have
not sought to expound the content of his thought so much as the course
of his debate with modern theology, the 'Copernican' revolution which
he has initiated, and his relentless probing into the nature of scientific
method in dogmatic thinking. Far less is it a manual of 'Barthian theology'. A 'Barthian theology' is just as impossible as an 'Einsteinian science',
but just as there is a pre-Einsteinian science and a post-Einsteinian
science, so there is a pre-Barthian and a post-Barthian theology, for the
contribution of Karl Barth to theology is, like that of Albert Einstein to
natural science, so deep-going and fundamental that it marks one of the
great eras of advance in the whole history of the subject.

The purpose of this work is to clear the ground of superficial interpretations and tendentious criticisms, and by setting out the development
of Barth's thought in his formative years, to let him speak for himself
within the frame of his own historical involvement and the immense
dialogue which he has conducted with modern theology and philosophy
for half a century. Karl Barth deserves from us the same sympathetic
study, and the same attempt to evaluate him in his own serious intention, as he has manifested in his interpretations of the great theologians
of the past, ancient, mediaeval, and modern. Because Barth has studied
so intensely and wrestled so mightily with the whole history of Christian
thought, his own theology cannot be appreciated in detachment from
that history. The history of theology cannot be isolated from the history
of culture, nor therefore from the history of philosophical and scientific
thought, and yet theology has its own proper concerns that must be distinguished and respected in every age. To clarify that relationship in
modern theology has been one of the chief interests of Barth, but for
that very reason his own thought is not to be understood except in its
involvement in and differentiation from the scientific and philosophical
movements of the twentieth century, in which he has played so notable
a role. Hence the development of Barth's theology from 1910 reflects
and reveals in an unparalleled way the history of twentieth-century
theology.

In this work no attempt has been made to criticise the theology of
Barth except within the logic of its own development. Barth is not a
theologian one can criticise until one has really listened to him and

grasped his work as a whole and discerned its place in the history of theology. It may be many decades before we can do that adequately, as it may well be centuries before we can measure sufficiently his contribution to the whole Church, but no one who really gets inside Barth's thinking and has learned to follow him in his persistent and profound inquiry into the Truth of God can remain unchanged or unmoved, or be ungrateful. No attempt to expound what he has to say can be a substitute for the experience of inquiring into the Truth along with Barth himself and of enjoying its divine beauty.

If this study only serves to set the stage, to open up the perspective, to point out the chief concerns, and then sends the student to read and reread and ponder the *Church Dogmatics*, then it fulfils its purpose. That is not to say that the earlier works of Barth can be neglected, for they help us to read the *Dogmatics* in their historical involvement, and so to discern their relevance for the immense problems theological communication in the twentieth century raises. Where these earlier works are not readily available or available in English I have given fuller account of them, e.g. *Die christliche Dogmatik* of 1927 and *Schicksal und Idee in der Theologie* of 1929. Special attention must also be given to Barth's study of Anselm, *Fides Quaerens Intellectum* of 1931, for that brought to a head his understanding of the fundamental attitude to the problem of the knowledge and existence of God and of the scientific method appropriate to the nature of the object proper to theology, and has ever since exercised a determining influence upon the inner structure of his dogmatic thinking.

I am very grateful to my brother, the Rev. James B. Torrance, for reading my typescript and offering valuable suggestions, and particularly for the help I derived from studying an unpublished essay of his on the theology of Anselm. My thanks are also due to Mrs E. S. K. Patterson and Mrs W. J. Klempa who assisted me with the typing.

T. F. T.

New College,
University of Edinburgh
May, 1961

PREFACE TO THE NEW EDITION

THIS book was originally published by the SCM Press in 1962, when it was read by Karl Barth himself, and met with his approval, but he pointed out firmly that he was not to be understood in terms of what he called his 'egg shells'. At the same time I wrote a long Introduction to the collection of his essays in *Theology and Church*, published by the SCM Press that same year. That was designed to accompany and supplement the SCM edition of this work. It was followed up years later by my book *Karl Barth. Biblical and Evangelical Theologian*, published by T&T Clark in 1990, in which I gave some account of my interaction with Barth. He was immensely pleased that I had organised, helped to translate, and co-edited with Geoffrey Bromiley the English edition of the *Kirchliche Dogmatik*, and thanked me warmly for my interpretation of his theology. Once when he asked me which of his volumes in the *Kirchliche Dogmatik* I thought best and valued most, I said at once *Die Gotteslehre* (KD II), which pleased him very much. He agreed. Not long after he sent me a copy of one of his recent books inscribed with *Karl Barth—Mit herzlichen Dank für viel Treue!*

Many books have now been written about Karl Barth, to several of which I would draw attention:- Eberhard Jüngel, *Gottes Sein ist Im Werden*, translated as *The Doctrine of the Trinity. God's Being Is In Becoming*, published by the Scottish Academic Press in 1966, and shortly to appear in a new translation under the title *God's Being Is in Becoming*, T&T Clark, 2001; two by George Hunsinger, *How to Read Karl Barth, The Shape of His Theology*, Oxford University Press, 1991, and *Disruptive Grace. Studies in the Theology of Karl Barth*, W. B. Eerdmans, 2000; *The Holy Spirit in the Theology of Karl Barth*, by John Thompson, Pickwick Publications, 1991; Gordon Watson, *God and the Creature. The Trinity and Creation in Karl Barth*, U.C. Print, Brisbane, 1995; Alan Torrance, *Persons in Communion. Trinitarian Description and Human Participation, with special reference to Volume One of Karl Barth's Church Dogmatics*, T&T Clark, 1996; Paul Molnar, *Karl Barth and The Theology of the Lord's Supper, A Systematic Investigation*, Peter Lang, New York, 1996. Special mention must be made of the work of Bruce L. McCormack, *Karl Barth's Realistic Dialectical Theology. Its Genesis and Development*

1909–1936, Oxford University Press, 1995. This concerns Barth's early lectures in Göttingen which he himself declined to publish (his 'egg shells'?!), but sent to the Press instead *Die christliche Dogmatik im Entwurf. Die Lehre vom Worte Gottes*, München, 1927, which I find to be particularly helpful and important, but which he left off to engage in the massive *Kirchliche Dogmatik*.

A Karl Barth Center has been established in Princeton Theological Seminary, New Jersey, presided over by George Hunsinger. With the fine copy-editing help of Frank McCombie of Newcastle, the thirteen volumes of the *Church Dogmatics* have all been thoroughly revised, including the *Index Volume with Aids for the Preacher*. I hope it will not be very long before the *Church Dogmatics* is available in a CD-Rom edition with the English and German texts in parallel columns, which will be immensely helpful.

This book, like the original edition, is dedicated to the memory of Hugh Ross Mackintosh, who first introduced me to the theology of Karl Barth.

T.F.T.

Edinburgh
Easter, 2000

ABBREVIATIONS

Ant. *Antwort. Karl Barth, zum siebzigsten Geburtstag am 10. Mai 1956*, Zürich 1956
ChrD *Christliche Dogmatik im Entwurf*
CD *Church Dogmatics*
FQI *Fides quaerens intellectum*
FuA *Theologische Fragen und Antworten*, Gesammelte Vorträge 3, Zürich 1957
Gd-Md *Gottesdienst-Menschendienst, Festschrift* for Thurneysen (Separatabdruck), 1958
GGG *God, Grace and Gospel*
ProtTh *Die Protestantische Theologie im 19. Jahrhundert*
Romans *The Epistle to the Romans*
SJT *Scottish Journal of Theology*
SuI 'Schicksal und Idee in der Theologie'
TC *Theology and Church*
TEh *Theologische Existenz heute*
WW *The Word of God and the Word of Man*
ZdZ *Zwischen den Zeiten*

Part One

KARL BARTH:
THE MAN AND HIS WORK

I

EARLY LIFE

In speaking of Karl Barth H. R. Mackintosh used to recall Creevey's words about Lord Grey: 'Take him all in all, I never saw his fellow; nor can I see any indication of him on the stocks.' In Barth, Mackintosh said, 'we have incontestably the greatest figure in Christian theology that has appeared for decades'.[1] That was written in 1935, but now after another quarter of a century in which Barth has published his greatest works, it is acknowledged by many in all quarters that Barth must be accorded an honoured position among the greatest theologians of the Church—Athanasius, Augustine, Anselm, Aquinas, Luther and Calvin.

Karl Barth was born in Basel, Switzerland, on May 10th, 1886, the son of a Swiss minister, a member of an old Basler family.

When Karl was only three years old, his father, Fritz Barth, was appointed professor in the University of Bern where he lectured in New Testament and Early Church History for many years, until his death in 1912. It was there that Karl grew up, went to school, and began his University training. There deep and lasting foundations were laid at home, in church, and at school, where his faith was nourished in positive evangelical theology, and there too sacred scholarship in the service of the Gospel entered, as it were, into his very blood. It was when he was sixteen, Barth has told us recently,[2] that he first became interested in systematic theology. During a course of instruction for Confirmation he learned, for example, that the five mediaeval proofs for the existence of God and the theory of the literal inspiration of the Bible advanced by the later orthodoxy were very doubtful undertakings. What was much more important, however, he learned how fine and good a thing it would be not only to know and affirm the great statements of the Creed, but to understand them from within. On the evening of his Confirmation day he boldly resolved to become a theologian, not with the thought yet of preaching and the pastoral care of a congregation, but with the hope

[1] H. R. Mackintosh, *Types of Modern Theology*, London 1937, p. 263.
[2] *Lehre und Forschung an der Universität Basel, zur Zeit der Feier ihres fünfhundertjährigen Bestehens*, 1960, p. 35f (ET by T. N. Tice, *SJT* 14.3, 1961, p. 225).

that through such a course of study he would reach real understanding of the Creed.

Eventually he came up to the University where before long he found in Kant, with his theoretical and practical philosophy, and Schleiermacher, with his analysis of religion and faith, his guiding lights. Like many other Continental students he studied in several Universities; beginning with Bern, he went to Germany spending a semester each in Berlin and Tübingen, and three semesters in Marburg, sitting at the feet of some of the most distinguished teachers. In Bern the most important were Fritz Barth, his own father, and Professors Steck, Marti, and Lüdemann; in Berlin, Harnack, Kaftan and Gunkel; in Tübingen, Schlatter his fellow-countryman, Haering and Fleiner; in Marburg, Herrmann[1], Jülicher and Heitmüller. He returned to Bern to take his final examinations, and was ordained by the Church of Bern in 1908.

The next year he spent assisting Prof. Martin Rade in Marburg in his editing of *Christliche Welt*, but soon returned to his native country and was appointed *Vikar* of the German-speaking congregation in Geneva where he remained for two years. By this time he had come to look upon himself as sharing to some extent in the dominant theological trend led by the younger followers of Albrecht Ritschl, yet not without growing alienation particularly in view of the *dénouement* of this school in the *Religionsphilosophie* of Ernst Troeltsch.[2] Although he could not see his way through this movement at the time, he realised it had turned up a blind alley and could offer little to satisfy his theological concern.[3] When Troeltsch in 1914 finally crossed over from the theological to the philosophical faculty, Barth felt more convinced than ever that theology was being led hopelessly astray. What was needed was a right-about turn.

There followed ten years of great importance, of ferment and discovery, in the agricultural and industrial parish of Safenwil in Aargau where he was appointed pastor, and where even more intensely than in his *Vikariat* in Geneva Barth was forced, in weekly preparation for the ministry of the Word, to wrestle with the Bible, as the root of all Christian thinking and teaching. For several years he carried through an exhaustive study of the Epistle to the Romans in the course of which St Paul came in a special way to be his guide into the truth and clarity of the biblical witness. Of special importance to Barth during these years was his friendship with Eduard Thurneysen, who has throughout

---

[1] In 1925 Barth wrote: 'Herrmann was the theological teacher of my student years. The day on which nearly 20 years ago in Berlin I read his *Ethik* for the first time, I remember as if it were today' *TC*, p. 238.   [2] *TC*, p. 60f.
[3] For the influence of Herrmann on Barth here, see *TC*, p. 244.

the years since been Barth's truest and most loyal friend, sharing with him in all his spiritual and theological developments. Thurneysen had charge of a parish on the other side of the mountain from Barth at Safenwil, but although they could not meet as often as they wished, they corresponded regularly with one another and thought out together their ministerial and theological problems; together they often journeyed to Bad Boll in Württemberg in their attraction to the preaching of Christoph Blumhardt and their desire to learn from his passionate concern to bring the message of the Kingdom and compassion of God to bear upon the daily life of man in all its redeeming power; and together they faced the fierce critical and indeed atheistic questions of modern man and sought for their answers in the Word of God.

It was in the midst of the daily pastoral activity at Safenwil and the daily exegetical work in which he engaged that Barth, as he says, 'tumbled himself into a conflict, the inward and outward significance of which he could not foresee',[1] but at last he broke through to an understanding of what theology as *fides quaerens intellectum* really is, and acquired the basic outlook which carried him out of and far beyond the tradition of the eighteenth and nineteenth centuries. And of course the years of wrestling with the Word bore fruit in the publication of the first edition of *Der Römerbrief* in 1919, and above all in its thorough rewriting and republication in 1921. It was this edition of the commentary which, as Karl Adam put it, 'fell like a bomb on the playground of the theologians'.[2]

Then two years later like a great stone flung into the pond came the call to be Professor of Reformed Theology in Göttingen. It took Barth entirely by surprise.[3] Were they so utterly blind in Göttingen to think of him in that way? Or did he have perhaps qualities, theological and scientific, which they saw but of which he himself was utterly ignorant?[4] Barth took his time over replying, for the invitation had uprooted him. He could not go back, and yet he could not see what way the road ahead took. He did not know whether he wanted to become a professor, for after all he was called as a preacher to announce a message from God, to proclaim his Word.[5] And yet the truth is that it was his profound concern for the positive content of that message, it was because he was

---

[1] Preface to the English edition of *The Epistle to the Romans*, p. v.
[2] Karl Adam, cited by J. McConnachie, *The Significance of Karl Barth*, London 1931, p. 43.
[3] Letter to Thurneysen of Feb. 1, 1921, *Ant.* p. 860.
[4] Letter to Thurneysen of 18 March, 1921, op. cit. p. 862.
[5] Letter to Thurneysen of 23 June, 1925, published in *Gd-Md*, p. 157.

so thoroughly a preacher of God's Word, that he could do no other than be a theologian in the service of the proclamation of the Gospel.

By October Barth was installed in Göttingen, and embarked upon his epoch-making theological career. He set himself at once to work through and come to terms with the whole historical development of theology in its earlier and in its later forms and tendencies, and at the centre to get to grips with the theology of the Reformers. He did not for a moment lose sight of the difficult task of a preacher confronted Sunday by Sunday by a congregation waiting to hear God's Word,[1] but rather bent all his rapidly developing powers and energies to make room again for a theology which would genuinely serve the preacher by establishing him upon the sure ground of God's Word and enabling him to reach an articulated understanding of its content.[2]

The professorship in Göttingen ran from 1921 to 1925, during which he worked night and day in the history of dogmatic theology, ancient and modern. Then he was appointed Professor *ordinarius* in Münster where he remained until 1930. That was the period in which he published his first attempt at dogmatics, *Die Lehre vom Worte Gottes, Prolegomena zur Christlichen Dogmatik*, 1927, and the essays which make up the volume, *Die Theologie und die Kirche*, 1928.

In 1930 Barth moved to Bonn to face overflowing classrooms, and after five crowded years which saw the rise of Hitler to power and tyranny he found himself ejected from Germany and taking refuge in the city of his birth, occupying the ancient chair of Theology in Basel. By this time he had fully developed his main position and had begun the publication of his monumental *Kirchliche Dogmatik*, the most formidable and massive work of theology since the *Summa Theologica* of Thomas Aquinas.

There is no need to describe here Barth's contribution to the German Church-struggle under the Nazi régime, his participation in the Swiss 'Resistance' during the second world-war, or the impact of his teaching upon Europe and indeed upon the world of Catholic and Evangelical Christendom since the war, for all that is well-known. Our concern is to confront Barth as theologian, to seek an understanding of his theology as a whole, to examine his theological development in order to see more clearly the setting in which to read both his early essays on theology and the Church, as well as his later *Church Dogmatics*.

[1] Even in the midst of his strenuous work on dogmatics at Göttingen he continued to think of the pulpit as 'the proper arena of the Kingdom of God'. See the exchange of letters between Barth and Thurneysen between 1921 and 1925 published in *Gd-Md*, p. 14.
[2] Cf. F. W. Camfield, *Reformation Old and New*, London 1947, p. 15f.

II

PERSONAL CHARACTERISTICS

It may be helpful to note right away some of Barth's outstanding
characteristics which have an intimate bearing upon all his life and work.

(1) Barth has the most searching, questioning mind I have ever
known. Never have I heard or read of anyone who asks questions so
relentlessly or who engages in such ruthless criticism, not with any
negative intention, but *in order to let the truth bespeak itself clearly and
positively*. This does not mean that for Barth theology is the answer to
man's questions about God or man or the creation, that is, general
questions that can be raised independently and then applied, as it were,
from without to the reality investigated, but rather the opposite. This
questioning is forced upon us because face to face with God's Word we
know ourselves to be questioned down to the very roots of our being,
and therefore in response to the impact of the Word we are thrown back
upon self-criticism, upon a repentant questioning and rethinking of all
that we have and are and claim to know. Hence questioning is the movement in which we seek to clear away all the unreality with which we
confront the objective Reality of God in his revelation, in order that we
may let God's Truth declare itself to us positively and clearly.

To illustrate that from Barth's own discussion, let us take a highly
illuminating page from the *Church Dogmatics* where he is discussing the
question aroused in us by the reality of revelation in Jesus Christ, a
question which he formulates as 'the objective possibility of revelation'.[1]

'By visualising the possibility presupposed and made available to
knowledge in the reality of the revelation of God, we regard the reality
as the answer to a question which we must put. We cannot regard this
as a general question, a question of theological anthropology which can
be raised independently and then applied, as it were, from without the
reality to Jesus Christ. It is, of course, the question aroused in us by the
reality of Jesus Christ, thrust at us by it, so to speak, and rendered
meaningful and necessary by its own relation to the question, i.e. the
question how far the existence of Jesus Christ is identical with God's
freedom for man. We cannot, and so we should not, do more than let

[1] *CD* I.2, p. 26 f.

ourselves be told quite simply that this is the case. We can and really ought to do that. We do that, however, only if we hear it as an answer embedded in the question which the thing itself puts to us, and if at the same time we hear it as the answer to this question. It would not be a genuine interpretation of the reality that is there, if it did not at the same time throw light upon its possibility as well. We have now genuinely to let ourselves be told, if we cannot also as a result tell ourselves what has been told to us—tell ourselves, not arbitrarily, but obediently. It would not be a serious awareness of this reality, were it not immediately to turn to understanding also. That would not be a *credere*, which did not force its way through to an *intelligere*. It is with God's revelation that we are concerned in this reality, that is, with God's relation to us, with His reality as it concerns us. If we would or could be merely aware without wanting to understand, merely let ourselves be told without also telling ourselves what had been told, merely have faith without knowledge, it would certainly not be God's revelation with which we had to do. If it were, such a refusal on our part would only reveal our disobedience, or our unwillingness to be involved in it. Obedience to revelation must invariably mean to let oneself be involved. To be involved must then mean to be questioned, in such a way that the question to which revelation is the answer becomes our own question, and so revelation as the answer acquires a direct relation to ourselves. We said that the question of fact must precede the question of interpretation of the fact. There is a reason for that. But just as definitely we must now state that the question of interpretation must follow the question of fact. The question of fact would certainly have been put and answered wrongly, did the question of interpretation not follow it. The indolence and futility, the lack of participation in which we would then remain in face of the reality of revelation, must never be confused with humility and awe towards it. And, on the other hand, the attempt to question ourselves and to receive what is told us as the answer to our own question must never be decried as rationalism, if it comes within its limits and its meaning, i.e. if it is undertaken with regard to the reality of revelation which precedes all questioning and answering and does not claim precedence over this reality.'

This lets us see why at every step forward in his *Church Dogmatics* Barth probes ruthlessly into the subject from different angles, going round and round the same point at different levels with different series of questions until he can see and understand the truth in its own reality and wholeness, and then he sets himself to find a way of expressing it in ways that are adequate and appropriate and faithful to the whole truth in its objectivity, in its manifoldness and in its native force. Thus in the *Church Dogmatics* one comes across page after page of questions following hard upon the heels of one another in order to clear the ground and to see what is actually there confronting us in the Word. Indeed, if all the questions of the *Church Dogmatics* were to be strung together they would fill hundreds and hundreds of pages. Behind all this questioning on Barth's part lies a deep humility before the face of the Truth: in his recognition that the Truth will not, and cannot be, mastered by our distinctions and formulations, that we cannot give shape or form to the Truth, but that we can only follow after it, inquire of it, listen to it, and seek to be obedient to it; and in his recognition that all our expressions and expositions of the Truth are human attempts that fall far short of the Truth itself, so that far from resting content with what we have already done, we are driven on by respect for the Truth and in unceasing obedience to it to continue our inquiry and to say again and again in ever new ways what we learn of the living and inexhaustible Truth of God.

It is this procedure which helps to explain Barth's style, for behind it lies not an indulgence in prolixity but sustained scientific intention of a mind hard at work in understanding and expressing the truth as far as possible out of itself. Thus in seeking to express the wholeness of the truth he refuses to break it up into parts thus dissolving its essential nature into unreal distinctions, and therefore he has to set it forth in long balanced sentences surrounded with careful clarifications and exact limitations in subordinate clauses so that the truth may come home to the reader as it has come home to Barth himself in the process of his own radical inquiry.[1]

(2) Barth has an uncanny ability to listen which is accompanied by an astonishing humility and childlikeness in which he is always ready to learn. That is what overwhelms the student as he enters into the great man's study for the first time. He goes in fear and propounds his questions with trembling, but soon finds that the Professor has turned the tables on him, and is asking him questions, drawing him out and listening to him as if he were the disciple and the student were the teacher. Few men are really able to listen like that, and fewer still are able to maintain a genuine listening attitude while posing such searching questions, but with Karl Barth *ruthless criticism is made the servant of his will to listen.*

[1] See the Editors' Preface to *CD* I.2, p. viif.

That is the secret of Barth's hermeneutics, whether he is interpreting Holy Scripture or interpreting the thought of another theologian. Perhaps here we may detect in Barth something of the influence of Schlatter who insisted that the supreme rule in exegesis is to read what is actually there, to see it in the light of its own theme and in the light of what it intends to denote.[1] Our greatest difficulty is with ourselves, for as Barth expresses it, 'our supposed listening is in fact a strange mixture of hearing and our own speaking, and, in accordance with the usual rule, it is most likely that our own speaking will be the really decisive event'.[2] Biblical exegesis takes place therefore in a strenuous disciplined attempt to lay ourselves open to hear the Word of God speaking to us, to read what the Word intends or denotes and to refrain from interrupting it or confusing it with our own speaking, for in faithful exegesis we have to let ourselves be told what we cannot tell ourselves. Therefore exegesis cannot be undertaken, especially when it has to break a way through the rigidity of our minds, through long-ingrained habits of thought and speech and outlook of our own which determine our hearing and reading, except through determined self-renunciation, courageous repentance and the most severe self-criticism, before the face of the Word of God.

The same qualities come out, as Professor Pelikan has recently pointed out in his introduction to *Protestant Thought: from Rousseau to Ritschl*, the English translation of eleven chapters of Barth's *Die Protestantische Theologie im 19. Jahrhundert*. 'Perhaps the most striking feature of the chapters presented here is their willingness to treat the theologians of the past on their own terms. Anyone who expects Karl Barth the dogmatician to become the judge of the quick and the dead when he functions as a historian of theology will find, to his surprise, that Barth has made a genuine effort to comprehend the theologians of the nineteenth century from within their own frame of reference.'[3] But what better instance of Barth's exact sympathetic exegesis of the writing of another theologian can we have than his examination and interpretation of Anselm's theology?[4]

(3) Another typical characteristic of Barth to which we must give

---

[1] Hence Barth was more than taken aback when the second edition of his *Römerbrief* met with a friendly reception by Bultmann, but with a friendly rejection by Schlatter—'the strangest episode in the history of the book': *Romans*, p. 16.

[2] *CD* I.2, p. 470, cf. also *TC*, p. 307f. For Barth's signal contribution to hermeneutics see *CD* I.2, especially pp. 464-72 and 710-40, and the preface to the second edition of *Romans*.   [3] Op. cit. p. 8.

[4] *Fides Quaerens Intellectum*, ET by Ian W. Robertson, 1960.

attention is his sheer creative power, his ability to produce something new. It is one of the characteristics of Beethoven's music that again and again there breaks into it a startlingly novel element which jolts you upright with a shock. You feel, 'He cannot do that. This is something illogical, a new theme that interrupts the symphony, that contradicts what we have just been hearing.' And then before you have recovered from your surprise you discover that with great profundity Beethoven has worked it into the texture of the whole symphony, and that far from being alien to the main theme it is perfectly integrated with it and wonderfully enriches it. Only a great genius can do that.

That is the genius of Karl Barth in the profundity and rich complexity of his *Church Dogmatics*. Even Emil Brunner was jolted into writing an article a few years ago on what he called 'The new Barth',[1] for in the third volume Barth appeared to convey quite new elements which Brunner welcomed warmly but which he could only interpret as a *volte face* or at least as out of harmony with what had preceded. But it was not so. The 'Christian humanism' of the new man expounded by Barth in the various parts of his third volume belonged to the very essence of his main theme. That is made particularly clear in the lecture Barth delivered to the Swiss Reformed Ministerial Fraternal in 1956,[2] which was published under the title 'The Humanity of God'. From first to last Barth's main theme has been the turning of God in utter grace in incredible condescension to man to be man's God, so that what we are concerned with in the Gospel is the sovereign togetherness of God with man and the exaltation of man to share in the divine life and love. To the superficial thinker this appears diametrically opposed to the message of Barth's *Romans*, but as the whole symphony is poured out in movement after movement we are lost in astonishment at the depth and complexity and yet the sheer simplicity and beauty of this theology in which elements are brought together in a profound and fertile economy of insight which in other minds fall apart into antagonistic positions or at best are only related to one another in some desperate artificial dialectic.

(4) There is one other aspect of Barth, both as a man and as a theologian, which we must select for mention: his joy and his humour.[3]

---

[1] *SJT* 4.2, 1951, pp. 123ff.

[2] ET in *God, Grace and Gospel, Scottish Journal of Theology Occasional Papers* No. 8, pp. 29-52. (Cf. the book *The Humanity of God*—another translation of two essays in *GGG*.) See also 'The Christian Message and the New Humanism', in *Against the Stream*, pp. 181-191.

[3] In this Barth is matched only by Heinrich Vogel who characteristically contributed to the 1956 *Festschrift* an essay entitled 'Der Lachende Barth', *Ant.*, p. 164f.

That is something that runs throughout all his writing and preaching,
though certain passages leap immediately to mind: the sparkling prefaces
to the different volumes of the *Church Dogmatics*, the discussion of the
phenomena of the human in volume three where he cannot repress his
chuckles at the frightful seriousness with which too many theologians
have set forth their picture of *homo sapiens*—'What a pity that none of
these apologists considers it worthy of mention that man is apparently
the only being accustomed to laugh and to smoke'[1]—, his obvious enjoyment of the *Insecto-theologia* of Christian Lesser, the merriment with
which he wrote at length about angels and cast his side-glances at the
demons (for they have a bad smell!), but also the silver thread of sheer
fun that runs throughout his account of the theologians of the eighteenth
and nineteenth centuries, his delight at giving Mozart, as it were, a place
among 'the Church fathers' (!), and not least the rich spice of humour
even in his angry *Nein* to Emil Brunner, which Anglo-Saxons seem
almost invariably to read with a Teutonic lack of humour.[2]

But what lies behind all this is not just his *Menschlichkeit*, his rich
humanity—in that Barth is more like Luther than any other figure in
the history of theology—but his doctrine of God, or rather his delight
in and enjoyment of the glory and beauty of God, and therefore in all
things he has made which echo and re-echo his eternal praises. The
glory of God is also 'His over-flowing self-communicating joy. By its
very nature it is that which gives joy . . . Are we saying something ex-
cessive or strange when we say that God also radiates this joy because
He is beautiful? We say "also" not forgetting that we are speaking only
of the form and manner of His glory, of the specifically persuasive and
convincing element in His revelation. The substance and content of His
glory is God Himself in the fulness of His perfection . . . The special
element to be noted and considered is that the glory of God is not only
great and sublime or holy and gracious, the overflowing of the sovereignty
in which God is love. In all this it is a glory that awakens joy and is itself
joyful. It is not merely a glory which is solemn and good and true, and
which, in its perfection and sublimity, might be gloomy or at least joy-
less. Joy in and before God—in its particular nature, distinct from what
we mean by awe, gratitude and the rest—has an objective basis. It is
something in God, the God of all perfections which justifies us in having

[1] *CD* III.2, p. 83.
[2] Barth has since likened his debate with Brunner, a dialogue between two
partners each speaking out of quite a different element, to an impossible conversation between an elephant and a whale. That is the way in which he had
earlier described the debate between Protestants and Romans.

joy, desire and pleasure towards Him, which indeed obliges, summons and attracts us to do this. That which attracts us to joy in Him, and our consequent attraction, is the inalienable form of His glory and the indispensable form of the knowledge of His glory. But this being the case, how can we dispense with the idea of the beautiful, and therefore with the statement that God is also beautiful? We shall not presume to try to interpret God's glory from the point of view of His beauty, as if it were the essence of His glory. But we cannot overlook the fact that God is glorious in such a way that He radiates joy, so that He is all He is with and not without beauty.'[1] From this Barth goes on to note that theology itself partakes of this divine beauty and joy, and claims that theology is 'a peculiarly beautiful science'. 'Indeed, we can confidently say that it is the most beautiful of all the sciences. To find the sciences distasteful is the mark of the Philistine. It is an extreme form of Philistinism to find, or to be able to find, theology distasteful. The theologian who has no joy in his work is not a theologian at all.'[2] There can be little doubt about the fact, that, if Barth's writing even when it is most serious ripples with laughter, if his ear is constantly tuned in to the care-free, joyous dialectic of Mozart, it is because he has been swept off his feet by the music of the angels announcing the Incarnation, *gloria in excelsis deo*, and has himself as a faithful servant entered into the joy of his Lord, for what describes him as man or theologian is above all the Augustinian expression *frui Deo*, the enjoyment of God.

[1] *CD* II.1, pp. 653 ff. [2] Ibid. Cf. also *God in Action*, p. 39 f.

Part Two

THE DEVELOPMENT OF
BARTH'S THEOLOGY

THE DEVELOPMENT OF
BARTH'S THEOLOGY

In seeking to understand the great thinkers one examines their historical context and the influences that have shaped and conditioned their outlook. But there arise from time to time men who tower above their immediate context, not only because they are men of genius, but because they are so steeped in the whole history of thought that they attain a breadth and comprehension reaching out beyond the *Zeitgeist* of any one age. That is very true, for example, of Calvin. In some respects he did not have the greatness or brilliant genius of Luther, and yet Calvin was far less a child of his own times than Luther, for all of his thinking was carried out in a dimension of great historical depth and his essential teaching far from being determined by any private inspiration was moulded in the rigorous school of historical exegesis and historico-theological dialogue with the Fathers. As Barth himself describes it, Calvin, having first established what stands in the text, set himself to wrestle with it, till the walls which separate the sixteenth century from the first become transparent.[1] It is for that reason that one can expound Calvin's theology more truthfully out of itself, and with reference to the Scriptures and the Fathers, but with less reference to his immediate historical context, than that of any other of the great modern theologians.

The same applies, although to a different extent, to Karl Barth. Immediate historical context and influence in his case cannot be neglected, for his thought is very much concerned with the great movements of the nineteenth and twentieth centuries, but here is a theologian who stands head and shoulders above it all and reaches back through it all in almost unparalleled fashion. The reason for that does not lie in any disregard for history, but, partly at least, in a consuming interest in history which he imbibed from his father, Fritz Barth.[2] The context of Barth's thought and the influences upon him can be measured only by measuring the whole history of Christian theology. That is supremely

---

[1] *Romans*, p. 7.
[2] 'The understanding of history is an uninterrupted conversation between the wisdom of yesterday and the wisdom of tomorrow. But it is a conversation always conducted honestly and with discernment. In this connexion I cannot fail to think with gratitude and respect of my father, Professor Fritz Barth, for such discernment he signally displayed throughout his whole active life' (*Romans*, p. 1).

evident in the massive volumes of the *Church Dogmatics* throughout which he carries on a discussion with the whole history of dogma, and indeed of philosophy, and often learns most from those with whom he disagrees most, such as Schleiermacher or Aquinas, but is concerned from first to last to be utterly faithful to the Holy Scriptures.

His comprehensive grasp and wrestling with the whole history of Christian thought makes him essentially a catholic theologian, but he is also very much of a European. By that is meant that he never forgets his immediate context in the Europe of the nineteenth century which produced so many great philosophers and thinkers, particularly in Protestant Germany. He has read, studied, and assimilated the great philosophical systems, above all those of Plato, Kant and Hegel, and subjected them to his relentless questions, and it is in and through all that that he has formulated his own theology and set it forth. In a very true sense the history of Karl Barth and the development of his thought is the history of European Theology for he recapitulates the whole of Evangelical Theology in Europe in himself, bringing it to its greatest and sharpest precision as well as giving it its most massive form. It is the verdict of Hans Urs von Balthasar, another Swiss, one of the most outstanding theologians of the Roman Church today, that Karl Barth has done for the whole of Protestant thought in modern times what Thomas Aquinas did for mediaeval thought.[1] Because von Balthasar reckons that Karl Barth has given Evangelical Theology its most consistent and supremely great expression, he insists that the Roman Church, in spite of the vast difference it inevitably has with Barth's theology, must nevertheless reckon with Barth as a partner in theological learning. It is significant that the Roman Church, which regards Barth in many respects as its mightiest opponent, has given him the most respectful study and yielded the greatest appreciation of his place in the history of Christian theology.[2]

To see the place of Karl Barth in the thought of modern Europe we may contrast him briefly with Søren Kierkegaard and Karl Marx. Both Kierkegaard and Marx reacted in different ways from the philosophy and religion of the nineteenth century which tended to escape into an unreal world of spiritualised ideas and romantic humanism. Kierkegaard

---

[1] Hans Urs von Balthasar, *Karl Barth. Darstellung und Deutung seiner Theologie*, 1951.

[2] See especially the works by Hans Küng, *Rechtfertigung. Die Lehre Karl Barths und eine Katholische Besinnung*, 1957, and by H. Bouillard, *Karl Barth*, I, *Genèse et évolution de la Théologie dialectique*, II and III, *Parole de Dieu et existence humaine*, 1958.

revolted against the static conception of the categories in Kantian philosophy and insisted in taking seriously the category of time, and he reacted even more violently against the abstraction of religion in Hegel and insisted upon taking seriously the concrete reality of men and women in their flesh and blood and in their actual day by day relation to God. Marx revolted from Hegel's abstract interpretation of history, and insisted upon taking seriously the concrete life of men and women in day to day society and economic involvement, and reacted equally from the spiritualistic pietism of the Church which through detaching men and women from the world numbed their sensitivities to the world of sordid oppression in the heart of human society. Both Kierkegaard and Marx sought to bring down the truth from the clouds and to earth it where men and women of flesh and blood live. But whereas Kierkegaard did that by returning to the Incarnation as the deed and presence of God in space and time in forgiveness and love, Karl Marx sought to do that by grounding all truth about man in the natural processes of social and economic evolution and so from the bottom upwards to transmute disorder into order, oppression into society.

Kierkegaard and Marx both lived in the mid-nineteenth century, but their thought only really became alive in the twentieth,[1] and the young Barth grew up in the midst of that developing situation, putting to it his tireless questions. But he did gain from it and share with it in various ways, learning above all the full import of the Incarnation of the Son of God in our flesh and blood, and the deepening concern for our social and political involvement on earth. In his early days he was by way of being a disciple of Kierkegaard and an admirer of Blumhardt and Ragaz and their social passion—but he could not rest content with their thought. Throughout all the tradition of the nineteenth century as it spilled over into the twentieth there was a morbid disease: modern philosophy and theology suffered from a cancerous subjectivism. Like a sheep overwhelmed in the snowdrift trying to keep itself alive by feeding on its own wool, religious man was trying to keep himself alive by feeding upon his own ideas. What he needed above all was to break through to concrete relations with the living God.

But there is another line of thought in which we have to estimate the place and contribution of Karl Barth—the attempt, which characterises all modern thought throughout the nineteenth and twentieth centuries,

---

[1] To complete the picture something should be said about the influence of Nietzsche upon the twentieth century, especially in German political and social thought—cf. R. D'O. Butler, *The Roots of National-Socialism, 1783-1933*, 1941, and A. Kolnai, *The War against the West*, 1938.

to be scientific, and to work out the appropriate scientific procedure in every field of investigation, not least a critical and truly scientific understanding of reason itself.[1] In the philosophical realm one thinks here above all perhaps of the neo-Kantians, Cohen and Natorp, for instance, and of men as different as Ernst Cassirer and Edmund Husserl, and the *strenge Wissenschaft* they pursued.[2] It is in this context that Barth has been so often and so radically misunderstood, when, for example, he has been accused either of Kantian subjectivism or of irrationalism.[3] Karl Barth belongs to the very centre of the great European tradition which has sought to give reason its fullest place in exact and careful thinking. The result of that was his *Kirchliche Dogmatik* which has met with a very interesting reception from a number of modern physicists who discern a close parallel between the scientific method of pure theology of this sort and that of pure physics. Of particular interest in this connection is the work of the so-called 'Göttingen circle' of physicists and theologians.[4]

To understand Barth's thinking we must look more closely at his development, at the three distinct stages which mark his wrestling with modern philosophy and his 'break-through' to the consistent Biblical Dogmatics of which he is the master exponent.

[1] See especially the essay 'Schicksal und Idee in der Theologie' (SuI) 1929, reprinted in *FuA*, pp. 54-92.
[2] Of not a little importance for Barth's thought in these realms is his close relationship to his brother Heinrich Barth, the philosopher, and to Heinrich Scholz, his colleague at the University of Münster. For an account of the views of Scholz see the article by Dieter Schellong, *Evangelische Theologie*, 1958, 1/2, pp. 1 ff. See also *Ant.*, p. 865 f.
[3] Contrast, for example, *CD* III.2, pp. 502 ff.
[4] Cf. Günter Howe, 'Parallelen zwischen der Theologie Karl Barths und der heutigen Physik', in *Ant.*, pp. 410 ff, and Howe's article in *Kerygma und Dogma* 4.1, 1957 ('Zu den Äusserungen von Nils Bohr über religiöse Fragen'), pp. 20 ff.

III

THE NEW STARTING-POINT

In his early period, it may be said, Karl Barth's theology falls within the thought-forms of Neo-Protestantism, as represented above all by the great Schleiermacher—that is, the liberal theology of religious individualism formulated under the impact of the Romantic Idealist philosophy of the nineteenth century and coordinated with the brilliant culture which it built up.

This 'liberal theology' Barth has recently described as: 'a theology in the succession of Descartes, primarily and definitely interested in human, and particularly the Christian, religion within the framework of our modern outlook on the world, considering God, His work, and His Word from this point of view, and adopting the critical attitude towards the message of the Bible and ecclesiastical tradition—to this extent, an anthropocentric theology'. In that sense, Barth admits, he was once a liberal theologian, even an enthusiastic one, in his youth.[1] We must not forget, however, his positive, evangelical upbringing, and his determination persisting from early years to penetrate into the fundamental ground of theology and to understand it from within its biblical roots and its own positive norms.[2] Although his University training threw him into the prevailing philosophical and scientific discussion pursued within the tradition of the eighteenth and nineteenth centuries so that he was forced to think within its universe of discourse, yet from the very start he felt deeply uneasy about it—it did not meet his theological hunger, for nowhere could he find a theology with radical clarity about its own positive task, but only one where the nature and function of theology were blurred through confusion with the subsidiary task of coming to grips with the spirit of the age. The whole tradition was dominated by the assumption that theology and even biblical exegesis could only be pursued within the framework of the accepted or prevailing *Weltanschauung* or a generally intelligible view of the totality of things, human, cosmic and divine. And so theologians tended in the end

[1] 'Liberal Theology: Some Alternatives', *The Hibbert Journal* 59, April 1961, p. 213 (reprinted from *Schweizerische Theologische Umschau*, July 1960).
[2] See the preface to the third edition of *Romans* (ET, p. 16f), and the *Briefwechsel* with Thurneysen 1921-25, *passim*.

c

to become merely servants of public opinion. Hence the startling, characteristic elements of the New Testament Message, which made it Gospel or Good News, the sheer divine reality of Revelation, the breaking-in of the supernatural Kingdom of grace from above, the participation of God himself in the agony of mankind, etc., all tended to be watered down and neutralised through their naturalisation and domestication in the bourgeois culture of the modern world. The 'Christianity' which Barth found around him in Switzerland and Germany, in the teaching or life of the Church, was indistinguishable in its manifestation from the mind or life of the world around it—it was all an expression of the same thing.

Barth's deep uneasiness was backed up by his inquiring mind which insisted on reflecting upon the questionableness of this whole proceeding, but the very fact that he had in some ways committed himself to the tradition of the eighteenth and nineteenth centuries,[1] made it hard for him to see his way through. Hence Barth's 'liberalism' and 'idealism' were of a strange sort, for even at this early period we find those searching questions directed to everything before him as the young theologian sought to probe down to the depths and upward and outward into clarity, and already we find the insistence that we must investigate down-to-earth historcial action, the concrete event and face up to its particularity and never apart from it reach knowledge of reality and the meaning of true being.[2]

Two things took a hand in his struggle toward understanding. The great theologians themselves, the inheritors and bearers of the tradition of the eighteenth and nineteenth century, took steps which opened Barth's eyes to the real nature of what they stood for, particularly Troeltsch and Harnack—to that we shall return later. The other and primary factor was his pastoral charge at Safenwil, and his discovery there of the new world within the Bible, as week by week he ploughed over the ground in careful laborious exegesis, like the farm-workers in his parish who from very early in the morning turned over the soil in assiduous husbandry acutely aware that each furrow was—of bitter necessity—a new furrow.

Thurneysen tells us that in this work he made use of many commentaries from those of Calvin through the works of the orthodox biblicists like Bengel and Tholuck to the modern critical volumes of von Hofmann,

---

[1] See, for example, his article 'Moderne Theologie und Reichgottesarbeit', in *Zeitschrift für Theologie und Kirche* 19, 1909, pp. 317 ff.

[2] See the illuminating discussion of elements of '*Liberalismus*' in Barth's thinking from 1909 to 1914 by H. U. von Balthasar, op. cit. pp. 220-29.

Beck, Lietzmann, Jülicher, and others.[1] It was out of this sermon-preparation and the fundamental encounter between the Word of God and modern theology into which he plunged, that the new direction and movement in theology associated with the name of Barth arose. 'Barth read out of the Scripture the message of the holy, gracious, righteous God, who stands in need of no defence, but who sends forth His Sovereign Word and who wills to be known and can be known through His Word alone. This Word of His is called and is Jesus Christ, the One around whom the centuries stand still, for He is the Centre of all time, the Bringer of the Kingdom which with Him breaks into the midst of this time as the new World of God.'[2]

It was here that Barth saw clearly that the preacher and theologian must be something quite different from a man trained in philosophy or history or psychology imbued with a spiritual outlook and capable of imparting spiritual insights. Writing later his preface to the second edition of the *Romans* Barth said: 'I myself know what it means year in year out to mount the steps of the pulpit, conscious of the responsibility to understand and interpret, and longing to fulfil it; and yet, utterly incapable, because at the University I had never been brought beyond that well-known "Awe in the presence of History" which means in the end no more than that all hope of engaging in the dignity of understanding and interpretation has been surrendered ... It was this miserable situation that compelled me as a pastor to undertake a more precise understanding and interpretation of the Bible.'[3] Hence Barth threw himself into a passionate struggle with the pages of the New Testament, involving much sweat and many groans, in order to release the matter contained in the text, to expose the Word in the words, and open up a way for the disclosure of its deepest meaning. He was determined to hear the Word of God out of itself, as it came straight from above, unfettered by a masterful culture, uncontrolled by the needs and satisfactions of bourgeois society, and before it had been sifted and diluted by being passed through some general frame of thought already worked out by modern man. Thus he made it his supreme task to penetrate into the new world of the New Testament, to make its deep inner dialectic, its fundamental outlook, his very own, and to bring this Word of God, with its redemptive, supernatural and eschatological message to bear upon the concrete work-a-day world of men and women. Under the

[1] Eduard Thurneysen, 'Die Anfänge Karl Barths Theologie der Frühzeit', *Ant.*, p. 831 f. See also the prefaces to the second and third editions of *Romans* (ET, pp. 6ff, 18f).   [2] Thurneysen, op cit. p. 832.   [3] *Romans*, p. 9.

theological tradition then dominant in the Churches, the life of the Church was being assimilated to the world, and theology was rapidly becoming secularised, when the whole meaning and intention of the Gospel lay in the opposite direction—that was the right-about turn which Barth found himself forced to take.

His thinking moved constantly between two poles, from the new world within the Bible where the Light and Word of God reigned and the concrete life of human beings around him. This forced Barth also to come to terms with the whole pietistic tradition of inwardness and its diluting to a purely individual hope of a future life for the soul the Gospel which announces that Christ has come and will come again to make all things new.[1] For Barth, the new world of the Bible, as he found it, was concerned with the whole of human existence, with man's outer as well as his inner life—for there is no area of human living and working which can exist for its own sake beyond the claim and operation of the Word of God.[2] And so in this stage in his ministry Barth joined the ranks of the social democrats and their activities in his parish, for his task was not only to confront men Sunday after Sunday with the Last Things, but to bring all that to bear upon their daily toil and suffering, for it is man in his totality whom God meets in his revelation.[3]

A powerful influence upon Barth at this stage was the eschatological teaching of Blumhardt[4] which helped to open up for Barth a fresh understanding of the Kingdom of God as the breaking into the world of God's unutterable compassion in a victorious grace which was both the judgment of the world and the great supernatural, saving event of the Gospel. God has poured himself out in love upon the world in Jesus Christ in order to take all its agony and hurt upon himself, and his purpose of Love will conquer, come what may. No doubt as yet that victory is visible only to faith and is hidden from our eyes. But the day will come, and indeed is near, when the time of the veiling or hiddenness of God's work will come to an end, and the victory of his Kingdom will be made clearly manifest. Because this supernatural Kingdom impinges upon the world even now, preaching has the task of relating it to the whole round of human life so that ethics and even politics are deeply involved in the eschatological message and are impregnated with new urgency.

In the younger (Christoph) Blumhardt the eschatological character of

---

[1] *CD* II.1, p. 633.   [2] See Thurneysen, *ZdZ*, 1927, pp. 515 ff.
[3] *Ant.*, p. 840. For a later description of a ministry of the word of God see *God in Action*, p. 58 f which can be read as an unconscious self-portrait on Barth's part.
[4] *Ant.*, p. 833. See the chapter on J. C. Blumhardt in *ProtTh*, pp. 588 ff.

the message of Jesus, realistically ackowledged, was related with corresponding realism to the rising socio-political movement, and he together with Leonhard Ragaz and Hermann Kutter became the fathers of the religious socialism in which Barth himself took part, yet not without strong reservations. Barth found he could not really come to terms with the teaching of Ragaz and Kutter for, much as he admired their social passion, he had to acknowledge that their 'fight for the Kingdom of God' which they contrasted with the Church, theology and Christendom, could not but lead back again into the deserts of secularisation. That is what actually happened, for example, in the case of H. M. Müller who found an inglorious end in the slough of the 'German-Christian' movement of 1933.[1]

Now let us look at the other side of the picture, at what appeared to Barth to be the collapse of the prevailing theology. Describing the rise of this theology in a lecture on 'Evangelical Theology in the nineteenth century', in 1957, Barth has this to say. 'For its inspiratioɪ. and instruction in the understanding of the Christian man and the Christian community, it went first to Herder and romanticism, to the religious and national awakening of the Napoleonic epoch. Then through speculative idealism, especially that of Hegel, it was able to acquire brilliant basic principles and terminology. It had, of course, to tolerate from that source also severe criticism and correction. Under the pressure of the positivism prevailing in the second half of the century—here the name of Albrecht Ritschl is to be remembered—it went back to the epistemology and ethics of the rediscovered Kant and to a Luther understood from that point of view, who likewise was then rediscovered. Finally, making the best of a scanty area for the sovereign religious experience of the individual, it became essentially a presentation and philosophy of the history of religion in general, and of the Christian religion in particular.'[2]

There were, of course, as Barth goes on to point out, exceptions and various mediating theologies, but without doubt it was the liberal theology that held the field, but then it too met its *dénouement*. 'The date of the exit of this theology is something about which it might be harder to find agreement. The year 1900, with which, according to the calendar, the nineteenth century ended represented, with the appearance of Harnack's *Das Wesen des Christentums* (ET *What is Christianity?*) a notable peak in its history. Yet even after that it continued to exist for a long time with proud bearing and undiminished strength, in spite of certain signs of dissolution. So much so that there could even develop around

[1] *CD* II.1, p. 33f.　　　[2] Karl Barth, *God, Grace and Gospel*, p. 56f.

1910 something in the nature of a Schleiermacher Renaissance, even if it was short and partial.[1] The actual end of the nineteenth century as the "good old days" falls for evangelical theology, as for other things, in the fateful year 1914. Fortuitously or not fortuitously, at any rate symptomatically, it happened just in that year that the recognised leading systematic theologian of the then most modern school, Ernst Troeltsch, finally crossed over from the theological to the philosophical faculty. For me personally one day at the beginning of August that year stamped itself as *dies ater*. It was that on which 93 German intellectuals came out with a manifesto supporting the war policy of Kaiser William II and his counsellors, and among them I found to my horror the names of nearly all my theological teachers whom up to then I had religiously honoured. Disillusioned by their conduct, I perceived that I should not be able any longer to accept their ethics and dogmatics, their biblical exegesis, their interpretation of history, that at least for me the theology of the nineteenth century had no future.'[2] The immediate reaction of Barth to this turn of events, and the collapse of any hope he had put in his famous theological teachers, was to dig down to bed-rock and look for new foundations. All through the first world-war these pressed hard upon him, giving him no peace, the urgent need at this very hour in the history of Christendom, to penetrate into the depths of the Christian faith, to make a new beginning, and to find a theological basis that would be really adequate and secure for the fulfilment of the Church's task in bringing the Word of God to mankind.

Describing the change that came over himself and the theological movement in which he participated, Barth has said in another lecture,[3] that though the revolution, materially regarded, was a sudden conversion, yet it had developed gradually in a movement which confronted the prevailing theology which had become religionistic, anthropocentric and humanistic, with a new and at the same time older and original Christian knowledge and language. What alarmed Barth and his friends was that even *God* had lost for this theology real depth and meaning, for to think of God meant for it, with scarcely any attempt to conceal the fact, to think of man, religious man to be sure, but *man*. To speak of God was to speak of this man with an elevated tone, while talk of dialogue with God tended to become but the mythical expression of

---

[1] Cf. especially the work of Heinrich Scholz, *Christentum und Wissenschaft in Schleiermachers Glaubenslehre*, 1909; and his critical edition (with introduction) of Schleiermacher's *Kurze Darstellung des theologischen Studiums zum Behuf einleitender Vorlesungen*, 1910.

[2] Op. cit. p. 57f.   [3] 'The Humanity of God', *GGG*, p. 32f.

something within man himself, of an inner monologue between his own heights and depths. We must let him speak again in his own words.

'Here some of us took fright—after having, with all the rest, drunk the various cups of this theology to the last dregs. Here (somewhere about the middle of the second decade of our century) they felt they had reached the parting of the ways. Had the pious man, had religion of whose history and present state we had at the University heard so much that was glorious and afterwards tried to say it ourselves, become, in our own person, problematical? Was it the encounter with socialism as interpreted by Kutter and Ragaz that opened our eyes to the fact that God might want to be God and to speak quite otherwise than in the fusty shrine of the Christian self-consciousness? Was it the aspect of the world, so suddenly darkened just then, compared with the preceding long peace period of our youth, which made us note that man's distress might be too great for him to find in the advice to turn to his religious possibilities a word that brought comfort and direction? Was it—and for me personally this played a decisive role—the failure of the ethics of modern theology at the outbreak of the First World War which led to our discontent with its exegesis, its conception of history and its dogmatics? Or, positively, was it the Blumhardt message of the Kingdom of God, which was only then, strange to relate, becoming actual? Was it Kierkegaard, Dostoevsky, Overbeck, read as commentaries to that message, through whom we found ourselves summoned to search out and to make for new shores? Or more fundamental than all that, was it the discovery that the theme of the Bible—contrary to the critical and the orthodox exegesis, in which we had been brought up—definitely could not possibly be man's religion and religious ethics—could not possibly be his own secret godliness, but—this was the *rocher de bronze* on which we first struck—the Godness of God, precisely God's Godness, God's own peculiar nature over against not only the natural, but also the spiritual cosmos, God's absolutely unique existence, power and initiative above all in His relationship to man? We felt that it was in this way, and only in this way, that we could understand the Voice of the Old and New Testaments, and that it was from here, and only from here, that we could from now on be theologians and particularly preachers, *ministri Verbi Divini*.'[1]

There can be no doubt that the tremendous factor in this development was the discovery that *God is God*, and that this is the God whose Word we hear in the Bible and whose Word the preacher has to take

[1] *GGG*, p. 33f.

upon his lips and announce to the congregation, an announcement which is accompanied at once by the lightning of the divine illumination and judgment and by the rainbow of the divine promise and faithfulness in everlasting mercy. God is really God and his Heaven is not some super-world but the Heaven of God. Man, however, is on earth and remains on earth—he is the creature of the flesh and of sin and of death and perdition. 'The relation between such a God and such a man, and the relation between such a man and such a God, is for me the theme of the Bible and the essence of philosophy.'[1] But God is the God who will not remain aloof but must and does come to man on this earth, in man's sin and in his death, in order to become his succour. This road from heaven to earth, from the exaltation of God down to the depth of man's need and hurt and guilt is the only way of man to God and to eternal life. There is no way from nature to grace but only the way of grace itself, that is, the way of Jesus Christ—it is the way of the unutterable compassion of God and the victory of Jesus Christ.

This led to a basic disagreement with the teaching of Schleiermacher, for not only was his theological kernel of an uneschatological 'Christian-ity-of-the-present' compatible neither with the Bible nor with the real world, but Schleiermacher's God was not a God who can have com-passion.[2] Likewise it led to a radical break with the movement repre-sented by the younger Blumhardt, Kutter and Ragaz which combined the Christian expectation of the Kingdom of God with the socialist expectation for the future.[3] And because this combination really in-volved at heart an identification between them, Barth felt compelled to stress the futurity of God as the limit and fulfilment of all human effort and of all time. Strangely enough, it was his insistence on preserving intact the positive compassion of God, and his fear of losing it again in a secularised Christianity, that pushed into the forefront the emphasis upon the divine *No* of judgment so that it came at times to be heard more clearly and loudly than the great positive *Yes* of God which was the basic content of all that Barth was now seeking to proclaim. The difficulty was that it could not be heard, and therefore could not be effectively proclaimed, until a way was cut through the confusion of God with man and man with God, and so the proclamation of the divine Grace had to take a critical form—and yet Barth admits that this aspect of his preaching and teaching could not unjustly be connected with the

[1] *Romans*, p. 10.
[2] See the letters of 1921-1925, *Gd-Md*, pp. 90f, 104, etc.
[3] See especially the illuminating correspondence between Barth and Thurney-sen in 1925 and Barth's comments on it, *Gd-Md*, pp. 137ff.

spiritual shaking experienced by European man through the world war.[1] This was the emphasis to which he gave such masterful expression in the first edition of his *Romans*, taking his cue from Romans 1.16 and 17 on the revelation of the wrath of God in the Gospel and the radical nature of the justifying righteousness of God.

It is worth noticing that although his emphasis at this stage was somewhat one-sided, probably necessarily so in the circumstances, the great issues with which Barth wrestled in his Safenwil days and the steps he took in putting and seeking answers to the fundamental questions are reflected all through the development of his theology. His primary concern then as now was the question as to what preaching really is as a task with its own independent right and action. There belongs to that the supreme question as to the true nature of interpretation—the proper concentration of exegesis which passes behind the many questions to the one cardinal question by which all are embraced—for true preaching cannot be anything else than an announcement of the Word of God grounded upon the exegesis of the Holy Scripture, and the theology that serves it can only take the form of fundamental dialogue with God, that is, the form of prayer and proclamation. Thus there arises the question how to expound the message of the Bible as the message of Christ and the coming of his Kingdom in such a way that the man of today can understand it, be moved by it and be changed through it. This again raises the question as to the nature of the Church as the living community addressed by, and responding in life and act to, the Word of God, rather than as the community concerned with its own religious feelings or inner spiritual experiences and meanings. Then there is the problem or the riddle of modern man whom we must try to understand anew in his actual existence, but understand from a centre in the Word of God as he with whom we are bound together in brotherly solidarity in Jesus Christ and his vicarious work for all men. No less difficult and puzzling is the question of the Church which instead of living continuously out of the creative impact of divine Revelation upon it, becomes entangled in its own institutions, imprisoned and torpid in its own existence, and so assimilated into the sphere of culture and civilisation that the world can only pass by unmoved in its own thoughtlessness and dreams. And yet the Church, this same Church, must awake and rise up again, for it is none other than the Church of Jesus Christ the Victor, whose conquering love will not be thwarted but will attain its end in making all things new.

[1] *CD* II.1, p. 634.

It was with this background and with thoughts like these that Barth read the writings of Franz Overbeck, and was able to appreciate his deep reverence for original Christianity and evaluate positively the intention behind their sharp attack upon historical Christianity.[1] When 'the remains' of Overbeck's work was published in 1919 under the title *Christentum und Kultur*, Barth gave to it an extended review which has considerable importance for our understanding of his thinking at this time.[2] What Overbeck had to say, together with what he had learned from Sören Kierkegaard, confirmed and sharpened Barth's analysis of the problem of Christendom, and at the same time put into Barth's hands weapons for his own attack which he was not slow to use in the commentary on Romans. Overbeck offered a severe and trenchant critique of all historical Christianity, which he contrasted with the original historic foundation of the Church in Christ and the apostles. 'Historical Christianity' as we know it, and as it has developed throughout the centuries, is a Christianity subordinated to time, to the time of this world, but originally, in its own history before 'historical Christianity' arose, Christianity was the product of the supernatural Kingdom of God, of the Last Things which bound and relativise all we know as 'world' and 'history'.[3] Thus the historicising of Christianity, its subordination to the time of this world, is its great betrayal, while the modern theologians of this historical Christianity simply perpetuate and advocate that betrayal—'Bismark-religion', Overbeck called it.[4] Hence, Overbeck launched his attack upon the Christendom that is identified with history, or as the manifestation of our conception of time, and sought to expose as impossible and worthless the historical and psychological evaluations of Christianity employed by modern theology. Indeed what is this modern, worldly-wise theology but 'the Satan of religion',[5] for what it does every day is 'to put God in the bag'?[6]

Overbeck's teaching was heartily disliked and linked to that of his friend Nietzsche,[7] but Barth saw beyond the devastating criticism to the desire on Overbeck's part for a real break-through in emancipation, from the shackles of historical Christendom and its worldly perversion in the Church, and return to the original history (*Urgeschichte*) of the

---

[1] See Thurneysen's comments upon Overbeck's influence on Barth, in *Ant.*, p. 836.
[2] This was republished as the first essay in *Die Theologie und die Kirche*, pp. 1-25 (ET, pp. 55-73). Cf. also Overbeck's essay, *Ueber die Christlichkeit unserer heutigen Theologie*, 1873.   [3] *TC*, pp. 58 ff, 61 f.   [4] *TC*, pp. 67, 69.
[5] *TC*, p. 69.   [6] *TC*, p. 70.   [7] *Ant.*, p. 836.

Church in the lifetime of Christ himself.[1] For Overbeck such a renewing of the foundations could only be achieved at the cost of historical Christianity, of all that hitherto we have called 'religion'—that is what Barth had to evaluate himself. In this Barth was undoubtedly influenced by Kierkegaard's attack on Christendom through contrasting a true Christianity with a false perversion of it, but also by the positive emphasis upon the grace of God he had found in the teaching of Blumhardt.[2] Two important points emerge out of Barth's critical appreciation of Overbeck. He sees more clearly than ever that the question of our presuppositions must be raised in a radical way, if theology is to forge ahead once again, but that means that we must take seriously Overbeck's dangerous, apocalyptic criticism of historical Christianity. A hiatus must be torn between Christianity and culture, between the Gospel and its worldly perversion, if we are to understand it adequately, but the critique must be undertaken in order to let the positive message sound forth. Thus in the circumstances, outer and inner, of his own day, there is only one thing to be done, to turn his back upon 'the flesh-pots of Egypt' and 'with clenched teeth to dare to go out into the wilderness'. It is impossible any longer to have genuine theology without determination and courage.[3] We must pass through the narrow doors of Overbeck's negation if we are to reach Blumhardt's affirmation, and then we will see Blumhardt's *Yes* to be the other, positive side of Overbeck's *No*. But that means that theology must face the Last Things, come up against the ultimate realities and judgments of God, and dare to go forward under their impact.[4] That is the significance of resurrection. 'It is sown in corruption; it is raised in incorruption: it is sown in dishonour; it is raised in glory: it is sown in weakness; it is raised in power.' That citation from I Corinthians 15 with which Barth ended his study of Overbeck pointed straight ahead not only to the lonely road out into the desert, but to the hope of a really new beginning beyond. Little did he know at that time what would actually come out of it all.

Barth has given us an essay on his appreciation of certain aspects of Overbeck's thought, but we do not have corresponding essays which reveal so clearly the influences of some others upon him, although that influence is undoubtedly strong, particularly that of Dostoevski[5] and Kierkegaard.[6] What he found in the thought of such men was a pro-

---

[1] Barth's evaluation of Overbeck met not a little opposition by those who could not see past the attack, but it was supported by Overbeck's widow—see *Ant.*, pp. 836, 856.   [2] *TC*, pp. 64, 55 f.   [3] *TC*, pp. 57, 72.
[4] *TC*, p. 73.   [5] Cf. E. Thurneysen, *Dostoevski*.
[6] See the preface to the second edition of *Romans* (ET, p. 4).

found sense of God, of reverence for his Majesty, awe before his deity (which Overbeck also had), hunger for his eternity (Dostoevski) and humility before his absoluteness and infinity (Kierkegaard),[1] and he linked it to the teaching of Calvin, and of Paul, Jeremiah, and Job.

Theologically and philosophically it was undoubtedly Kierkegaard who had the greatest impact upon him, far greater than the actual mentioning of his name, in the *Romans*, for example, indicates. That is obviously apparent in the indebtedness of his thinking to Kierkegaard's attack upon all direct communication and all living on easy, comfortable terms with God. 'May we be preserved from the blasphemy of men who "without being terrified and afraid in the presence of God, without the agony of death which is the birthpang of faith, without the trembling which is the first requirement of adoration, without the panic of the possibility of scandal, hope to have direct knowledge of that which cannot be directly known . . . and do not rather say that He was truly and verily God, because He was beyond our comprehension" (Kierkegaard).'[2]

What interested Barth in Kierkegaard's teaching was the emphasis upon the explosive force that the invasion of God in his Godness into time and human existence meant, which Kierkegaard sought to express by the paradox and dialectic. This is a point that has often been misunderstood in both Kierkegaard and Barth—for the emphasis upon the infinite qualitative difference between time and eternity (which Barth tells us he kept always in mind in the second edition of the *Romans*[3]) was not upon some abstract and distant Deity, but precisely upon the nearness, the impact of God in all his Majesty and Godness upon man —that is the significance of Jesus that had been lost, and which Barth as well as Kierkegaard sought to recover.

Commenting upon the statement that the Father is not revealed by flesh and blood (Matt. 16.17) Barth says: 'The revelation which is in Jesus, because it is the revelation of the righteousness of God, must be the most complete veiling of His incomprehensibility. In Jesus, God becomes veritably a secret: He is made known as the Unknown, speaking in eternal silence: He protects Himself from every intimate companionship and from all the impertinence of religion. He becomes a scandal to the Jews and to the Greeks foolishness. In Jesus the communication of God begins with a rebuff, with the exposure of a vast chasm, with the clear revelation of a great stumbling-block. "Remove

---

[1] *Romans*, p. 252, where Barth speaks of 'the relentlessness of Calvin, the dialectical audacity of Kierkegaard, Overbeck's sense of awe, Dostoevski's hunger for eternity, Blumhardt's optimism', which sums up very well Barth's appreciation of these men.   [2] *Romans*, p. 279.   [3] *Romans*, p. 5.

from the Christian Religion, as Christendom has done, its ability to shock, and Christianity, by becoming a direct communication, is altogether destroyed. It then becomes a tiny, superficial thing, capable neither of inflicting deep wounds nor of healing them; by discovering an unreal and merely human compassion, it forgets the qualitative distinction between God and man" (Kierkegaard). Faith in Jesus, like its theme, the righteousness of God, is the radical "Nevertheless".[1]

Like Kierkegaard, and in a different way, like Kutter, Barth sought to measure the Church, and the world, and above all to measure religious and ethical man, by the absolute standards of God and the Gospel. But that is just what produces *crisis* and upheaval, for it turns upside down all our beloved human erections and institutions. Overbeck saw that it meant the rending of the whole husk of historical Christianity, and its 'death', but with Kierkegaard Barth sees that the whole realm of humanity is confronted and dissolved, and indeed the whole form of this world is threatened.[2] To think that through is to think dangerously and requires courage and determination—that was where the challenge of Kierkegaard and Overbeck coincided—the need for a theology that 'comes up against the wind', and that 'sets itself heroically against the time', that was prepared for 'the absurd', the presence of God in space and time, and therefore the apocalyptic relevance of Jesus in our existence.

Much of the influence of Kierkegaard on him Barth sought later to tone down and sometimes to cut out altogether, but there is one important point which we must not fail to note: Kierkegaard's doctrine of the *Truth in the form of personal being*, Truth as Subject (not Truth as subjectivity, but as Subject-ivity). In Kierkegaard that was a product of his understanding of the Incarnation, the Truth of God incarnate, encountering us objectively, which therefore calls in question the illusion that truth arises from within us, from the depths of our own memories. In Barth that is related also to the sovereignty of God, to the *Lordship* of Christ, and it is also related to the command of God to love our neighbour. At this point, Barth felt, Kierkegaard needed some correction lest his stress upon 'the single one' should lead back into the religious individualism that had dominated romantic idealism, but Kierkegaard's

[1] *Romans*, p. 98 f. Cf. *Romans*, p. 38: 'The Gospel requires *faith*. Only for those who believe is it the *power of God unto salvation*. It can therefore be neither directly communicated nor directly apprehended. Christ has been appointed to be the Son of God—*according to the Spirit* (Rom. 1.4). "Now, Spirit is the denial of immediacy. If Christ be very God, He must be unknown, for to be known directly is the characteristic mark of an idol" (Kierkegaard).'

[2] Cf. *Romans*, pp. 278, 395, 440, etc.

stress upon the objectivity (not in the sense of a dead 'object') of the living Subject, and his attack upon every attempt to retreat backwards by some Ariadne's thread of immanent continuity or *anamnesis* (*analogia entis*, as Barth called it) into eternity, helped Barth to see that modern Christianity, as in Pietism or in Schleiermacher, had 'read the New Testament Gospel backwards',[1] for instead of taking the way of Calvin or Kierkegaard from God to man (and only then from man to God) it had reversed the Gospel of election and grace, and had sought to take a private road from the depths of human experience and consciousness to God. That was the great reversal that Barth set himself to overturn, in order to let the Gospel take with us the way it had originally taken in the Incarnation of the Son of God.

We may conclude this section of our examination of Barth's thinking with a self-revealing passage from 1922. 'Those who accept the thoughts I have brought forward as germane to the essential facts thereby acknowledge themselves descendants of an ancestral line which runs back through *Kierkegaard* to *Luther* and *Calvin*, and so to *Paul* and *Jeremiah*. There are others, to be sure, who claim the same ancestry. Perhaps, therefore, for the sake of clearness I ought to add that our line does *not* run back through Martensen to Erasmus, and through those against whom the fifteenth chapter of First Corinthians was directed, to the prophet Hananiah, who took the yoke from the neck of the prophet Jeremiah and broke it.

'And so to leave nothing unsaid, I might explicitly point out that this ancestral line does *not include Schleiermacher*. With all due respect to the genius shown in his work I cannot consider Schleiermacher a good teacher in the realm of theology, because, so far as I can see, he is disastrously dim-sighted in regard to the fact that man as man is not only in *need* but beyond all hope of saving himself; that the whole of so-called religion, and not least the Christian religion, *shares* in this need; and that one can *not* speak of God simply by speaking of man in a loud voice. There are those to whom Schleiermacher's peculiar excellence lies in his having discovered a conception of religion by which he overcame Luther's so-called dualism and connected earth and heaven by a much-needed bridge, upon which we may reverently cross. Those who hold this view will finally turn their backs, if they have not done so already, upon the considerations I have presented. I ask only that they do not appeal *both* to Schleiermacher *and* to the Reformers, *both* to Schleiermacher *and* to the New Testament, *both* to Schleiermacher *and* to the

[1] Cf. *WW*, p. 286.

Old Testament prophets, but that from Schleiermacher back they look for another ancestral line. In such a line the next representative might possibly be Melanchthon. The very names Kierkegaard, Luther, Calvin, Paul, and Jeremiah suggest what Schleiermacher never possessed, a clear and direct apprehension of the truth that man is made to serve *God* and not God to serve man. The negation and loneliness of the life of Jeremiah in contrast to that of the kings, princes, priests and prophets of Judah, the keen unremitting opposition of Paul to *religion* as it was exemplified in Judaism, Luther's break, not with the impiety, but with the *piety* of the Middle Ages, Kierkegaard's attack on *Christianity*—all are characteristic of a certain way of speaking of *God* which Schleiermacher never arrived at.'[1]

As we look back, then, over the first stage of Barth's development, we can see that the master-questions and themes were already being hammered out in the exegesis of Romans, Ephesians, and Corinthians, face to face both with 'the world' within which the minister is called to fulfil his task, and with 'the Church' that has itself become only too much 'world'. One focus of his thinking is to be found in the new world within the Bible, the eschatological message of the Kingdom and grace of Christ, and the other focus in the rigorous application of scientific exegesis in order to let the profound themes of the Word of God, under the guidance of St Paul, break forth and take living control of preaching and theological activity and of the concrete life and work of man in the whole round of his existence. On the one hand, this involves achieving distance, separation, a boundary line, as it were, between Christianity and the Church's involvement in the world, in order that the Gospel may be heard as *Gospel*, but on the other hand, it involves concrete involvement in the world and in the times in which the preacher or theologian lives, that he may bring the Gospel to bear upon the world in all the power of its newness as message *from* God *to* men. It is because he is a preacher that the preacher has forced upon him the critical task of theology, but because he is a preacher he must also go on to take up the positive task of theology, in seeking to unfold and develop the content of the Church's message by the rigorous control of exegesis and under the guidance of the historic confessions of the Church.

[1] *WW*, pp. 195 ff.

IV

FROM DIALECTICAL TO DOGMATIC THINKING

1. Dialectical Theology

THE second principal stage in Barth's development began with the re-writing of the commentary on Romans. That task fell within his ministry at Safenwil, although the manuscript was finished just as he migrated to Göttingen. For its rewriting Barth had learned immensely from the reception of the first edition, for the criticism directed to it and especially the favourable reviews compelled him to criticise himself severely. But above all it was his persistent listening to the mighty voice of Paul, which had been so new to him when he first went to Safenwil, that made it necessary for him completely to rewrite and reform the work in an energetic and creative attempt to rethink through the whole material of the epistle and expose it to view in its native and explosive force.

That meant for Barth that he had to abjure entirely the exegetical method of men like Jülicher and Lietzmann[1] who in their different ways brought to the text a prior understanding in terms of which they distinguished in the raw material of the Bible what they approved from what they rejected, and so instead of wrestling with the difficult and scandalous passages, set them aside as 'Jewish' or 'popular Christian' or 'Hellenistic' or some other kind of material of no concern to modern men. Barth rejected that as a flight from the given realities, as an avoidance of the hard work of genuine interpretation, and as a failure to apply the rigorous methods of exact science. True interpretation involves the determination to face up to what the text is actually saying whether we like it or not, and whether it agrees with our presuppositions or not, and especially a struggle with it at the uncomfortable points until we let it yield what it really has to say to us without any attempt on our part to chop it down or to foreclose the dialogue before we have gone through with it to the end. As a matter of fact,

---

[1] Barth gained a better impression of Lietzmann's exegetical work later through direct contact with him—see the letter to Thurneysen of Nov. 26, 1924, *Gd-Md*, p. 123.

Barth confessed—and this is what had such an impact on him—he found that it was in his wrestling with those elements in the Epistle which were 'scandals to modern thought' that he really broke through to the characteristic and veritable discernment of St Paul. Faithful exegesis entailed a ruthless, radical self-criticism, but that was the very thing the older and contemporary commentators avoided. For Barth it meant the shaking and shattering of his own frame of reference, the tearing down of his own scaffolding, in fact, a radical repentance.

Thus the encounter with modern thought begun in the first edition of the *Romans* was to have far-reaching effects. If it can be said that in his first period Barth's theology fell in some measure, at least, within the thought-forms of Neo-Protestantism, it must be said that the second period was one in which he set out to break loose from them, in which quite deliberately he swam against the current and beat upon the bolted doors of prevailing tradition. He set himself to show that the teaching of St Paul cannot be made to fit into our man-made syntheses, or coordinated with our philosophical or cultural presuppositions, or be interpreted in line with the striving of mankind for its own betterment. Rather does the Gospel as proclaimed by St Paul cut against the grain of man's own vaunted needs and desires and against the so-called upward evolution of the human spirit, for the Gospel comes plumb down from above as a judgment cutting into man's life, setting it into crisis, and it comes above all as grace setting man's existence on a wholly new basis, but is therefore of the most disturbing and critical significance for all human achievement and so-called civilisation. The Gospel falls upon man as God's own mighty Word, questioning him down to the bottom of his being, uprooting him from his securities and satisfactions, and therefore tearing clean asunder all the relations that keep him a prisoner within his own ideals in order that he may be genuinely free for God and for his wonderful new work of grace in Jesus Christ. The emphasis was quite definitely upon what became known as *diastasis*, the distance, the separation, between God's ways and man's ways, God's thoughts and man's thoughts, between Christianity and culture, between Gospel and humanism, between Word of God and word of man.[1]

That was the explosive significance of the new edition of his commentary, for in it Barth struck away as far as he could all that remained of immanent evolutionary notions, and while he learned from his brother Heinrich Barth considerably more of the philosophies of Plato and Kant

---

[1] This is what Barth has called 'the great Calvinist distance between heaven and earth', *Briefwechsel* 1921-1925, *Gd-Md*, p. 42.

D

he determined to renounce the use of all idealistic and neo-Kantian conceptions in exegesis. He cast aside any attempt to speak of the difference between God and man, heaven and earth, in terms of the finite and infinite, and scrapped every vestige of an attempt to bolster up his theological statements by giving them some sort of ontological substructure or a setting in any kind of *Weltanschauung* or basic philosophical outlook upon the universe, and all this in an even more radical attempt to let the message of the Gospel speak for itself and throw its light and healing upon the dark mysteries of human existence, which he considered to be the most important task of all, the task of preacher and theologian alike.

The first edition of the *Römerbrief* had not received undue notice, but the second edition raised a storm in the theological and philosophical thought of Germany and Switzerland, going through many editions. In it Barth expressed his deep dissatisfaction with the insidious subjectivism of Protestant theology which confounded man with God and put man in the place of God. 'Thinking of ourselves what can only be thought of God, we are unable to think of Him more highly than we think of ourselves. Being to ourselves what God ought to be to us, He is no more to us than we are to ourselves. This secret identification of ourselves with God carries with it our isolation from him.'[1]

The new edition was deliberately intended to create an upheaval. Barth threw all his powers into the attack, his remarkably vivid, dramatic use of language and metaphor, exaggerated but effective artistry, cutting irony and shrewd humour, and yet not a little friendly and reconciling laughter, all in order to break open the rigid mind and outlook of his contemporaries, to shatter the peace of their easy, comfortable religion moulded to their self-chosen ends, and to tear to shreds the web of self-deception in which modern theology and philosophy had become entangled. Barth likened it to the web which the spider spins out of its own inner self. The *Romans* is to be understood, therefore, in the light of Barth's own particular situation at the time and the general situation which he confronted in the theological and cultured world of his day, in terms of the great mass of nineteenth- and twentieth-century literature in philosophy, art, music, romance, as well as theology. The commentary contains thousands of allusions and references to the whole round of modern culture. From beginning to the end of the book twentieth-century man is planted face to face with Almighty God in his infinite Majesty and Holiness and incredible, inscrutable Grace.

This is an extraordinary work, for just as a bomb can only have its

---

[1] *Romans*, p. 45.

intended effect if it explodes and shatters itself, so the *Romans*, as it were, blows itself up and the reader along with it. If it is an all-out attack upon immanentism and relativism, arrogant scepticism and idolatry, it takes the most radical of all roads, for it places all human undertakings and formulations, theological and ecclesiastical as well, under the total judgment of grace, under the *krisis* of the Spirit of Christ—and therefore, of course, Barth's own Commentary falls under the judgment of the same axe that is laid to the root of the whole tree. *All flesh is as grass.*[1] It is a sort of relativism from above downward; before the absolute grace of God all else is relative, precisely by relation to it. That is the radical consequence of the Pauline doctrine of justification by grace alone which Barth seeks to reveal at every point in the exposition. It is just because God puts us in the right with himself in the entire freedom and sovereignty of his grace, that he calls us utterly in question, revealing to us that before him we are always in the wrong, always unprofitable servants, in that we are those upon whom he has complete compassion and unlimited grace.

Barth admits that there may well be wrong-headedness and even arrogance in the way which he sought to get this across, and that the book may even have a fatal influence upon immature minds, but his intention was to bring out into the open what has to be heard, as it were, by forensic justification. That is the reason why the cutting edges of the Gospel are sharpened and laid bare, and God's saving action is spoken of as limit and boundary and crisis and suspension and question-mark directed to man, even to moral and religious man. There can be no doubt that the great positive theme of the *Romans* is the saving grace and compassion of God, the grace that is equated with the definite saving action of God, grace that is both the forgiveness of God and the self-consciousness of the new man, grace that is therefore the deepest answer to the question concerning human existence. But how is that to be conveyed in such a way that it can be really understood and not identified with 'something' which man has in himself and is to be assimilated to his possibilities?[2]

Barth's answer is clear. 'We are not in a position to say anything which is relevant concerning grace and sin, until our perception has been sharpened and we are protected from pantheism by being reminded of the critical significance of the death of Christ; until we have been liber-

---

[1] *Romans*, p. 276.
[2] 'So long as we endeavour to speak about grace, our speech must labour under a necessary obscurity', *Romans*, p. 224. See also p. 103.

ated from obsession with the problem concerning what we can do or not do. Grace is the Kingdom of God, His rule and power and dominion. Grace is radically contrasted with the whole realm of human possibility, yet nevertheless, for the same reason, it judges human life and launches a disturbing attack upon it. In so far as in this contrast God is encountered, human life is refashioned and provided with a new hope and a new promise.'[1]

Hence it was inevitable, Barth felt, that in the inner and outer circumstances of those years grace should be presented, if presented at all, in an essentially critical form if it is to perform its function; it must be permitted to make an absolute assault upon man, and to question man down to the roots of his being. It is only under that divine questioning that we will be able to put genuine questions, the right questions, and yet because the divine question in the Gospel is still put to our questioning, the answer to the question implies a still greater emphasis upon the question. 'May God never relieve us of this questioning. May He enclose us with questions on every side. May He defend us from every answer which is not itself a question. May He bar every exit and cut us off from all simplifications. May the cavity at the cart-wheel's centre, which Lao-Tse perceived long ago, be delimited by a ring of questions. In that central void the answer to our questioning is hidden; but since the void is defined by the questions, they must never for one moment cease.'[2]

There can be no doubt that the *Romans* was an epoch-making work, because of the alarm it sounded throughout the theological world, because of the content of its message and because of the effective way in which Barth got it across through his critical freedom of exegesis and masterly handling of the questioning method combined with his own creative energy, which succeeded beyond all expectation in letting the Scriptures speak out, unhindered by what we want them to say, the very Word of God.[3] The main theme can be described as: Let God be God, and let man learn again to be man, instead of trying to be as God. The supreme sin of man is that he is always identifying God with the depths of his own self-consciousness, always twisting the truth to suit his own selfish and private ideas. Hence the ruthless criticism so necessary in exegesis must be mainly in the form of self-criticism, precisely because

[1] *Romans*, p. 215.　　[2] Op. cit. p. 254.
[3] See the comments of Thurneysen in *ZdZ*, 1927, p. 517 about the new way in which Barth and he began to read the Bible with fewer presuppositions than before; and also Barth's own remarks in *Kirchenblatt für die reformierte Schweiz*, 96.7, April 1940, p. 99.

it has to struggle with sin as the will of man to be independent of God. Its whole purpose must be to make room again for the holy and transcendent God of the Bible, of Jeremiah and Paul—and, Barth could add, of Luther and Calvin and Kierkegaard.

When man is confronted with God like that, there is crisis, collision, crucifixion. The Cross is seen to be the supreme and unique event of the meeting between holy God and sinful man, and at the Cross all the subtle attempts of man at self-deification and self-aggrandisement are exposed. That is particularly true of religious man, for it is primarily religious man who is the sinner, and it is in the clothing of religion that sin can achieve its most terrible form. It was, after all, religious man who crucified Jesus. And yet the breath-taking fact about the Cross is the pure grace and infinite love of God which, while tearing away from man his rags of self-deceit, clothes him in the righteousness of God in order to stand him on his feet again as a child of the heavenly Father.

Barth was revealed in the *Römerbrief* to be a real genius in theological penetration and expression, for with the most powerful and dramatic strokes of his pen that analysis was driven into all aspects of modern life and thought. It shattered the selfish individualism of theological liberalism or else made it bitterly peevish and even hysterically angry. In many ways Barth himself was alarmed at the success of the work, both at the enthusiasm with which it was greeted in some quarters, and at the appallingly negative impression it made on others, and he hastened in his succeeding prefaces to warn against both reactions. There was little point, however, in rewriting the work—although the whole thing would have to be recast again to avoid false impressions—for the purpose of the work was to sound the alarm at the critical moment, not to lay the basis of a new theology in itself but to point the way far beyond to the recovery of theological exegesis and of a positive theology orientated upon the Word of God—and to that work he dedicated his energies.

To read the *Romans* in the light of what happened later is most revealing, for then it becomes evident that behind all the negatives and sharp distinctions there was hard at work a great new positive theology struggling to be born. If everywhere the old husk was being rent it was because everywhere after a hard winter new life was pushing forth and beginning to unfold its new foliage, or, to change the metaphor, the new wine was bursting the old wine-skins; but it is the new *Ansatz*, the new starting-point, the new direction, the new basis, that shines through and stands out in contrapuntal response to the understanding of the Gospel as the absolute *Novum* of God among men. The teaching of *Romans* was

more than Barth claimed, more than 'a corrective' or 'a marginal note':
it pointed out, if not the actual road ahead, at least the direction in which
it lay.[1]

In Göttingen and then at Münster Barth was free to pursue this task
through laborious study on his own in the whole history of dogma, and
in daily confrontation with his students in lectures and seminars, and in
almost continuous debates with his theological colleagues in Germany,
not excluding the Romans whose interest he had aroused so sharply that
genuine theological discussion with them became possible.[2] This is the
period in which his earlier study of the Reformation, particularly in its
exegetical works, was vastly deepened by a study of Lutheran and Reformed theology, in which he both developed a profound sympathy for
the great theologians of the sixteenth and seventeenth centuries, and
acquired a masterly knowledge of Reformed and Lutheran scholasticism.[3] It soon became evident that he was to stand forth as a great
champion of Reformed dogmatic theology in the tradition of John Calvin, learning from but critical of Scholastic Calvinism, because learning
again from the patristic tradition and above all from fresh theological
exegesis and from fresh appreciation of the problems of the Reformation.[4]

Thinking of what he learned when he was called from the parish to
an academic post and had to face the problem of systematic exposition
and Reformed theology, Barth has recently given us the following suc-
cinct statement. 'The view of the role of investigation in systematic
theology which I acquired at that time, and subsequently more thoroughly developed, is this: with all the previous course of Christian
thinking and teaching fixed before one's eyes, to trace out the message
of the Old and New Testaments, as analysed in its particulars by biblical-
exegetical theology, in its unity and totality (and to that extent to trace
it out "systematically"). In this message systematic theology has not
only its real but also its epistemological ground. It has not to anticipate
it, therefore, with any general metaphysics, theory of knowledge, ontology or even philosophy of religion taken as bearing upon it normatively.
Nor has it even to subject it to the law of any churchly tradition. In no

---

[1] Cf. Heinrich Vogel, *Verkündigung und Forschung*, 1951, p. 121 f.

[2] See *Theology and Church*, 'Roman Catholicism: a question to the Protestant
Church', *TC*, pp. 307 ff.

[3] See the letters to Thurneysen of Jan. 22, March 26, April 2, May 9, June 8,
28, 1922 and Jan. 23, etc. 1923 in *Gd-Md*.

[4] See his address on 'The doctrinal task of the Reformed Churches' to the
General Assembly of the Union of Reformed Churches at Emden, 1923 (in *The
Word of God and the Word of Man*, pp. 218-71) and to the Presbyterian Alliance
of 1925, and his discussion of the thesis of E. Peterson (*TC*, pp. 112 ff and pp.
286 ff. respectively).

sense has it to dominate this message. It has to serve it. It has to recount its utterance completely, coherently and consistently (and, again, to this extent "systematically"). It has to allow it the first word and the last, so that by reflex action from the exposition it may speak for itself. It asks (as "Church *Dogmatics*") after *the* "dogma", i.e. the *norm* of Christian thought and speech which is supreme over dogmatics as it is supreme over the entire Church. In the measure that it respects the message which is its object and source and in this very freedom pertaining to its work, it is itself (over against the Christian as well as the non-Christian world) really *free* science.'[1]

Although that was written by Barth as he looked back from the *Church Dogmatics*, there can be no doubt that it describes well the direction into which his thinking and teaching moved in the Göttingen and Münster professoriates, as we can judge from the various essays collected in *Theology and Church* and republished in 1928. To this period also belongs another collection of lectures, *The Word of God and the Word of Man*, 1924, in which we are given the fruit in more theological form of his discovery of the strange new world within the Bible and the bearing of it upon the life and work of the Church; *The Resurrection of the Dead*, and not least, what Barth has called his 'well-known false start', the volume of prolegomena to a '*Christian Dogmatics*', 1927.

In order to point the way through the development of Barth's theology during these years, it may be best to select several of the principal themes that engaged his attention and discern something of their significance for his work as a whole.

(*a*) Perhaps the first theme we must note in this essentially polemical era in Barth's thinking is his questioning of the deep-seated immanentism, reductionism, and anthropocentricism of Neo-Protestantism. His studies impressed him with the fact that the great achievements of the nineteenth century had to be questioned at their roots, for the criticisms that had so far been launched against it operated within premises common to it; hence what was called for was a complete counter-movement, a *positive* reconsideration of the basic Christian tenets on their own ground and in terms of their own inner, objective logic, along with a *critical* probing into the foundations of nineteenth-century theology in order to free theology from its procrustean bed in the ideological structures of modern man, and deliver it from the falsification that befalls it when it is used as the expression of, and therefore a cover for, latent

---

[1] *Lehre und Forschung an der Universität Basel, zur Zeit der Feier ihres fünfhundertjährigen Bestehens*, 1960 (ET in *SJT* 14.3, p. 226 f).

social and cultural interests. Theology must be purged of the fatal ideological twist that has marred it so badly in modern times. That is what
Barth set himself to do, the positive task had to move more slowly, but
the ground had to be cleared in continuous engagements with the great
thinkers and theologians of modernity.[1]

Barth realised that this was a colossal task, for the theology he had to
attack was intertwined with the thinking and outlook of the greatest
intellectual achievements of modern Europe in philosophy and literature and music and all the *Geisteswissenschaften* of brilliant European
culture. Therefore he had to come to grips with it all, not through
piecemeal cavilling criticisms but through a fundamental *Auseinandersetzung*. The difficulties of this task, however, led Barth to appreciate
and respect the immense difficulty that confronted the preaching and
teaching of the Christian faith in the nineteenth and twentieth centuries,
for the understanding of Christianity had to be unfolded and expressed
within an era of the greatest brilliance and genius of the triumph of the
human spirit over nature in the advances of the natural sciences and the
power of modern thought. The Christian leaders and thinkers of the
nineteenth century had to be admired and given their full due, Schleiermacher above all, for their deep sense of responsibility for modernity,
and their will to match in power and intellectual vigour the communication of the Christian faith with the power and vigour of contemporary
civilisation and culture. There can be no doubt also that they achieved
great success in their own way, for they succeeded in expounding Christianity as an essential part of that culture and indeed as its highest and
finest expression, but in so doing, they presented a Christianity which
was but a particular form of the development of the human spirit, and
so betrayed it. The measure of their achievement thus became also the
measure of their aberration.

The charge that Barth sought to bring against that theology was that
it made its primary task the need to address itself to discussion with the
age by allowing the age itself to dictate the questions which it sought to
answer, and which it answered therefore on the same ground on which
the questions were put to Christianity, i.e. from outside the Gospel and
the Church. The basic purpose of that theology was to satisfy the human
intelligence at the heart of nineteenth-century culture, rather than to
convey to it the positive message of the Gospel, or the results of a theological investigation carried out scientifically for its own sake. Thus the

[1] This is nowhere better revealed than in the letters of 1921-1925 republished
in the 1958 *Festschrift* for Thurneysen, *Gd-Md*.

nineteenth-century theology was basically apologetic in the sense that it set out to demonstrate the possibility of faith within the cardinal assumptions and within the limits of the world-view that prevailed at the time, and so it subordinated the validity of the Christian faith to the accepted canons and norms of intelligibility and taste of contemporary civilisation. In other words, it renounced its own fundamental frame of reference, its own right to formulate its questions scientifically in a way appropriate to its own subject-matter and as arising directly out of it, and assimilated itself to the framework constructed by the human spirit in its advancing triumph over nature.

This meant that theology had to rethink its own content and embark upon a process of reductions and simplifications in order to transpose the message of the Gospel into forms acceptable to modern man, but all this involved as Kierkegaard felt so keenly, and as Barth was not slow to press home, a μετάβασις εἰς ἄλλο γένος, that is, not only a transition to another universe of discourse but a transposition of the inner substance of the faith into something altogether different and alien to it. The process of reduction and simplification involved not simply individual doctrines, especially those which were particularly offensive or scandalous to the age, but it reached down to what was the most fundamental of all, the doctrine of God. Ultimately, for all his will to maintain the objectivity of God, Barth held, Schleiermacher only speaks of God 'by speaking of man in a loud voice', for he 'never possessed a clear and direct apprehension of the truth that man is made to serve God and not God to serve man'.[1] In other words, what Schleiermacher and his contemporaries and followers were concerned with was not the living God, holy and transcendent above and beyond man who condescends to him in his compassion, not an Infinite above man and really coming to him, but an Infinite within the finite, an Eternal immanent within the human spirit, who cannot be disentangled from the religious self-consciousness for it is one with it and native to it, and indeed cannot be disentangled even from man's consciousness of the world.[2]

Apart altogether from the scientifically questionable method which this theology pursued,[3] it worked with an ultimate premise that Barth insisted on calling in question, namely, that religion is rooted in the

[1] *WW*, p. 196.
[2] Cf. the statement of Schleiermacher: 'We have only to do with God-consciousness given in our self-consciousness along with our consciousness of the world; hence we have no formula for the being of God in Himself as distinct from the being of God in the world . . .' *The Christian Faith*, § 172, p. 748. See also p. 17.   [3] See *CD* II.1, p. 813 for a brief critique of this.

general structure of the spiritual life of man and is but a particular form of it. It was the assumption that the human spirit which inspires all man's great endeavours and pervades the whole of civilisation as its soul has a universal tendency or disposition, a sense of the infinite, a religious *a priori*, giving rise to one of the essential ingredients of culture, namely, religion, and that each religion is but a particular realisation of it, although Christianity must be reckoned its highest and greatest manifestation. If that is so, then what theology is concerned with, is with one of the deepest aspects of human culture, and must be expounded in such a way that its essential relation to the whole life of the human spirit pervading and inspiring man's great achievements is brought out. It follows also that the interpretation of the Christian faith must be carried out in such a way that it is shown to be fundamentally in continuity with the evolution of the human spirit, and therefore its basic tenets and doctrines must be reinterpreted or re-edited to pare away from them any inherited characteristics which might bring them into conflict with the results of the other great *Geisteswissenschaften* and their principles.

In other words, the theology of the nineteenth century carried through on a massive scale the assimilation of Christianity to the prevailing culture of Europe and sought to justify it as part of its full flowering. Writing later of Schleiermacher Karl Barth has said this. 'By birth and upbringing in its innermost sanctuary his theology is cultural theology: in religion itself which is the true object of his theology, it is the exaltation of life in the most comprehensive sense, the exaltation, unfolding, transfiguration, ennobling of the individual and social human life which is at stake. Civilisation as the triumph of the spirit over nature is the most peculiar work of Christianity, just as the quality of being a Christian is for its own part the crown of a thoroughly civilised consciousness.'[1]

Against this Barth directed, among others, two principal charges.

In the first place, he insisted, that by making this apologetic its primary function, that is, by defending the Christian religion as necessary to the development of the human spirit, this theology renounced its proper theological function and indeed made it impossible. That is to say, by making its own theological task subsidiary to the general and major task of civilisation and culture, it failed to take theology seriously as a matter to be pursued for its own sake, as having a subject-matter rational and thinkable in itself and to be investigated in the light of its own interior logic and necessity. Hence it had very little that was positive of

[1] *From Rousseau to Ritschl*, p. 315 f. See also the essay 'The Word in Theology from Schleiermacher to Ritschl', *TC*, pp. 200-216.

its own to offer to the age, and failed to see that an apologetics with scientific integrity could only be one which operated with a mode of rational activity appropriate to the nature of its own subject-matter and therefore one that relied upon its own self-evidence without seeking for justification for itself at the bar of other and different sciences. Hence for all its great productivity the theology of the nineteenth century achieved very little in the long run by way of advancing our positive understanding of Christian doctrine, while on the other hand its apologetic programme which sought to justify the Christian faith within the framework of the validities and conditions of general culture, operated against it and contributed immeasurably to widespread alienation from the Christian Church. The subjection of the Christian message to the interpretation of a general philosophy of the world and of life, and its assimilation to the development of Western culture, so deprived it of its essential character and so thoroughly secularised it, that it became easy to regard it as but a phase of human evolution and then, as the human spirit marched on, as an anachronism to be tolerated in the interests of historical culture or to be put away as a useless survival of the past.

In the second place, Barth pressed home the charge that ultimately the theology of the nineteenth century, and its twentieth-century champions, were more interested in faith than the object and content of faith, more interested in the religious self-awareness than in God.[1] Nineteenth-century theology realised that all theology is concerned with God and man, with man and God, neither with God *in abstracto* nor with man *in abstracto*, but whereas in the classical positive theology of the Fathers and Reformers God was worshipped as God and man regarded as his child and servant, in Neo-Protestantism the central focus of attention and the primary subject of theology was man's own spirit and piety, and God ultimately became little more than the co-determinant of religious feeling or awareness, or the transcendentalised symbol of the religious *a priori* in man, or even the objectification of man's own highest experiences.[2]

In other words, this theology failed to see that theology as man's conversation with God is based absolutely on God's conversation with man, and not the reverse.[3] Therefore even when we take the human pole of that relation seriously we are forced to reach beyond and above

[1] But cf. Barth's appreciation of I. A. Dorner in this respect, *TC*, p. 214f, and *ProtTh*, pp. 526 ff.
[2] See Schleiermacher's *Glaubenslehre* (ET *The Christian Faith*) § 4.
[3] *GGG*, p. 67.

ourselves because we are grasped from above and beyond by One who is not identical with the depth of our own soul but who is none other than God himself. But the nineteenth-century theology grounded its theological activity in the analysis of the human spirit, and in the exploration of personal religious self-consciousness. It sought to move from below upward, but it was ultimately unable to transcend its starting-point, for its very mode of starting, its isolation of man's self-understanding as its primary security and ultimate criterion, deprived it of the Archimedean point whereby it could be lifted above and beyond itself. It became the autonomous judge of its own case and lost the proper criterion of truth. By seeking the meaning of faith in self-comprehension, the Christian message was transposed into an expression of the creative spirituality of man; then God, the real, masterful, living God, who confronts us objectively in Jesus Christ, who actively intervenes in history, coming to us to save and forgive, disappeared behind the clouds of subjectivity and what took his place was a mythical projection out of the depths of religious anthropocentrism.

That is the supreme charge that Barth brought against the theology of Neo-Protestantism, the reduction of all theology to some form of anthropology. The same charge, from quite a different point of view, had already been made by Feuerbach, whose reaction to the idealist Christianity of his age was that it was nothing more than the projection of man's own wishes and of himself into the infinite.[1] The tragedy was that nineteenth-century Christianity had been unable to heed the warning, and even if it had taken Feuerbach seriously it would have been quite unable, on its own premises, to rebut his attack, for it was only too guilty of what he accused it. It was natural knowledge, human religion, the universal spirit of man which constituted for it the presupposition, criterion, and the necessary framework for all understanding of God, of his revelation or reconciliation. Hence all knowledge of God became, as it were, the predicate of what is essentially and universally human, and hence even Revelation could only be acknowledged and handled as a confirmation of man's own latent possibilities or of his own analysis and self-understanding. But in this way nineteenth-century theology made it impossible to derive any benefit from a genuinely transcendent and objective Revelation, for from its very starting-point it stripped the Christian Religion of the specifically *Christian* elements which militated against its humanistic and rationalistic presuppositions,

[1] L. Feuerbach, *The Essence of Christianity*. Cf. the discussion of Barth in *TC*, pp. 217 ff, 212f; and in *From Rousseau to Ritschl*, pp. 355 ff.

so that it could only fall back into the morass of spiritualistic anthropomorphism.

The one point where it could have met that attack was the very point where it was weakest and most confused, in Christology. Barth notes that Christology was the great disturbing element in Schleiermacher's theology—Jesus of Nazareth fitted desperately badly into his theology of the historical 'composite life' of humanity which was after all fundamentally self-sufficient. It was, therefore, at this point that Barth sought to 'have it out' with Schleiermacher and his followers, that is, at the point where our encounter with God is concrete, in decisive historical acts, in the message of forgiveness through the death of Christ, in the seriousness with which God treated man and affirmed him in his creaturely existence and reality, for it is here above all that we can see clearly and decisively that God is not what stands at the end of some human way—of self-analysis or self-consciousness or self-understanding but the God who comes to man and establishes him in an act of divine Grace.

'Jesus is *not* the crowning keystone in the arch of *our* thinking. Jesus is *not* a supernatural miracle that we may or may not consider true. Jesus Christ is *not* the goal which we hope to reach after conversion, at the end of the history of our heart and conscience. Jesus Christ is not a figure of our history to which we may "relate" ourselves. And Jesus Christ is *least of all* an object of religious and mystical experience. So far as He is this to us, He is not Jesus Christ. He is God who becomes man, the Creator of all things who lies as a babe in the manger. But as such He is to be understood by the other fact that He is the one who was crucified, dead, buried, who descended into hell, but rose again from the dead.'[1]

That is the way of forgiveness, the way that God takes with us, the way from God to man and not otherwise. It is there, face to face with Jesus Christ where God's grace assaults us, searches us, questions us, condemns us precisely by forgiving us, that we are confronted by the holy and masterful God whom we cannot subdue to forms of our own self-understanding or domesticate within the realisations of our own religious consciousness, but before whom all our own forms of consciousness and understanding, religious though they be, fall under his judgment and are disqualified—in short, God in his sheer Godness.[2] If it is

---

[1] *WW*, p. 181.
[2] As Thurneysen has recently pointed out (*Ant.*, p. 835 f), it was the teaching of Barth at this stage which first had such a powerful influence on Bonhoeffer: the teaching that God's grace is total in its judgment and that sin is at last contra-

really God whom we confront, can we confront him in any other way? If it is really God who comes to us, does he come to us in any other way than—as God? Jesus, Jesus of Nazareth, is the place we really believe in God, i.e. God who really is God and not just the mythical symbol of what goes on in the depths of our own spirit, for in him we meet with the concrete self-revelation of God in a mighty fulness which cannot be fitted within the general framework of human thought, but which rather constitutes the place where true thinking of God is grounded and moves upward.

The final answer that Barth gave to the anthropocentric theology of the nineteenth century, and to the charge of mythological anthropomorphism levelled against it, was his Christology, that is, his doctrine of God who comes to us in this way, from God to man, in election, and incarnation and salvation—that is, not just Christology as such, but Christology as opening up for us of the *doctrine of God*, Christology as *election*.[1] The concrete action of God in Jesus Christ which is the outgoing of God's own Being is the guarantee that what is subjective will not displace the objective in our human thinking of God. It is the unfolding of that concrete action of God over against us in the humanity of Christ that is the sustained answer to the charges of mythology. Here we may let F. W. Camfield express that for us.

'The doctrine of election alone, as it stands in Barth's exposition, can secure Christology from the reproach of mythology. Mythology arises from man's projection of himself and his world into the sphere of the divine; and it is often asserted that the doctrine of Incarnation is a signal instance of the mythologising process. Here, it is said, is an outstanding case of man being exalted to divine heights. Christology, it is contended, is mythology *par excellence*. And the kind of Christology which would represent the divinity of Christ as a full or exemplary expression of the divinity latent in all men must ever be exposed to the accusation of mythologising. But the conception of the God-man, as it stands in the Biblical doctrine of election, means not the projection of the human into the divine, but the projection of the divine into the human. So far from the God-man establishing man's divinity, it decisively denies it and

---

diction of grace, that grace is therefore the grace of God through the blood of Christ, costly grace, and that all men, religious or secular, within the Church or of the world, come under the same total judgment of grace, that religious man is sinner in the supreme sense of the term, and therefore the Church must recognise its profound solidarity with the world in sin and under grace.

[1] For the philosophical or epistemological significance of this see *FuA*, p. 90 f. See also the valuable discussion of this by Charles West, *Communism and the Theologians*, London 1958, pp. 223 ff.

brings it under a radical judgment. God is manifested, not as the extension to infinity of man's being, but as the entire rejection of man in his empirical actuality. In fact, all mythologising is unmasked as such in the conception of the God-man, and branded as idolatry. And it may very well be asked whether all human thinking which rejects the conception of the God-man can be anything but mythology at last.'[1]

That was written with Barth's great account of election in view, an account which was published years later in the *Church Dogmatics*, but it is precisely that fundamental point that he seized upon and made his own at this stage in his *Auseinandersetzung* with Neo-Protestantism.

(b) Another powerful element in Barth's teaching is the profound and realistic conception of *sin*. The influences upon Barth are obvious and clearly acknowledged, Luther's notion of sin *coram Deo*, Kierkegaard's teaching in *Either/Or, Sickness unto Death, The Concept of Dread, Fear and Trembling* and *Training into Christianity*, J. Müller's *The Christian Doctrine of Sin*, one of the best works from the nineteenth century on the subject, the trenchant novels of Dostoevski burdened with the awareness of guilt and also, it would appear (although it is not mentioned) Kähler's doctrine of the irrational, surd-like, element in sin. And yet to read the sections in the *Römerbrief* makes it clear that Barth's teaching here is derived above all from facing up to the blunt, uncompromising message of St Paul.

Barth began his academic thinking, as we saw, under the guiding lights of Kant and Schleiermacher—that is the context in which he had, in part at least, to think about sin. That is to say, on the one hand, the question of ethics, even the problem of radical evil, was the question in which the nineteenth century saw expressed the peculiar greatness and dignity of man, but on the other hand, the problem it involved required 'explanation' and, inevitably within the context of romantic idealism, aided and abetted by evolutionism, it was explained naturally. Kant and Schleiermacher stood for those two things, but Barth's questioning of them took him down to the bed-rock, and in that he was aided on his part by Kierkegaard's insistence that these questions must be examined *sub specie aeterni*, or, to use Luther's terminology, *coram Deo*.

On the one hand, then, Barth faced up to the problem of ethics as posed by Kant, but sharpened it by looking at it from the ultimate perspective of eternity. This meant that the ethical question was not cut short by relating it to this or that proximate end or goal, but to the end or goal beyond all these, to the standard which is not a part of our

[1] F. W. Camfield, *Reformation Old and New*, p. 85.

existence as we know or conceive it but to the absolute presupposition of our existence, to the truth about Truth—in that light the good as well as the evil became problematic, for all actual and possible forms of conduct were called in question. That is what happens when we look at the question of ethics in God's sight. But that means that instead of finding a witness to man's peculiar greatness and dignity we are confronted unavoidably with the ultimate character of the perplexity and embarrassment and uncertainty under which man is placed by the ethical question —that is the cardinal question of man's existence. It is not only the question about evil but the question about the good which always entails a judgment on man as we know him, even about moral man. But what is more, man is not only questioned here, he must himself ask the question, and in so doing annihilates himself. 'Man condemns himself to death by his question about the good, because the only certain answer is that he, man, is *not* good, and from the view-point of the good, is powerless.'[1] Or, to use Kierkegaard's language, the problem of ethics is not only of the sickness of man but of a sickness unto death.[2]

Looked at in that light, the whole of modern Protestantism was utterly questionable, and the Christianity it advocated, for it was fused to an ethic which could not stand up to questioning, and was indeed already tumbling down before the scepticism of modern man about himself and his moral goals. Thus the ethics of Ritschlianism was obviously the ethics of the bourgeoisie growing prosperous, and the ethics of Troeltsch the ethics of the new economic civilisation.[3] But behind all that the ethical question made religious man in any and every form utterly problematic, for it was concerned with the very roots of his existence. And yet, in ethics itself, there is no answer at all to the cardinal question it entails. That was discerned even by Kant, Barth notes, who saw man claimed by a demand upon his natural will which he is wholly unable to realise except by a still more amazing act of faith.[4] Kant himself does not seem to have wrestled adequately with the difficulty it involved, which is, according to Barth, the fact that ethics cannot exist without the notion of the millennium but by that Barth means something very different from Kant's kingdom of the practical reason or the kingdom of ends advocated by the neo-Kantians and Ritschlians; rather is it, as we see all over the pages of the *Romans*, the sheer eschatological kingdom of the grace of God which is yet hope as reality here *on earth*.[5]

In other words, the only answer to all our questions here is God

---

[1] *WW*, p. 167; cf. 140, 147.   [2] *WW*, p. 150.
[3] P. 145.   [4] P. 155.   [5] Pp. 156ff.

himself, and *God's conduct* toward us—that is, in *grace* and the way it takes with our concrete existence on earth, the justification of the ungodly.[1] Hence in Barth's dialectical questioning, he is forced in the nature of the case before him to turn about and let his questions be those directed to him by God, that is, to let God's positive relation to man be both the supreme question and the supreme answer to human existence. This is the most radical and profound approach of all, from the side of grace alone. There is no doubt that Kierkegaard's break-through from ethics to grace, that is to forgiveness and Christianity, and his analysis of man's sin as the dread wound in his existence which he cannot heal, but which is both revealed and healed by grace, lies behind much of Barth's thinking, especially as it comes out in the sustained exposition of man's existence in sin, that is, of sin as a determination of fallen man's existence before God. And there cannot be any doubt about it, that here the whole question of sin is approached in the most profound way from the side of grace, so that for all his emphasis upon its total and radical nature and upon the completely lost condition of man, there is no trace of any misanthropic tendencies, but rather of the reverse. If evil and sin are understood only in the light of grace, then the last word, the last triumphant word, is undoubtedly that of grace and of new creation, a word of immense optimism.[2]

Looked at from this, the theological point of view, sin is seen to be essentially a *religious category*—and here at once, the blind-alleys of Neo-Protestant ethics as reposing in man's higher nature and therefore as intrinsically intelligible to him, and of the Neo-Protestant doctrine of sin as the 'not-yet', or of evil as anachronism, and therefore as explainable naturally, are by-passed and a road is opened with a real goal in view. But the road of grace is a very difficult road for man, for grace lays the axe to the root of the whole of human existence; it slays man in order that he may be made alive. Such is the way in which God has conducted himself toward us in the crucifixion and resurrection of Jesus Christ, and that is the way that really opens the road for ethics, for a *true* way of human life before God. 'In point of fact, it is grace alone that is competent to provide men with a truly ethical disturbance; and if grace is to perform this function, it must be treated as covering the whole field of human life, and must be permitted to make that absolute assault upon men without which ethics are completely meaningless.'[3]

[1] Pp. 169ff.
[2] Here again Barth's thought coincides with the message of Blumhardt. Cf. here G. C. Berkouwer, *The Triumph of Grace in the Theology of Karl Barth*, ET London 1956. [3] *Romans*, p. 430.

E

Looked at from the point of view of grace, sin is seen as a totality over against the totality of grace, and sin is seen to affect at its root the fundamental relation that makes man man, namely his relation with God. Hence here we have a really profound as well as a deeply moving account of sin and man's existence in sin, that is, of sin as the fundamental determination of man as we actually find him in the fallen world, and as God has actually dealt with him in Jesus Christ.

Man is not only one who sins, but he *is* a sinner—sinful man is the old kind of man we know in this world. Sin is thus a power in actual human existence as such, controlling and shaping man's being and life. Man's actual sins are the means whereby his fundamental status or condition is made manifest, and from that point of view it may be said that the particular forms sin takes are irrelevant, for they all reveal that man *is* a sinner before God. But this sinful state Barth describes, borrowed in a way of speaking from Anselm, as *robbery of God*. 'Clearly—and this lies already in the word "Fall"—God is here deserted and denied by men; He suffers and is robbed. Sin is robbing God of what He is: and because it is a robbing of God, sin is essentially the appearance in the world of a power-like God. Sin is an invisible negative occurrence encountered by God.'[1] This is 'a robbery which becomes apparent in our arrogant endeavour to cross the line of death by which we are bounded; in our drunken blurring of the distance which separates us from God; in our forgetfulness of His invisibility; in our investing of men with the form of God and of God with the form of man; and in our devotion to some romantic infinity, some "No-God" of this world, which we have created for ourselves. And all the time we are oblivious that we must die in ungodliness and unrighteousness. In its visible and concrete form sin is the disturbing of the relationship with God which is defined by death. However, this concrete and historical aspect of sin points to another aspect which is neither historical nor concrete. Death forms the limit of our life and marks the boundary between us and God. But since God is not death, but the life of the Coming Day, there is a different way of looking at sin. In its non-concrete and non-historical aspect, sin is robbery, in the sense that it is the falling of men out of direct relationship with God, the rending asunder of the spiritual band which unites God with the world and with men, the Creator with His creation. It is an assumption of independence in which God is forgotten. It is the sophisticated, pretentious, unchildlike, wisdom of the serpent: Hath God said?—a wisdom to which men attend, and which produces an

[1] *Romans*, p. 177.

unreal aloofness from God who is the Life of our life. In its concrete form sin is no more than the ever-widening appearance and the expression and abounding in time of this Original Fall. But there is also another invisible significance attaching to sin. It is *ungodliness and unrighteousness* of men, since it damages the living relationship between God and man, and appropriates to itself the madness of the devil—*eritis sicut deus (ye shall be as God)*.'[1]

Barth wishes to stress several things about this account of sin revealed by the Gospel of the righteousness of God.

(1) Sin has become a world power—that is to say, the whole of our existence is conditioned by sin, so that there has come into being a *cosmos* determined by the fact that it has somehow broken loose from God. And that is reflected within us in that we live in contradiction, in this breaking-apart of a 'world without' from a 'world within'; we live our life in a cosmic movement towards independence from God, of a world in which things try to exist in their own right, a world of principalities and thrones and dominations. This may take the form of divinised worldliness or worldly divinity, but whichever way we take it, it is a perversion of what God made. 'The only glory of the Creator which remains is that by which this independent validity is limited, for these things do in fact contain their own criticism. They are in fact open to question; for the possibility, even the necessity, of their dissolution is latent in them. That is to say, what they are points to what they are not; and the only possibility of perceiving the glory of God is that perception which operates *sub specie mortis*.'[2]

(2) That is another aspect of the matter that Barth stresses, the fact that death is the reverse of sin, and so shows where man's life is broken off from God, where it is bounded in its guilt, and imprisoned within its self-will. But if so, it is death which makes clear the relationship of man to God—the negative, broken relationship under judgment. Looked at in this light man is seen to have an existence that is bounded by non-existence, limited by divine judgment, and therefore relative. But this negative relationship points to God, by relating the temporality and relativity of man's existence to what is beyond it and limits it. The very perplexity of man, the wound in his existence, arises from the fact of God, against whom man has rebelled. 'Our life is confronted with a steep precipice, towering above us, hemming us in on every side, and on it are hewn the words: *All things come to an end*. And yet in all their

---

[1] *Romans*, p. 167f.   [2] *Romans*, p. 169.

negativity there is no point which does not bear witness to the summit
—"whence Adam fell" (Luther). There is no relativity which does not
reflect a vanished absolute which can never be wholly obliterated, since
it is this absolute which makes relativity relative. Death never occurs
but it calls attention to our participation in the Life of God and to that
relationship of His with us which is not broken by sin. The thought of
Life and of God is stirred in us by death—by the reality of death, not
by our experience of it.'[1]

(3) But further, man's sin, as revealed in death, is bounded and
limited by the judgment of God, man's temporal existence by eternity.
Therefore sin must be looked at from the side of *God's* action—that is
from the side of predestination, of an inescapable presupposition which
underlies every human event and conditions every human status. It is the
Fall as seen from the divine judgment over and on it, the Fall meeting
a *prius* in God upon which it pivots and from which it derives a fateful,
unavoidable character; it is a past under judgment which determines the
present, an outer and inner situation under which man has fallen prisoner, and which confronts him as *anangkē* or a necessary destiny.[2]

In other words, this is the law of sin which brings forth death, and
which reveals that the whole of our concrete and observable existence is
sinful. The recognition of that fact, together with the recognition of our
finiteness and brokenness over against God is what Barth calls *religion*—
and to religion he contrasts *grace*.[3] Religion, here, describes, for the
most part, the negative relation of man to God, and grace describes the
positive relation between them which arises from the side of God. Religion carries us to the very brink of human possibilities, but there it calls
a halt at the frontier of existence enclosed by a final and unresolved
question, in terrible awareness of the reality of death and its visible
sovereignty that points backward to the invisible sovereignty of sin.
'It is religion, then, which sets a question-mark against every system of
human culture; and religion is a genuine experience. But what do men
experience in religion? In religion men know themselves to be conditioned invisibly by sin. In religion the Fall of mankind out of its primal
union with God becomes the presupposition of all human vitality.'[4]

It is precisely within religion that sin takes on its supreme form, so
that Barth can speak of religion as the loftiest summit in the land of sin.
Religion is both the expression of man's utmost possibility and of his
limitation, and therefore it halts us in order that God may confront us

---

[1] *Romans*, p. 170.   [2] *Romans*, pp. 173 f, 179.
[3] See further *ChrD*, pp. 301 ff.   [4] *Romans*, p. 244.

on the other side of the frontier of religion. But here the vitality of man presses forward into the sphere of religion, and there takes place a rebellion of creatures against the Creator, for in pressing over the boundary they become to themselves what God ought to be to them. 'Transforming time into eternity, and therefore eternity into time, they stretch themselves beyond the boundary of death, rob the Unknown God of what He is, push themselves into His domain, and depress Him to their own level. Forgetting the awful gulf by which they are separated from Him, they enter upon a relation with Him which would be possible only if He were not God. They make Him a thing of this world, and set Him in the midst of other things. All this occurs quite manifestly and observably within the possibility of religion.'[1]

Grace, on the other hand, means that God reckons man's whole existence to be his and claims it for himself and therefore constitutes the positive re-ligio or re-binding of man to God. As such grace is the divine possibility for man that breaks into his life, but it is not in any sense a human possibility for men side by side with other human possibilities, but is rather the divine possibility which reveals to man that he has no human possibility for God, and therefore robs him of any possibility of his in that direction. 'Grace as the power and authority of God over men, can never be identified with the actions or with the passivity of the men of the world. Grace is the unobservable truth of men: it is their impossibility, which constitutes the veritable possibility of their acting or not acting; it is their veritable existence, which can be defined as non-existence. The man who is under grace has this contradiction in himself. Grace is not "something" which man has in himself, it is that which God has in him, by which the man of sin is contradicted. Since, however, we know only the man of sin, this contradiction contradicts all men, and it contradicts ourselves. We are therefore compelled to say quite definitely that to possess grace does not mean to be this or that, or to do or not to do this or that. The possession of grace means the existential submission to God's contradiction of all that we ourselves are or are not, of all that we do or do not do.'[2]

In this event, the worst thing that man could do would be to try and construct a religion of his own out of grace, for that would be an attempt to convert grace, which by its very nature is man's divine possibility lying beyond all human possibility, into something within the realm of human possibilities—then it would not be grace at all. But that is just what modern Protestant theology sought to do—to treat the experience

[1] *Romans*, p. 216.   [2] *Romans*, p. 216.

of grace as the prolongation of an already existing religious experience,[1] or as something that can be dovetailed in with other human possibilities and understood within the frontiers of finite existence fenced in by death and shut out from God, and where any movement to cross the frontier on man's part is robbery of God, and the titanism of sin. Barth cannot, therefore, avoid the conclusion that this kind of religion and this kind of theology are forms of sin, and are modern manifestations of what Paul found in Judaism when he said that the Law could be the very strength of sin, and that with the coming of the Law, that is, with religion, and indeed ethical religion, sin burst forth. It is, however, only under grace that we can know this, for grace is the crisis of religion; by breaking in upon man as the only possibility for man and his salvation, it exposes all religion that contains at its heart the essential notion of sin: *eritis sicut Deus*.

And yet grace is the divine possibility for man, and therefore it not only reveals the positive truth of religion in the operation of God's Spirit, but also breaks through both mysticism and morality to bring man under the divine claim and so bring what is impossible within the realm of the possible for man. Grace is the establishment of the positive truth of religion. It is the establishment of the Law. It is the establishment of ethics.[2]

There are two points in Barth's discussion of sin within the dialectic of religion and grace that we must note, for they were later repudiated by him entirely. The *first* is the idea that the sin which entered the world through Adam is timeless and transcendental, the doctrine of a non-temporal Fall of all men from their union with God (Kant), as the backward movement of the race, while in Christ the Second Adam goes forward victoriously (Schleiermacher); the *second* is the existentialist conception of religion as a determination of man's wounded and perplexed existence, of sin as bound up with temporality and finiteness over against the lost God, and of the negative determinant in man as pointing to a positive or of the relative to the absolute which limits it. Similar views were held by Brunner, Gogarten, and Bultmann, in their several ways, and it is not surprising that in their critique of prevailing tendencies they were often regarded as belonging to the same movement. Both of these ideas, however, represent an appreciable element in Barth's, confessedly

---

[1] Cf. the *Briefwechsel* between Harnack and Peterson in 1928 (republished by Peterson in 1950) in which Peterson points out that it is this element in Protestant pietism which led him into the Roman Church, i.e. the stress on *indwelling-grace, Theologische Traktate*, p. 316 f.

[2] See Barth's discussion of 'the power of obedience', *Romans*, pp. 207-228.

misguided, contribution to existentialist theology, which he was forced to eradicate when he had to think through the problems he made for himself in the *Christliche Dogmatik*. Brunner, of course, stood much closer to Barth than either Gogarten or Bultmann, and, after all, the negative point of contact which Brunner employed in his eristic theology is already apparent in Barth's analysis of man's existence in the *Römerbrief*.

(c) Another dominant motif in Barth's thinking which it will be instructive for us to examine is *eschatology*. As we have already seen, the immediate influence upon Barth which helped to open his eyes to this masterful aspect of the biblical witness was that of Blumhardt and of Overbeck: Blumhardt's teaching about the supernatural Kingdom of God which had invaded this world in Jesus Christ in divine compassion for our humanity, and Overbeck's insistence on the essentially eschatological character of Christian faith which had been persistently obscured in the history of the Christian Church through its assimilation into the secular sphere of civilisation and culture. Nor must we forget the contribution to this eschatology of Johannes Weiss's notion of the life of the Church 'between the times'.[1] This strong eschatological note Barth had also found, among other earlier theologians and commentators, in the writings of J. A. Bengel. Once he committed himself to it a whole new world opened for him in the Bible, and he found he was carried far beyond anything he had dreamed or could grasp—the volcanic effect of that was expressed in such publications as the *Romans* and *The Resurrection from the Dead*.

This new direction of Barth's thought must also be looked on as part of a wider movement in which he came to share, which was bound up particularly with the application of scientific exegesis to the New Testament which forced scholars and interpreters to acknowledge, no doubt often against their own will, the thoroughly eschatological nature of the Message of Jesus. In addition to the work of Overbeck, there must also be mentioned particularly the influential writings of Johannes Weiss, especially his work on *The Preaching of Jesus concerning the Kingdom of God*, published in 1892, and of Albert Schweitzer in his famous *Quest of the Historical Jesus*, as it is called in English, first published in 1906.

In order to understand the significance of this rediscovery of eschatology for Barth's thinking and his own contribution to it, we must glance

---

[1] *Zwischen den Zeiten*, 'Between the Times' was the name given to the periodical to which Barth and many of his friends or would-be friends contributed in the early years until it was superseded by *Theologische Existenz heute* in 1933.

back at Schleiermacher and the attitude of the nineteenth-century theology, and its twentieth-century continuation, to eschatology. The astonishing thing about it, as we look back upon it, is that it was so uneschatological, partly because it was quite blind to it, but partly because it deeply resented certain aspects of the biblical and early Christian witness bound up with it.

It is Schleiermacher who provides us with the key to understanding this tradition. Basic to all his thinking was a radical dichotomy between the *sensuous* and the *spiritual*, the realm of physical events and the realm of consciousness. It was the realm of the spirit and of consciousness that was fundamentally and ultimately real, and from within that realm the world of sense appeared to lack reality and required interpretation and transvaluation through being taken up into the realm of the spirit and consciousness. This determination to transmute the sensuous into the spiritual affected every aspect of Schleiermacher's thought; Ethics,[1] for example, in which he saw sin and evil to be the opposition of the flesh to the spirit, and so demanded its spiritualisation; or *Hermeneutics*,[2] where the hiatus in the New Testament texts between the grammatical and the spiritual required to be bridged through psychological penetration and a divining and reconstructing of its meaning. This was particularly the problem of the theologian at work upon the tenets of the Christian faith and the traditional doctrines and dogmas of the Church. In the biblical tradition the spiritual is presented to us in forms that are bound up with the physical, the sensuous and the concrete, but from within the realm of the spirit and of purified self-consciousness, sensuous thinking is regarded as rather crude and as giving rise to mythological notions which require to be reinterpreted as determinations of the religious self-consciousness. Hence doctrines are to be defined as accounts of these determinations set forth in speech.[3] In *The Christian Faith* this was given careful exposition working with an epistemology which carried over in Schleiermacher's peculiar way Kantian presuppositions, in a distinction between objectifiable and non-objectifiable being, or objective and non-objective consciousness. All comprehension

---

[1] See *Philosophische Ethik*, § 46.

[2] *Hermeneutik und Kritik, mit besonderer Beziehung auf das Neue Testament*, especially part 2, 'Die Psychologische Auslegung'. Cf. *TC*, p. 168 f; and Barth's letter of Feb. 5, 1924, *Gd-Md*.

[3] *The Christian Faith*, Introduction, ch. I. See especially the exposition of this given by F. Flückiger, *Philosophie und Theologie bei Schleiermacher*, 1947, and the article by P. Löffler, 'Selbstbewusstsein und Selbstverständnis als theologische Principien bei Schleiermacher und Bultmann' in *Kerygma und Dogma*, 2.4, 1956, pp. 304ff.

of God beyond the self-consciousness is only possible *symbolically* and is to be taken as the reflection of self-consciousness. Schleiermacher will allow no concept of the objective reality of God to be formed, for there are no objective acts of God vis-à-vis faith—the only reality we are concerned with is that which is a co-determinate of the human spirit, and co-existent with it in its self-consciousness.[1]

The sequel to this is clear. If the great acts of God proclaimed in the New Testament *kerygma* and articulated in the *dogmas* of the Church are to be reinterpreted as determinations of the religious self-consciousness, and their objective elements are to be understood only symbolically, then the historical, sensuous elements inhering in both kerygma and dogma have to be transposed into 'spiritual' forms; but this carries with it the elimination from Christian thinking of the action of God in history, the breaking of the eternal into time and space, and betokens a docetic flight from the concrete existence and historical involvement of man realistically conceived. Hence in the heirs of this thoroughly idealistic reinterpretation of Christianity we find a consistent animus against what they term the 'mythological' from the point of view of those who operate with such a radical (but false) dichotomy between a realm of sense and event, and a realm of spirit and idea.

That is particularly apparent in the great scion of this movement in the twentieth century, Adolf von Harnack, who obviously had a horror of all corporeality, and so both misunderstood and vigorously attacked the realistic emphasis in the New Testament and in the Early Church upon externality and somatic existence. Hence some of the great terms of the faith such as *sōma, physis, sarx, thanatos, zōē, anastasis*, etc. were offensive to him. Belief in miracles, that is in the action of God in our flesh and blood existence, was painful—but behind it all, as Barth has pointed out, Harnack had a horror of the being of God in his revelation, of the being and action of God in history and in the midst of humanity.[2]

This is both a refusal to acknowledge the historico-ontological element in the biblical message, and an evasion of the actuality of divine revelation on the ground that it is an 'unscientific conception', and so Harnack's exegesis, historical interpretation and theology were all designed to strip away the realism of the New Testament, but that is to strip away from it entirely all possibility of eschatology and ultimately all relevance of the Gospel to human existence in the flesh.

---

[1] *The Christian Faith*, § 4.
[2] *CD* I.2, p. 130f. See again the illuminating exchange of letters between Harnack and Barth in 1923, republished in *FuA*, pp. 22ff and p. 31.

The publication by Harnack of his Berlin lectures of 1900 (*What is Christianity ?*) marked perhaps the height of the uneschatological interpretation of the Gospel, and the beginning of its end. The contrast with Barth could hardly be greater with his realistic proclamation of the incarnation and of the resurrection as a *new corporeality*, and upon Revelation as absolute actuality, behind which lay a new determination to take with the utmost seriousness the doctrine of God as Creator and Redeemer of men, and to relate the ends and actions of God fully and realistically to concrete human existence and history.[1] That is, in many ways, the antithesis of idealism. It is significant, therefore, that it was through his sharp conflict with the *ethic* of his Neo-Protestant teachers that Barth was forced to question radically all their exegetical, historical and dogmatic interpretations of the Gospel.[2]

It will be helpful now to describe on a wide front the change in European theology toward an appreciation of eschatology in order to see the place of Barth's thought in the midst of it—and here it will be necessary to carry our discussion of his own development beyond this second stage which engages our attention at the moment.[3]

In the forefront of the return to the understanding of the eschatological character of the New Testament stand the names of Overbeck, Johannes Weiss and Schweitzer, though the influence of the last named has been most potent in the English-speaking world. The 'discovery' associated with these scholars was that the New Testament teaching is lodged within an eschatological scheme which gives to each doctrine its peculiar form. Or to put it the other way round, the New Testament thought-world has a pattern or framework which gives its otherwise varied character an essential unity, so that the individual ideas and doctrines that come up fall within its orbit and have their deepest meaning in relation to its central point. This central point is declared to be a specially modified form of late-Jewish apocalyptic eschatology. This means that as against the uneschatological views of men like von Harnack the New Testament must be interpreted in a thorough-going or consistent eschatological fashion. And further as late-Jewish apocalyptic eschatology was essentially futurist and catastrophic in character, we must regard the Kingdom of God in the Gospel as purely future and abruptly supernatural. Jesus, it is said, expected only an eschatological realisation of the Kingdom, and therefore in our interpreta-

---

[1] Cf. *The Resurrection of the Dead*, pp. 123f, 201, etc.
[2] Cf. *WW*, 'The Problem of Ethics Today', pp. 136ff.
[3] For the following see *The Evangelical Quarterly*, 1953, pp. 45ff, 94ff, 167ff, 224ff 'The Modern Eschatological Debate'.

tion of his message everything must be projected into the coming age.

Schweitzer's views have had enormous influence, particularly in destroying those reconstructions of the Gospel which chose to ignore the eschatological sayings of Jesus in an attempt to set him forth as the central figure of the Kingdom of God on earth regarded merely as a social and ethical movement in history and reaching out through human progress to an end in some idealistic Utopia. But there can be no doubt that Schweitzer overstated his case, and gave a very one-sided account of the New Testament. He ignored almost entirely the element of teleology in the teaching of Jesus with its roots in the prophetic teaching of the Kingdom. At the same time it is simply not true that the teaching of Jesus had only a future reference, as William Manson, Edwyn Hoskins, C. H. Dodd and others have in their various ways made very clear, for there is a constant insistence upon the fact that the Kingdom has already broken in upon humanity, while throughout the New Testament, as both the Blumhardts were not slow to point out, there is a joyful sense of the victorious presence of God among men in Jesus Christ and in the pouring out of his Spirit upon them. He is the King of the Kingdom, and is here now through his Spirit to redeem and save by the finger of God. What is at stake ultimately in Schweitzer's view is the doctrine of Christ, for a Jesus who is so utterly deluded as the figure of Schweitzer's reconstruction, who dies with a despairing cry when events take an unforeseen course, bears little relation either to the New Testament witness or the faith of the Church in him as very Son of God.

But behind all this, it must be said that Schweitzer misunderstood the nature of eschatology itself when he thought of it only in a narrow apocalyptist sense. Indeed again and again it would appear that in eschatology Schweitzer saw little more than a primitive cosmology. Therefore, when he set the Gospels in a thoroughly eschatological setting that really meant that it was set in the midst of an apocalyptic scenery which, so far as he could see, was simply bound up with unscientific views of the world. It is not surprising, therefore, that he rejected eschatology almost *in toto* as primitive mythology, nor surprising that if his scholarship forced him to declare the New Testament to be eschatological from end to end that he should think of the story of the Church as the story of a progressive elimination of eschatology—a view which was taken up and developed by Martin Werner. Schweitzer himself carried that position to its ultimate conclusion which significantly ends—in the amazing contrast with his own superb Christian life and service—in the rather trivial declaration of faith as reverence for life.

Schweitzer's interpretation of the New Testament was elaborated in opposition to the uneschatological views of the nineteenth-century theology and of von Harnack, but it is all too apparent that Schweitzer failed because he operated with similar romantic-idealist and rationalist assumptions which prevented him from thinking through the eschatological message of the New Testament radically.[1] Two chief presuppositions inherited from the nineteenth century must be noted. The first is manifest in the influence of impressionistic art upon hermeneutics —the influence of men like Herder, and Lessing and Schleiermacher. Until modern times the interpreter confronted with a text sought to look with the author at what he was observing, and if he succeeded in doing that, through following what he found in the text, he claimed to understand him. But in the nineteenth century, men began to be interested in a text as a work of art, and they studied it to see what it revealed in the soul of the author, not primarily for what he was trying to communicate but for what he revealed of himself. Thus hermeneutics tended to be called an *art*, as by Schleiermacher, and empathy, fellow-feeling, the endeavour to reproduce in one's own soul the vitality and creative spirituality out of which the author's work arose, were to be employed in interpreting it. They constitute the art of breaking through the veil of sense into the realm of spirit. Applied to the interpretation of the New Testament, to the writings of St Paul, or even to the Gospels, ultimately the important thing was not to look with the writers at what they were looking at or claimed to look at, that is, at the objective subject-matter, but to see what was going on in their souls which led them to express themselves in this exciting and daring way. What they were doing was to use already existing methods of expression in order to break a way through to an entirely different conception of life, and therefore we have to interpret them as employing an impressionistic use of archaisms. We cannot get any value out of their communication unless we pass through and beyond their archaisms and share in the new direction of life and thought which they opened up. It was only in this way, Schweitzer felt, that we could get across to Jesus or let Jesus get across to us without secretly turning him into a nineteenth- or twentieth-century figure who is only too harmless and familiar. Our task as interpreters of the Evangelists, then, to use Schweitzer's musical metaphor, is 'to tune in' to

[1] Schweitzer's views are worth comparing at this point with Bergson's Vitalism and his theory of art.

their spirit, to assimilate their outlook, and so reproduce in ourselves, and in our modern conditions as they did in theirs, the creative spirituality revealed in their presentation or portrait of Jesus.

The second presupposition goes back to the radical dichotomy between the sensuous and the spiritual which we noted in Schleiermacher, and which goes back ultimately to the thoroughly Hellenic distinction between the sensible world and the intelligible world of the real that has dominated modern European philosophy. Applied to the interpretation of the New Testament, this did not mean for Schweitzer as it did for von Harnack that we have to strip away from the New Testament message what is impossible and incompatible with our rational and scientific assumptions, but rather that we must face the New Testament as it confronts us in all its stark realism, but while we cannot accept for ourselves what is described so vividly as the coming of God into space and time, and of God's agony on the Cross, of God's mighty acts in resurrection, ascension, and *parousia* and the like, we must treat it like a painting of Van Gogh and let it speak to us out of its sheer dramatic force, until we tune in to it, and so leap across the centuries to participate in the basic *Weltanschauung* of the early Christians—it does not matter whether we can put that into words or formulate it in rational propositions; what is important is to be assimilated to the spirit of the anonymous 'Jesus'; and live and act accordingly. The function of the New Testament on this view is not really to offer teaching or doctrine, not to communicate a word which we can fully understand, but so to present things that we may act on them in a specific way, that is, to change the idiom to that used by Bultmann, that we may find 'authentic existence'.

According to Schweitzer the great stubborn fact upon which everything turns is the failure of the Kingdom of God to come in the first generation as the Gospels said it would. The recognition of that fact opens our eyes to see that the stark realism of the New Testament is not to be taken literally but is to be reinterpreted, as we have expressed it, impressionistically. Hence the great problem that faces the Church, and has always faced the Church throughout its long history, is to adjust itself to the actual fact that the Kingdom of God did not come as the early Christians expected. Unfortunately Schweitzer's way of propounding the problem has set a great deal of the modern discussion off upon a false scent, but even when we see that his conclusion and his problem derive from false premises, we must nevertheless acknowledge that he has done very great service to biblical studies in calling attention to the thoroughly eschatological nature of early Christian faith, and exposing the traditional reconstructions of 'the historical Jesus' as but a 'Jesus' dressed up in the philosophy and culture of modern man.

The great turning-point in modern understanding of eschatology after Schweitzer came undoubtedly with the publication of Barth's *Romans*. Here the problem of Schweitzer was solved by what appeared to be a 'timeless eschatology'. It was pointed out that in Schweitzer's sense the New Testament is not eschatological in a thorough-going way for the stress is as much upon the present as upon the future. The end of history is not to be interpreted as an end within time as we know it, for no end within time can be a real or complete end. The end is also the beginning, and so the nearness of the end is interpreted as the transcendental relation of the present to its origin in the eternal.[1]

Barth has described his own teaching at that time in this way: 'When I came to expound a passage like Rom. 13.11 f ("Now it is high time to awake out of sleep; for now is our salvation nearer than when we believed. The night is far spent, the day is at hand."), in spite of every precaution I interpreted it as if it referred only to the moment which confronts all moments in time as the eternal "transcendental meaning" of all moments in time. The tension between the "then" which we believed and the "now" of "disturbing recollection", a new awareness of Christ's *parousia*, was only a continual tension, having no connexion with the tension of the two points in time and the time of Church history. The "last" hour, the time of eternity, was not an hour which followed time. Rather at every moment in time we stood before the frontier of all time, the frontier of "qualified time". . . . I missed the distinctive feature of the passage, the teleology which it ascribes to time as it moves towards a real end.'[2]

In spite of Barth's own self-criticism, it must be noted that the notion of a near *parousia*, far from being part of the mythological element that must be left behind, was regarded as an essential part of the content of faith itself. It depends upon the infinite qualitative distinction between time and eternity and is just as essential and real for faith as time and eternity. Such a view of eschatology as timeless crisis appeared to empty history of its worth, that is, of its teleology, and there was definite reaction against it even by those who like Althaus learned from it. Over against Schweitzer, however, the significance of Barth's early view was this, that whereas for Schweitzer eschatology was only the time-conditioned mould in which the thought of the New Testament was expressed, for Barth eschatology has to do with the very roots of faith and

[1] See *The Resurrection of the Dead*, pp. 110ff.   [2] *CD* II.1, p. 635.

belongs to the inner core of the Gospel. We cannot therefore slough it off either in Harnackian or Schweitzerian fashion in favour of some essence which remains uncontaminated by it or some anonymous spirit to which we may tune in by means of it. In this respect Barth completed the revolution made by Weiss and Schweitzer in biblical studies, and indeed it can be said that it is just because he took it full circle that his thought did not run out at last into triviality.

Then came another change on Barth's part. He soon discovered that the position he had formulated in his commentary on Romans and other early writings, necessary as it was at that stage in several ways, was actually untenable, both because it did not square with the New Testament emphasis upon Incarnation, and space and time, and because it involved contradictorily enough a dialectic between time and eternity that cut across the essentially eschatological tension of faith. The result was that Barth gave up what was called a 'timeless eschatology', and set himself to take seriously the New Testament teaching of an imminent advent of the Kingdom in time and yet to see that as belonging to the inner core of faith. This meant that the real eschatological tension was not interpreted in terms of an eternity/time dialectic, which always means in the end a refusal to take time seriously, but rather in terms of tension between the new and the old, of a *new time* in reconciliation and union with the eternal and an *old time* which is the time of this fallen world and which through sin exists in mysterious contradiction to God. Here the whole content of eschatology is thought through Christologically in terms of the Incarnation, the God-Manhood of Christ, the events of the Crucifixion, Resurrection, Ascension and final Advent. In this way eschatology is a thorough-going expression of the doctrine of grace as it concerns history, while the important word is not *eschaton* but *Eschatos*, that is, Christ who is both *Prōtos* and *Eschatos*, the First and the Last.[1]

As we look back over his early writings, it is difficult to say that this Christological understanding of eschatology was not there in some measure from early in the Safenwil period, but there can be no doubt about the fact that it was during the Göttingen and Münster period that he came to carry through a Christological correction of the whole of his thinking and so to think through again his early emphasis upon the relation of the Gospel to the concrete existence of man realistically in the light of the new corporeality of the resurrection. Or to put it the other way round, this anchored eschatology for Barth more securely

[1] This is already apparent in *The Resurrection of the Dead.*

than ever in the very heart of his theology and at the same time gave eschatology greater and more urgent bearing upon the whole of man's life in his concrete embodiment in space and time here and now as well as in the fulfilment of God's creative and redemptive purposes.

It is of considerable interest to note the impact of Barth's early eschatology upon the history of thought on the subject. Tillich with his *kairos*-philosophy, and later Bultmann with his reduction of New Testament anthropology to the terms of an existentialist philosophy, considered Barth an ally to their own views, and appropriated not a little from his eschatological dialectic of crisis, while others, starting at the stage of the *Römerbrief*, and often in reaction against important parts of it, took over some of the very elements which Barth cast off, and continued to develop an eschatology which was mainly concerned with the dialectic between time and eternity, not always with the sharpness of Barth's early 'infinite qualitative distinction between time and eternity', but nevertheless in a doctrine of timeless crisis, which is anti-evolutionary and non-teleological. It is difficult not to see the advocates of 'realised eschatology' as well as Bultmann, Tillich, and the Niebuhrs falling within this general category. From Barth's point of view, however, the gulf that separates his teaching from the view of these men is as great as, and not fundamentally different from, that which separates him from the theology of romantic-idealist Neo-Protestantism. The core of the difference lies in the realism of his Christology, and therefore in *the doctrine of God*—for it is in Jesus that he has learned to believe as he does in the *Father* who so cares for man that he will not live without him and who so loves him that he insists on respecting and affirming man in his creaturely existence in space and time, even when sharing with him his own divine life.

(*d*) A fourth aspect of Barth's theology in this second and transitional stage was the *dialectical thinking* he employed which became so notorious that it gave rise to the description of his position as 'dialectical theology'. This was the form Barth found his theology taking as, on the one hand, he tried to give serious attention to divine revelation, and as, on the other hand, he directed his searching inquiries into the roots of the nineteenth-century theology and also into the roots of scholasticism, Protestant as well as Roman. Dialectical thinking indicates the basic reversal that takes place in our thinking as we are confronted by God: we know God or *rather are known by God*. It is God who speaks, man who hears, and therefore man may only speak of God in obedience to what he hears from God.

The primary factor that gave rise to dialectical thinking is well brought out by the debate between Barth and Harnack in 1923.[1] It was the new attempt to do justice to the witness of the Holy Scriptures to *revelation*, that is, not to the uncovering of some religious potentiality hidden in human nature, but to genuine Revelation as the act of God himself among men. The New Testament bears witness to the fact that the Word became flesh, that God himself became human, historical actuality in Jesus Christ. That is the fact that our thinking has to face up to, and the problem of the offence it entails: even though the divine act, the happening of the Incarnation, was historical event, it cannot as such become the object of historical investigation and knowledge. We cannot identify the act of God in his revelation with the existence of one Jesus of Nazareth considered merely as the object of historical investigation; or, to put it the other way round, no amount of historical research into the existence of Jesus carried out on the mere plane of human history can carry us through to the actuality of divine revelation. The so-called 'historical Jesus' constructed out of the records is not identical with Revelation, for revelation is the act of God himself which cannot be directly read off the face of history. To imagine that 'the historical Jesus' we can construct by our historico-scientific research is Revelation, would be simply to identify revelation with the realisation of some religious potentiality in man; it would be to turn what is essentially relative into something absolute, to confound man with God. But what the New Testament bears witness to is a revelation that is and remains in the most exclusive sense God's own affair, and in so doing it insists that the New Testament Scriptures themselves are only witness to that act of God; they themselves are only relative, for it is their function to point a way to the absolute reality of God.[2]

The problem that Barth had to face can be expressed in this way: If in Revelation we are concerned with the being and act of God himself in space and time, then we cannot know it directly as if we could read it off by historical and critical reflection, for that would be to posit a direct continuity between the divine being and act and historico-psychological realities. If we do posit such a continuity between history and revelation, between human knowledge and faith (which answers to the act of God in his revelation), then we empty Revelation and faith of all but their human, historico-psychological content. That does not mean, however, Barth maintains, that we must cut the connexion between the two, even though we must call in question the continuity posited by

---

[1] Republished in *FuA*, pp. 7-31.   [2] *FuA*, pp. 22ff.

F

theologians like Harnack from the side of man to God; rather must we affirm a dialectical relation, which seeks to do justice to the connexion which God himself establishes, without attempting on our part to turn it into some form of an identity between the creature and the Creator. Only if we insist rigorously that God is not the creature and the creature is not God, will it be possible in this *No* really to acknowledge the creature as God's own creation, and really to acknowledge God as God, and as the source and goal even of the thoughts which man in the darkness of his culture or lack of it is wont to form about God, for underneath and above this *No* that derives from God's revelation there is the divine *Yes* which we hear in his Word of justification.[1]

Barth's dialectical thinking sought, therefore, to make sharp and clear both the separation and the connexion which the act of revelation effects, because Revelation is God himself coming to man, God in his Godness coming to man in his humanity. This has another aspect which we must not fail to note.

In Revelation God gives himself to us as the object of our faith and knowledge, but because he remains God the Lord, he does not give himself into our hands, as it were; he does not resign himself to our mastery or our control as if he were a dead object. He remains the living Lord, unqualified in his freedom, whom we can only know in accordance with his acts upon us, by following his movement of grace, and by renouncing on our part any attempt to master him by adapting him to our own schemes of thought or structures of existence; that is, whom we can know only by knowing him out of himself as an objective reality (*Gegenstand*) standing over against us, as the divine Partner and Lord of our knowing of him. A favourite term that Barth uses to describe this unique object of knowledge, which we cannot bring under our own control, is *mystery*. By 'mystery' Barth does not refer to anything a-logical or irrational, but on the contrary to full, complete and self-sufficient rationality, the rationality of God, who is so fully rational that he does not need to be interpreted in terms of anything outside of himself. That is the supreme rationality that confronts us when God gives himself to us to be known as a reality whose possibility resides absolutely within himself, and whom we cannot understand, far less derive or substantiate, except out of himself. He reveals himself to us in such a way that we can know him only if our thinking begins with his revelation, and follows it through, if it is grounded entirely upon it, and never subjected to any other truth or criterion outside of it.

[1] *FuA* 'p. 27f.

Theological thinking, then, is inescapably dialectical because it must be a thinking by *man* not from a centre in himself but from a centre in *God*, and yet never seeks to usurp God's own standpoint.[1] It is dialogical thinking in which man remains man but in which he meets God, listens to him, answers him, and speaks of him in such a way that at every point he gives God the glory. Because it is dialogical it can only be fragmented on his side, for it does not carry its co-ordinating principle in itself, but derives it from beyond itself in God's Word.

It is obvious how much this dialectical thinking of the early Barth owes to Kierkegaard: to his conceptions of 'indirect communication', 'the paradox', and 'fragments' which Kierkegaard found forced upon him through his efforts to take in deadly earnest the fact that, as he put it, the absolute fact had become a historical fact.[2] It all hinges upon the concrete historical reality of God in Jesus Christ.

It is at this point that we can see the contrast between the dialectic of Barth and the dialectic of Hegel. While the dialectic of Kierkegaard and Barth is a dialectic of humility, which renounces the possibility of thinking of God's revelation *sub specie aeternitatis*, Hegel's dialectic is rather the masterful stroke of the reason whereby it seeks to overcome the antitheses which confront it by transcending them in a higher synthesis, thus insinuating itself, as it were, into God's own self-consciousness or arrogating to itself God's own point of view. Barth's dialectic, however, does not seek to achieve a synthesis, but on the contrary attacks the syntheses forged by man, out of a proper respect for the synthesis which God in his grace throws over all our contradictions in order to bind us to himself. It is because his thinking takes its rise from within this synthesis of grace and revelation, of forgiveness and justification and regeneration, that Barth's thinking did not need to achieve a synthesis, while in the face of the false syntheses of man usurping the synthesis of grace it could only take the radically dialectical form of *diastasis*. It was particularly through his attack upon the immanentist thinking that this came about, for what he called in question was the deep-lying philosophy of identity, the basic pantheism, the axiomatic use of continuity which it involved, every attempt to erect a synthesis between man and God from the side of man. Neo-Protestant theology was impregnated with an instinctive abhorrence of all discontinuity so that it was consciously and unconsciously determined to break down barriers, to pare away the edges of difference, and to bring everything within one continuous dimension of reality. Hence the great differences between God

[1] See *TC*, p. 302.   [2] *Philosophical Fragments*, p. 84.

and man, eternity and time, Christianity and humanism, were eaten away until the precipice that separated them was transformed into a slope leading gradually from one to the other.[1] The consequence of that was that 'God' suffered sacrilegiously from a profound anthropomorphosis through assimilation to the human spirit, and man suffered inhumanly from a divinisation that attacked his humanity.

In face of that Barth called for a return to sober thinking which really let God be God and let man be man. But in order to provoke that, and to impel theology toward achieving it, Barth had to expose and attack the deep unconscious canons of thought, the basic attitudes of romanticism and pantheistic humanism, and destroy the conviction that they were necessary and inevitable and axiomatic, and so he employed all his powers to reveal to theology its own false assumptions, accusing it of a naïve lack of self-criticism and laughing at the frightful seriousness with which it took itself. But above all he confronted it with the radical discontinuity, the absolute difference between God and man, and so an absolute and not a relative difference between Christianity and humanism.

Behind modern theology there lay a basic naturalistic *Weltanschauung* which was always diluting and transforming Christianity from behind, making it incapable of critical and creative impact upon the world and so rendering it harmless; rather did it bend Christianity to serve man's own natural satisfactions and desires. Against this Barth put forward a radically different outlook marked by the seriousness with which it took original sin, and the courage with which it looked into and faced deep desperate disharmonies in man's existence revealed in the agonies of his guilt, and failure, and death. And therefore against the evolution and immanentism of that theology he opposed a dynamic eschatology of death and resurrection, of judgment and grace, and called to his aid the teaching of the early Luther of the God who slays us and makes us alive, who takes us to heaven but only by first taking us down to hell, the God of the Yes and the NO and of the NO by the Yes as of the Yes through the No.

In other words, Barth's theology took a dialectical form because he had to shatter the basic axiom of an immanent continuity between man and God, and yet affirm man just as really and realistically as he affirmed God. In all his attempt to break down the false continuity between God and man there was no attempt to sacrifice either of the two poles of thought, God or man. But in this essentially polemical period when the

---

[1] Cf. T. E. Hulme, *Speculations*, London 1924, p. 10.

ground had to be cleared of false conceptions, and the positive relation between man and God had yet to be worked out dogmatically, it was inevitable that the two poles should be held together only in a dialectical relationship, and that in that dialectical relationship the No should sound louder than the Yes. Until the No had done its work, until the whole root of pantheism was pulled up and cast aside, there could be no fruitful or positive affirmation of the union of God and man and of man and God, for it would no sooner be said than the acids of immanentism would start to eat it all away. Dialectical theology is therefore the attempt to affirm both God and man in their utter difference, that God may be God and man may be man, and at the same time to suspend (at least, full) positive account of their relation to one another.[1]

It was in aid of this that Barth employed Luther's exaggerated metaphors of the 'mathematical point', the 'tangential relation', Kierkegaard's 'wholly other', 'the leap of faith', Overbeck's *Urgeschichte*, eschatological 'death', and added to them some of his own such as 'boundary', 'deathline', 'knife-edge', 'empty-space', 'crisis' etc., and also employed Luther's and Kierkegaard's paradoxical method of arguing *sub contraria specie*. Looking back over his passionate thinking and writing of those days, and while admitting that it was one-sided and gave an all-too negative impression, Barth claims that he still thinks he was right ten times over as against those who then passed judgment on his views and resisted them. 'Those who can still hear what was said then by both the religious and the worldlings, and especially by religious worldlings, and especially the most up-to-date among them, cannot but admit that it was necessary to speak in this way. The sentences I then uttered were not hazardous (in the sense of precarious) on account of their content. They were hazardous because to be legitimate exposition of the Bible they needed others no less sharp and direct to compensate and therefore genuinely to substantiate their total claim. But these were lacking. If we claim to have too perfect an understanding of the Gospel, we at once lose our understanding. In our exposition we cannot claim to be wholly right over against others, or we are at once in the wrong.'[2]

Barth's own self-criticism is always instructive, and carries us deeply into his thinking.

'It must now be asserted equally openly that we were then—even vis-à-vis the theology from which we derived and from which we had to detach ourselves—only to a limited extent in the right. Limited in the sense in which all movements, attitudes, and positions that are pre-

[1] Cf. *WW*, pp. 206ff.   [2] *CD* II.1, p. 635.

dominantly critical and polemical, however significant they may be, are accustomed to be right only to a limited extent. What mighty formulations are then partly taken over, partly newly fabricated. In the forefront of them all—"and as they bled, a thousand voices struck up and echoed them in the field"—the famous *totaliter aliter* breaking in "vertically from above" and the no less famous "infinite qualitative difference' between God and man; the vacuum; the mathematical point and the tangent, in which alone they were supposed to touch each other; the bold assertion that there is generally only one theological interest in the Bible, that there is visible in it only one way, namely, that from above downwards, and that there is audible only one message, namely that of forgiveness of sins—immediate, without before or after—while the problem of ethics as such is identical with man's sickness unto death; the view of redemption which consists in the cancellation of the creatureliness of the creature, in the swallowing up of this world by the world beyond; correspondingly the summons, to faith as to a leap into the abyss and the like. All, no matter how well meant it was, and how much was to be said for it, yet somewhat cruelly inhuman, and itself also— only on the other side—running to some extent in a heretical direction. What a clearance was made—and almost nothing else. Everything that even from afar smelt of mysticism and morals, of pietism and romanticism or even of idealism, how suspect it was and how strictly prohibited or confined in the strait-jacket of restrictions that sounded prohibitive. What derisive laughter there was where there need only have been a sad and friendly smile. Might not the whole appear more like the news of an enormous execution than the message of the Resurrection which was indeed its aim? Was there no foundation for the impression of many contemporaries that it all might amount to making Schleiermacher, for a change, stand on his head, that is, making God, for a change, great at the expense of man: so here not so very much fundamentally would be gained, perhaps in the last resort only a new titanism be at work? Was it only obduracy when alongside the many who listened and took part with a sense of emancipation, so many others preferred to shake their heads, dumbfounded or even—as Harnack then—angry at such innovation? Did that attitude not proclaim the dim suspicion that something indispensable might be at stake in the religionism, the anthropocentrism, the doubtful humanism of that theology of the proceeding period— namely, the humanity of God which in all the unmistakable weakness, indeed, perversity of its conception did not get justice when we—immersed in the spectacle of the mighty deployment of Leviathan and

Behemoth in the book of Job—focused all attention on His Godness.'[1]

In spite of this sustained self-criticism of Barth so far as the positive content and emphasis of his thought at that time was concerned, two further points must be made.

In the first place, in his dialectical thinking Barth was faced with a fundamental problem of all theology and all thinking about God. It is *man* who thinks, *man* who asks searching questions about God, *man* who is hungry to know God, to speak about him, and make judgments about him; but when that man stands face to face with God, he discovers that he stands at the bar of *God's* judgment and it is *God* who speaks to him and questions him. Man begins by investigating God but discovers that God is all the time investigating him—and when he tries to express that, theologically, he finds that all his grammar gets upset—for God is always indissolubly Subject—and all he can do is to stammer 'yes' and 'no' in very fragmentary utterances. 'I believe; help thou my unbelief.'[2]

As H. R. Mackintosh once wrote, 'Barth contends that so long as we are here on earth, we can do no otherwise in theology than proceed by using the method of statement and counter-statement; we dare not pronounce absolutely "the last word", at least if we are not to incur the guilt of presuming to identify what as sinners we say of God "with the dogmatic of the saints in heaven". The Word of God itself cannot be broken or refracted. But our human word about God *is* broken, and only in this "brokenness"—this absence of limpidly clear self-evidencing terms—can it bear witness to the truth of God. "We know that we are unable to comprehend except by means of dialectical dualism, in which one must become two in order that it may be veritably one".... "If you ask me about God", Barth once wrote, "If you ask me about *God*, and if I am ready to tell about Him, dialectic is all that can be expected of *me*. Neither my affirmation nor my denial lays claim to being God's truth. Neither is more than a *witness* to that Truth which stands in the centre between every Yes and No." '[3] Dialectical theology stands for the fact that toward the Truth itself all our statements must remain essentially *open*, in humble acknowledgment of the fact that it is not in our competence to capture the Truth or to enclose it in our formulations, in frank admission that our thinking and speaking of God have their finite boundaries over which they cannot transgress.[4]

[1] *GGG*, p. 35 f. See also the *Grundfragen*, 1935, p. 24.
[2] *The Resurrection of the Dead*, pp. 18, 49, 85 f, etc.
[3] H. R. Mackintosh, *Types of Modern Theology*, p. 26 f. See *WW*, p. 209; and *TC*, 'Church and Theology', § 7.   [4] *TC*, pp. 298-302.

In this sense, dialectical thinking is a correlate of justification by grace alone, in its epistemological reference. That is to say, it is a form of thinking which acknowledges that the only legitimate justification or demonstration of Christian truth is that which is in accordance with its nature, as truth and grace of God, and that to seek justification of it on any other ground is to falsify knowing at its very basis. Dialectical thinking is therefore thinking which combines statement and inquiry, for it makes its statements not from a vantage point above the truth where it is the master but from a point below it where it never leaves its position of humble inquiry. Hence in dialectical thinking we let our knowledge, our statements, or our theological formulations be called into question by the very God toward whom they point or are directed in inquiry, for he alone is the Truth. Hence theological doctrines or formulations are essentially contingent; they do not claim to have the truth in themselves for by their very nature they point beyond themselves to the Truth in God. Dialectical thinking, therefore, as Barth employed it, is to be considered as a form of combining statement and inquiry with the intention of letting the Truth declare itself to us, and therefore it indulges in a deliberate abstention from final judgments lest by breaking off or foreclosing the inquiry we should block our vision of the truth or be tempted to imagine that we have caught it in the net of our formulations.[1]

In the second place, in his dialectical thinking Barth was engaging in a terrific struggle with theological and philosophical language. As Schleiermacher showed in his *Hermeneutik und Kritik*[2] every language (whether we mean by that the language of a race or the language of some particular region of discourse) has its own web of meaning, its own network of conventions and its communal qualities. Any use of words involves in some measure or other a compromise with, or a manipulation of, the communal meaning in which they share, and must therefore come to terms with the culture or the philosophy or the tradition from which they derive and into which they quickly and easily slip back. Thus any attempt to break a way through into a new direction of thought, or any attempt to set our thought on a new basis, involves a passionate and creative effort to wrest the words we use from their original web of meaning, and then great power of concentration to hold them in their new context until they become sufficiently assimilated to the new direction to be habituated to it. What makes this particularly difficult is that we not only express ourselves in words but for the most part actually

---

[1] Cf. *ChrD*, I, p. 454ff; *WW*, p. 211f; *TC*, pp. 299ff.
[2] See the scientific edition of H. Kimmerle, *Hermeneutik*, Heidelberg 1959.

think in words, so that it is very difficult indeed in using words to get away from the philosophies or outlooks with which they are already so deeply impregnated.

This means that any attempt to carry through a piece of radically new thinking must make room for it through a severely critical revision of previous habits of thought and speech, in order to break through and break down the mental and linguistic barriers these habits have erected, and then exert the constructive power necessary for the composing of new forms of thought and speech. It has to hack a way through the concatenation of meaning in which the words to be used already carry with them, and then to thrust them back upon the objective realities they are to serve that they may acquire material modes or forms adequate to their communication. At its initial stage such a movement of thought is bound to offer the appearance of a new scholasticism or even to incur the suspicion of a new nominalism, but all this is properly to be regarded as the preliminary skirmishing leading up to the full engagement with the objective realities in question.

This is the sort of struggle we have to see in the thinking of Barth throughout his dialectical period. This is clearly a struggle that has gone on ever since, and must ever go on if theological terms are not to become debased, but it is equally clear in Barth's case that once the break-through was achieved, and the ground was cleared for fresh thinking, the severely dialectical form of his thinking could be dropped and a less austere and more positive and reconciling form of thinking could be taken up in its place. That is indeed what happened. So much is that the case that it would now be a misnomer to speak of his theology as 'dialectical', for the emphasis is no longer upon *diastasis* but upon *analogy*—i.e. it is no longer a movement of thought setting men apart from God, but a movement referring man back to his source in the grace of God the Creator and Redeemer.

To be sure, the dialectic continues, but now it is rather the movement of inquiry which penetrates into the interior dialectic of the subject-matter, into the logic of the Logos. In biblical interpretation that takes the form of theological exegesis, the whole intention of which is to let the Word be heard in and through the words. In dogmatic activity it is the questioning which seeks to penetrate into the deep inner forms which the Word of God takes in his communication, and our assimilation, of divine revelation; it is, so to speak, the wielding of a theological 'Occam's razor' which lays bare the deep and comprehensive simplicities of the one Truth of God in which we learn, in obedience to the divine condescension and economy, to think the truths of God after him, and to be thankful.

(e) Before we pass on, we must glance at the bearing of Barth's early dialectical thinking upon his doctrine of the Church, for, as we would expect, it is essentially a dialectical concept for him at this stage. In its primal sense, and in its ultimate divine reality the Church is the counterpart to sheer, abrupt revelation, to the ingression of the Kingdom of God into existence and history, the counterpart to the *Urgeschichte* which is its primal origin in Christ. The Church in history, the historical Church in which we find ourselves, and from which we can never escape, Barth speaks of as 'the canalisation in history of that divine transaction in men which can never become a matter of history.'[1] In its primal sense the Church remains pure Event, the eschatological miracle that happens ever and ever again under the impact of revelation, in the creative operation of the Spirit. 'The Holy Spirit is the operation of God in faith, the creative and redemptive power of the Kingdom of Heaven, which is nigh at hand. As a tumbler sings when it is touched, so we and our world are touched in faith by the Spirit of God, who is the eternal "Yes". He provides faith with a content which is not a thing in time; if it were a thing, it would be nothing but a void and a negation. He is the miraculous factor in faith, its beginning and its end. He is equal with God, and on His account God reckons righteousness to the believer. He is invisible, outside the continuity of the visible human subject and beyond all psychological analysis. He creates the new subject of the man who stands upright in the presence of God. He is the subject of faith which "religious experience" longs for, but never finds. He is the subject by whom we are enabled to speak unspeakable things: to say that we have peace with God, that we have entered into grace and that we glory in the hope of the glory of God. He is the presupposition of all human being and having; but to us He is comprehensible and conspicuous only in what is not given.'[2]

That is the invisible, supernatural, inner reality of the Church, but the historical Church is the visible manifestation where humanity in the world becomes conscious of itself, is religious, and suffers from God, suffers because it has to be uprooted from the concrete and the temporal or at least from finding its security there to find it beyond all possibilities and tangible securities in God alone. Nevertheless the Church as the canalisation of that divine transaction in history is 'that visibility which forces invisibility upon our notice, that humanity which directs our

---

[1] *Romans*, p. 129.　　　　　　[2] *Romans*, p. 129.

attention towards God. To suppose that a direct road leads from art, or morals or science, or even from religion, to God is sentimental, liberal self-deception. Such roads lead directly to the Church, to Churches, and to all kinds of religious communities—of this the experiences of so-called "religious" socialism provide an instructive illustration. Only when the end of the blind alley of ecclesiastical humanity has been reached is it possible to raise radically and seriously the problem of God. All that occurs up to this point is harmless illusion.'[1]

This is where the *diastasis* comes in in Barth's diacritical doctrine of the Church. The Church cannot fulfil its function in the hands of God except by being broken, in repentance and suffering and dissolution in the hands of God, but then it is made to point beyond itself and finds its essential life in witness and mission. The tragedy of the Church is that it clutches itself and nurses itself, and regards itself as the prolongation of grace, as the extension of religious experience, and so makes itself into an existential denial of grace and the supernatural Kingdom of God. But that is the way that has been taken by Neo-Protestantism which has attempted to construct a religion out of the Gospel, and so to set it as one human possibility in the midst of others—but that is precisely to fall from grace.[2] 'The Church which sings its triumphs and trims and popularises and modernises itself, in order to minister to and satisfy every need except the one; the Church which, in spite of many exposures, is still satisfied with itself, and, like quicksilver, still seeks and finds its own level; such a Church can never succeed, be it never so zealous, never so active in ridding itself of its failings and blemishes. With or without its offences, it can never be the Church of God, because it is ignorant of the meaning of repentance.'[3]

That is the Church that Barth is attacking all through the *Commentary on Romans*—he is intent on hurling the thunderbolts of the Pauline Gospel at the Church, on letting grace be the supreme question-mark set by God against it, in the hope that the Church may wake up to its divine self-crucifying mission. Thus Barth's powerful sense of the eschatological Kingdom, of the absolute miracle of God, had the effect of disclosing rather ruthlessly and throwing into high relief the Church's failures and weaknesses, its ambiguity, its worldliness and indeed its profanity as work of man, and therefore as falling under the judgment of God. 'Where the Church ends—not of course by a human act of will, but by a divine decree—there is its beginning. Where its unrighteousness is altogether exposed, there its righteousness dawns. The divine

---

[1] *Romans*, p. 337. [2] *Romans*, pp. 225, 240, etc. [3] *Romans*, p. 370.

demolition of any Church means that every Church arises as signpost, threshold, and door of hope. It is then that the Church appears, as it were, as an arrow shot from the other bank; it appears as the messenger of Christ and the tabernacle of God with men.'[1]

From this citation, it is apparent that the aim and intention of the dialectic is to make room for hope, to create a space in the Church for participation in the resurrection, yet the weight of the exposition falls upon the diastasis, upon the Church that belongs to God and suffers from him because God is God and he is against it, upon the Church as the counterpart to the divine purgation, the sphere of the great disturbance, where the judgments of God are a great deep.[2] 'Regarded from a purely human point of view, the Gospel of Christ and the human work of the Church operate in diametrically opposite fashions. In the Church the hostility of men against God is brought to a head; for there human indifference, misunderstanding, and opposition attain their most sublime and almost their most naïve form. In the Church the dead no-man's-land between the two opposing forces becomes visible; for there the advance of human achievement, even though it imagine itself to be invested with divine power, is finally checked . . . And so room is made in the Church for the forensic justification of the Gentiles. For the Church is the communion of saints seeking forgiveness, of the lost who are saved, of the dead who are alive.'[3]

Barth's teaching here is put into the right perspective once again by his own self-criticism. 'One of the exaggerations of which we made ourselves guilty around 1920 was that we were able to see the theological relevance of the Church properly only in its character as negative counterpart to the Kingdom of God, then so fortunately rediscovered by us. We were inclined then to regard as "not so very important", because "human all too human", the form of its teaching, of its public worship, of its legal arrangements. We declared all earnestness or zeal directed to them as superfluous or even pernicious. In all this we, at least, came near to the theory and practice of a spiritual insurgency and of an esoteric *gnosis*. At the present moment, in view of the unceasingly actual Roman temptation, as well as the ecclesiastical, clericalistic and liturgistic restoration and reaction going around in the Germany of today and perhaps one day encroaching on our own territory, it would certainly not be fitting to silence or even to subdue today the note sounding

---

[1] *Romans*, p. 416.
[2] His protest against the Church was, Barth claimed, *gerade kirchlich gemeint*, letter of March 4, 1925, *Gd-Md*, p. 142.   [3] *Romans*, pp. 417ff.

ultimately through the whole Bible of the judgment beginning at the house of God. And it was and is definitely no good undertaking to reverse the order, *événement-institution*, which is likewise secured in the Bible. But we had and have to see and understand that, in maintaining this order and remembering this judgment, there can be no neglect or renunciation of our solidarity with the Church. Criticism of the Church can be significant and fruitful only when it comes from insight into— I am not exaggerating—the necessity for salvation of the existence and function of the Church, and when it is uttered to further its ministry in its fathering, upbuilding and mission.... We believe the Church as the place namely where in the Christocratic brotherhood the crown of humanity, man's co-humanity, can become visible—and more than that, as the place where God's glory will dwell on earth, where, namely, the humanity of God will assume palpable form already in time and here on earth.'[1]

This advance from the teaching of his *Römerbrief* to a fuller and more positive doctrine of the Church is evident in several of the essays republished in *Die Theologie und die Kirche*, particularly where Barth is wrestling with the nature of theology as an activity of the Church[2] and is concerned to clarify the Protestant doctrine of the Church over against that of Rome.[3] The decisive point of difference Barth finds in the God/man, grace/faith relationship. It is the grace of God that creates in man the capacity to receive and grasp it, but it is never put at the disposal of man—he is never in a position to control grace. Thus in the God/man relationship created by grace, there does not arise a reciprocity which enables man to lay his hand upon God as God lays his hand upon man. The Church is the place where that God/man relationship in grace takes place. The Church is the divine institution in space and time where God is active in his grace, but where God is present in his sovereign freedom—therefore although the Church as the earthly body of the heavenly Lord is the place and means of his grace, it is itself never patron or lord, but servant and even 'beggar' that lives from day to day out of the hand of God alone. In other words the God/man relationship established in the Church is an *irreversible relationship*, which does not

---

[1] *GGG*, p. 50f, from the lecture on 'The Humanity of God', delivered in Sept. 1956. By 'the humanity of God', Barth refers to God's relationship and approach to man and his sovereign togetherness with man based on his grace. In this sense 'God's Godness rightly understood includes His humanity', op. cit. p. 37.

[2] The influence of Vilmar on the development of Barth's thought is to be noted at this point, cf. *TC*, pp. 214, 303ff, etc.

[3] 'The concept of the Church', 1927, pp. 272ff; 'Church and Theology', 1925, pp. 286ff; and 'Roman Catholicism: a question to the Protestant Church', pp. 307ff.

give man any claim over God or allow him in any way to assume the place of master. The Church remains the Church of forgiven sinners in whose midst Jesus Christ dwells in his grace making it his body and instrument and the means of his grace to the world, but as such it lives as the Church for which Christ died, under the judgment and promise of God, and lives by taking up the Cross and following its Lord.[1]

Because the Church has its source and ground only in the grace of God, it is not to be regarded as a human way of salvation, nor the result of human actions and decisions. It is solely a divine foundation and arises from election and revelation. On the other hand, the Church cannot be regarded as institutionalised election or as extended revelation; that is to say, it cannot be related directly and absolutely to the act and revelation of God, as if its history were revelation, as if its nature were grace, as if its life in the world were as such the life of God. The Church is the place where God's revelation and grace have entered into the time and history of this world without abroga ing it, and meets us within our darkness and estrangement, within the form and existence of a lost world, that is, the place where God really comes to man and meets him in his desperate plight and need. We cannot escape the fact, therefore, that the Church on earth partakes of the ambiguities, relativities, and the questionableness of history, and as such it will remain the Church under the judgment of God's grace waiting for the Parousia.[2]

It is precisely because the Church derives from revelation that it is bounded by eschatological limits over which it cannot trespass without *hybris*, without self-glorification or the apotheosis of its own life, without setting up in itself 'a divine I'.[3] Barth is concerned, therefore, to oppose the Roman teaching about the Church as a condition of the Logos, the divine '*Ego Eimi*', as the 'extension' or 'prolongation' of Christ or the Incarnation, and therefore the Roman identification of the mind of the Church with the mind of Christ, of the dogma of the Church with the Word of God, of the authority of the Church with the authority of the Holy Spirit.[4] Important and necessary as is the place we must give to the mind of the historical Church and its dogmas and authority and to its tradition and institution, nevertheless the Church lives not out of these, not out of itself or its own past, but it lives solely from beyond itself in the miracle of the Kingdom, in the ever-new event of God's grace, out of constant hearing of God's Word—and therefore what it must avoid is any attempt to identify or relate directly its own historical

[1] *TC*, p. 280f.   [2] *TC*, pp. 281f, 327f.
[3] *TC*, p. 314f.   [4] *TC*, pp. 113, 286f, 293ff, 298f, 312ff.

institution or tradition with the indwelling Christ, and so make revelation a predicate of its own history. Institution and tradition are to be regarded rather as the counterpart to the creative impact of God's presence—but apart from that, it is but an empty canal or a burnt-out crater where once God had spoken and the fiery miracle had taken place.

This teaching of Barth about the Church as the counterpart in history to the ever-recurring new event of grace brought upon it from the side of Roman theology the charge of 'occasionalism', but there can be little doubt that that is a serious misunderstanding.[1] Superficially regarded, it may be granted that it offered something similar to that in its appearance, just as the struggle with the forms of thought and speech he had inherited from Neo-Protestantism gave rise to the accusation of 'nominalism'.[2] But as this so-called 'nominalism' was the clearing of the ground required by the epistemological relevance of justification by grace alone, in order to make room for a realist understanding of the objective reality of the Truth, that is from the side of the Being and Act of God, so this so-called 'occasionalism' made room for the real being of the Church as grounded in the Word made flesh and as teleologically participant in the Life of the risen Lord.[3] It called into question and exposed the false objectivities in order that the real objectivity of the Church might be revealed in 'the humanity of God'. It called into question and exposed the false identification of the continuity of the Church with the contingencies and relativities and ambiguities of historical succession in order that its real continuity in history might be revealed in the Covenant of Grace interpreted as the inner presupposition and ground of creation, and in union with the Incarnate and ever-living risen Lord—that is to say, it is God's grace alone that throws a bond over the contingencies, relativities and ambiguities of the Church's historical life, co-ordinating it and grounding it in the enduring reality of his Kingdom and the new Humanity of Jesus Christ, the same yesterday, today, and forever.

2. The Theology of the Word

We come now to consider the element in Barth's theology which has become more and more deeply characteristic throughout the years, his

---

[1] See Jérôme Hamer, L'occasionalism théologique de Karl Barth, 1949, and cf. H. U. von Balthasar, Karl Barth, Darstellung und Deutung seiner Theologie, p. 69.
[2] E.g. E. Brunner, Natur und Gnade, p. 39 (ET in Natural Theology, 1946, p. 54).
[3] The charge of occasionalism shatters itself on Barth's doctrine of creation (CD III.1), and of the creature as given its own distinct mode of being, continuity and activity over against God (CD III.2; CD IV.3.1, especially pp. 120ff).

understanding of theology as *theology of the Word of God*.[1] Here it is apparent that Barth stands in the great tradition of the Reformation, both Lutheran and Calvinist,[2] in sharp distinction from that of Romanism and Neo-Protestantism, and from first to last his theology is a plunge into the absolute objectivity and actuality of divine Revelation.

We have already seen that Barth broke through to this early in his life when he had to face the task of bearing the Word of God to a waiting congregation. In his struggles to fulfil his ministry,[3] in which Calvin's commentaries obviously offered him considerable help, and then in his energetic efforts to discharge his office as a teacher of Reformed Theology in Göttingen, when he made use of Calvin's *Institutes*[1] and Heppe's *Reformed Dogmatics*,[5] he both found a new world within the Bible and discovered the depth of the Reformation insights into biblical theology. But all this had yet to be released for him in its fulness, and he had to make it really his own, by finding the tools with which to assimilate and shape understanding of it in his mind. That took a long time, for it is not until his second attempt at writing prolegomena to theology on the doctrine of the Word of God that he won his struggle. Our task now is to characterise his thought at this stage when he is still struggling forward, and to assess the far-reaching significance of his chief insights.

(*a*) It is all-important to realise that for Barth the Word of God refers to the most completely objective reality there is, for it is the Word of *God* backed with God's own ultimate Being.[6] It is not only God's Word but God's Word as God himself says it—that is the Word which comes breaking into the circle of our own subjectivity, our questioning and our own answering, and assaults us as the great question of God to us.[7] If it can be said that in the questions which we direct even toward God, it is ultimately we ourselves who are the question, then it can be said even with greater force that the question which God directs to us in his

---

[1] See especially the essay 'The Word in Theology from Schleiermacher to Ritschl' in *TC*, pp. 200-216.

[2] His teachers were above all, Barth has said, Luther and Calvin and the confessional documents of the Reformation century. 'Die Neuorientierung der prot. Theologie in den letzten dreissig Jahren', *Kirchenblatt für die Reformierte Schweiz* 96.7, April 1940, p. 100.

[3] Cf. the essay 'The Word of God and the Task of the Ministry', in *WW*, pp. 183 ff.

[4] The letters of 1921-1923 reveal the immense impact of Calvin on Barth at this all-important period.

[5] A new German edition of this work, *Die Dogmatik der evangelischreformierten Kirche*, was brought out by Ernst Bizer in 1935. For it Barth wrote an illuminating foreword. The English edition, translated by G. T. Thomson, appeared in 1950. Cf. Barth's foreword, p. v.

[6] *Christliche Dogmatik im Entwurf*, pp. 137 ff.   [7] *ChrD*, pp. 73 ff.

Word is his own Being, the downright actuality of God, the ultimate objectivity, the infinite obstacle which confronts us and which we cannot subdue to any form of our own subjectivity. This really transcendent, sovereignly free, objective Word of God, filled and backed up with all the Godness of God, is the positive answer to immanentism.

This Word of God is the proper object of theological activity, whether of the preacher or of the professor. That is affirmed by Barth in direct antithesis to the conception of *Glaubenslehre* in Neo-Protestantism.[1] That is to say, theology is not concerned with determinations of the consciousness or the analysis of religion or experience—there may well be a place for that sort of thing, but that is not theology. Theological thinking is not thinking from a centre in ourselves, in our own faith or piety, but a thinking from a centre beyond ourselves, in God. Of course it is never a thinking *in abstracto*, or *in vacuo*, for it is we who think, in a definite situation and context, we who carry with us in our conceptions and words a whole conglomerate of notions and philosophies, and it would be deluding ourselves to imagine that we come to theological activity without that, but in theological activity we come up against the reality of God who gives himself to us as the object of our knowledge, and we yield ourselves to the determination of the object, in a movement of theological repentance in obedient response to God addressing us in person, to God interrogating and investigating us, and revealing himself to us. We let ourselves be questioned, we let ourselves be told, we listen in the obedience of faith and learn. Our greatest hindrance is ourself, our own individuality which we keep obtruding as an obstacle between us and God, and yet it is just because this obstacle meets with God himself, confronting us like a huge boulder in the path which we cannot climb over or get past, that we awaken to the objective reality of his Word. Then it is not our right human thoughts about God that occupy us but God's thoughts about us which we are summoned to think and repeat after him until our whole way of thinking of him is governed and established by the relationship which he has established between himself and us, and which he has set forth for us in the Holy Scriptures.[2]

Two things must be said here. Both against Roman Catholicism and against Neo-Protestantism, Barth asserts the ultimate reality of the Word of God as *Word*. The only God whom we know is this God who

---

[1] Cf. also the *Glaubenslehre* of Schleiermacher or of Troeltsch. See also 'The Word in Theology . . .', *TC*, pp. 200ff; 'The principles of dogmatics according to Wilhelm Herrmann', *TC*, pp. 238ff; and *ChrD*, pp. 82ff, 429ff, 447f.

[2] *WW*, p. 43f. See also H. R. Mackintosh, *Types of Modern Theology*, pp. 272ff, and 287ff.

comes to us in his Word, not a God without his Word, not a Word without the reality and actuality of God, but a Word who is God, and a God who as Word has become Man.[1] Barth will have nothing to do, therefore, with some imaginary realm above and beyond the Word where there takes place some wordless vision or a-logical experience of God; nor will he have anything to do with the God who is defined as Schleiermacher defined him, a God who is ultimately dumb, and whom we know only through examining and analysing our own feelings and determinations of soul, and so put words into God's mouth through interpreting our religious sensations. No, God comes to us as Word himself, Word who is independent of our awareness and mystical experiences, who is not the correlate or determinant of our feeling of absolute dependence, who is sovereignly free from the circle of our subjectivity and exalted above it all. Rather is he the Word who assaults our subjectivity, who tears it wide open by his address, and relates us to himself beyond ourselves, to a real Word of address, a genuine objective communication, who breaks into our monologue with ourselves and assumes us into dialogue with himself.[2]

It is because of the ultimate objectivity of this Word that Barth insists on speaking of its encounter with us as *Ereignis* or event. It is pure act of God unqualified by anything outside of it. The Word of God, as God himself utters it, is not something we can possess or master, or upon which we can impose *our* conceptual forms, for we can never know the Word, far less speak the Word from the side of God, that is, from the side of his own divine Being or Act which the Word is. When we hear the Word, it is the Word confronting us, impinging upon us from beyond, from moment to moment in actual address and concrete communication, in ever new event or unexpected happening which is itself the creative source of every possible response on man's part, and which conveys to him the rational forms for his understanding of it. Hence Barth speaks of our hearing of the Word correspondingly as a hearing that is ever new over against the Word, and of our experience of the Word as one in which we acknowledge the coming of the Word to us, in its concrete act in time and history, in its 'contingent contemporaneousness', there and then, and which is indeed Word to us in the actual event of its address. In that sense the Word continuously becomes Word of God to us in ever-new encounter.[3]

---

[1] *ChrD*, p. 137 f.
[2] *The Holy Ghost and the Christian Life*, pp. 18 ff, p. 456 f.
[3] *ChrD*, pp. 75 f, 79 f.

The intention of all this on Barth's part is to stress with unheard-of emphasis the objectivity of the Word, for it is so objective that we can never, never drag it within the ellipse of our own subjectivity, just as the Word never resigns its exalted and sovereign freedom in order to become the prisoner of our religious consciousness or theological formulations.[1] And yet it is strange that both from the side of scholastic Romanism and scholastic Protestantism it was accused of Kantian subjectivism, when, in point of fact, it is the exact antithesis of that. It is the assertion of the Lordship of the Word, of God in his freedom and grace, who gives himself to us to be known by us, but who does not resign himself to our control. That is fully expounded in the later *Church Dogmatics*, but it is important to see that even in this period of his thinking, the insistence upon the Word as ever new *Ereignis*, breaking through our syntheses and continuities and opening them up in *diastasis*, is Barth's dynamic way of speaking of the Word of God in its living objectivity and concrete actuality, in its ultimate Godness and Eternity.

In his studies in the history of nineteenth-century theology Barth came to see that it is the omission of eschatology that renders easy the disappearance of the object behind the subjectivity of the believer, and the concentration, to which modern theology is so prone, upon an objectless faith. But when the object of theological knowledge is God in his act upon us, God in his finality, in his judgments, in the impact of his royal grace, and when confronted with the object we are confronted with the last things, with the ultimate reality of God himself, God in his own personal Being, then we cannot confuse it with our own faith. It was a recovery of this eschatological orientation that Barth discerned in the thinking of Dorner which in Barth's eyes gave Dorner a place over against Ritschl which had not yet been appreciated.[2] Barth's insistence that the Word is *Ereignis*, God's act, eschatological and ontological event, is also what he means by saying that the Word of God even as the object of our knowledge is always and indissolubly *Subject*.[3] But before we turn to that, we must note another side to Barth's theology of the Word.

(*b*) God's Word is a *concretissimum*, so to speak, a concrete universal.[4] The Word of God is not only event, it comes to us with eternal content, with God's message—it comes as real Word. It does not come to us, then, as mere Event which throws us back upon ourselves to interpret it

---

[1] *ChrD*, p. 313f.   [2] *TC*, p. 215.
[3] *ChrD*, pp. 149ff, 215f, 454. See also *Gd-Md*, p. 114.
[4] See H. U. von Balthasar, op. cit. p. 203f.

out of some schematism of our own, nor does it come as a body of propositions or truths the reality of which we are obliged to authenticate. Rather does the Word come to us as both Event and Truth, authenticating itself as ontological Reality and bringing to us the concrete form through which it is actually to be understood. In the language we noted earlier, Barth speaks of the Word as the Word who is God, not as Word without God, not as God without Word. It is not a Word which *we* can form any more than *we* can form God, nor is it a Word which *we* can utter any more than *we* can utter God, for God's Word is the Word as God utters it. Yet it is not only Word which God utters to himself, but Word which he utters for us and communicates to us, and enables *us* to receive and know and utter, human beings though we are.[1]

In order to assert this teaching Barth had to conduct a polemical engagement on a double front. On the one hand he distinguished his position sharply from the romantic, impressionistic theologies which like to think of the divine revelation as the impartation of life rather than as the communication of truth.[2] Revelation or Word of God in that sense has no rationality of its own, for it is not *logos* in its own nature, and therefore it has to borrow rationality in order to be interpreted and handled in theological or dogmatic activity. Hence the dogmatics of Neo-Protestantism was inevitably bound up with contemporary philosophies, and it was *their* pattern that they imposed upon the Christian faith in seeking to give it systematic articulation. Barth insisted, however, that the form which we employ in our dogmatic activity must be taken from the object itself, the Word of God; theology must engage in active and constant exegesis in order to make sure that its dogmatic thinking is grounded in and determined by the fundamental forms proper to the Word of God itself.[3] Hence Barth will have nothing to do with any free thinking or romancing in theology or any kind of loose arbitrary speculation or autonomous thinking, but insists upon a heteronomous theology bound to the Word and articulated firmly and solidly in doctrine derived from and determined by the forms inherent in the Word. *The Word of God is rational Event.* It is the form in which Reason communicates itself to reason, Person to person. A theology of the Word has its own inherent rationality (i.e. deriving from the Word), which it is the task of dogmatics to draw out and elucidate in order to insure that our thinking of God's Word is in faithful conformity to it.[4]

---

[1] *The Holy Ghost and the Christian Life*, p. 18 f; *ChrD*, pp. 6 2 f, 65 ff, 137 f.
[2] Cf. Barth's critique of Herrmann's insistent idea that Revelation is *nicht Lehre*, *TC*, p. 248 f.
[3] *ChrD*, pp. 432 f, 437 f, 448 f, 454.   [4] *ChrD*, p. 62 f.

On the other hand, Barth distinguished his position also from those of scholasticism and so-called orthodoxy. The great weakness of this orthodoxy, he pointed out, is not its supernaturalism. That is its strength. It is rather the fact that orthodoxy has a way of regarding some objective description of an element as the element itself.[1] The Word of God does indeed convey to us objective truth which requires of us rational assimilation and articulation but it cannot be embodied in objective sentences, so to speak, for that would be to obstruct the objective truth by substituting a false objectivity in its place. Even as Truth the Word of God remains eternal Event and is ever again Truth for us in its living and active encounter with us, and is always sovereignly superior to *our* statements and conceptions of it, and can never be included in our systematic constructions. Our theological formulations, therefore, do not embody their own standard of reference, do not become self-explanatory, nor do they carry within themselves the proper criterion of their truthfulness. Rather do they themselves fall under the judgment of the Truth and testify to the Word of God as their sole and proper criterion. That means, of course, that only theological 'common places' or *loci* are possible, not a theological system.[2]

Once again, it must be said that the temptation of orthodoxy, and all scholasticism, for all their appearance of objectivity, is to fall a prey to their own subjectivities through converting the truths of the Word of God into rationalised objects. In so far as the objective descriptions of the Truth are confounded with or mistaken for the Truth, and do not fall under its questioning and judgment, they easily become assimilated to the prevailing intellectual trends and fall under the power of its patterns of thought and speech and their philosophical presuppositions. That is what happened, for example, in the mediaeval world, when Roman theology made extensive use of neo-Aristotelian thought-forms in which to express and articulate its doctrine, for in point of fact the philosophical presuppositions carried by those thought-forms triumphed over the doctrine and have permanently influenced and altered it. Barth's studies in the history of Protestant theology convinced him that when it took over so much of the mediaeval intellectual apparatus with which to articulate doctrine in the sixteenth and seventeenth centuries it became overloaded with philosophical presuppositions, and so compromised itself with natural theology, and a supposedly enlightened understanding, that it easily fell in with the stream of philosophical development, at length assimilating into itself or becoming assimilated

[1] *WW*, p. 201 f.   [2] *ChrD*, p. 451 f.

to Cartesian subjectivism, in which the objective truths of the Word of God were converted into psychological objects, to a much greater degree than many modern champions of seventeenth- and eighteenth-century orthodoxy would care to admit.[1]

This was one of the reasons for Barth's ruthless attack upon the *analogia entis* or the reversibility of the God/man relationship, whether in its Roman or its Protestant form, for it is through it that this confusion of the objective Truth of God with the supposedly objective formulations of theology takes place, so that instead of propounding a theology in which thought is brought into obedient conformity with objective being, men developed a theology in which objective being was brought into conformity with their thought, or at least one which operated with a relation of reversibility and reciprocity between them.[2] In Protestantism that reached its supreme expression in the romantic-idealist theology of the nineteenth century, but its roots went back by clear and straight lines through pietistic rationalism into the orthodoxy of the sixteenth century. What had to be asserted again was the transcendence of God over all our conceptions and formulations, his freedom from the control of all *our* analogical constructs and arbitrary impositions, his refusal to be bound within any frame of reference we can desire, and his implacable opposition to every form of idolatry.

It is understandable, therefore, that during this period of intense historico-theological study of dogma, Barth was determined to be on his guard not only against the dangers of Neo-Protestantism and Romanism, which were more obvious, but even of the classical Protestant orthodoxy, with which he felt himself in many ways in such very deep sympathy.[3] This was the stage when Barth found considerable reinforcement in the teaching of Kohlbrügge, particularly in his radical doctrine of justification by grace and of his understanding of the objective basis of the Christian life in Jesus Christ, for it helped Barth to affirm more profoundly the fact that all our theological formulations and works are under the judgment of God, precisely because it is only in him that we are put in the right with the Truth.[4] It is justification by the grace of God alone, in its epistemological relevance, that is the answer to every

---

[1] See Barth's foreword to Heppe, *Reformed Dogmatics*, p. vi f; and *CD* I.2, pp. 285 ff and *ChrD*, pp. 302 ff.

[2] Compare in *Theology and Church* Barth's critique of Neo-Protestantism (pp. 200 ff) with that of Romanism (pp. 281 ff).

[3] 'He who has some intimate knowledge of the very respectable theological work of the seventeenth century, will never be ashamed to be reckoned to belong to that so-called orthodoxy' *Kirchenblatt für die reformierte Schweiz*, 96.7, p. 100.

[4] See *ProtTh*, pp. 579 ff; and *ZdZ*, 1927, p. 297 ff.

false objectivity or subjectivity, for it reveals that no idealistic appercep-
tion, no transcendental deduction on our part can carry us across the
gap between the word of man and the Word of God or justify the claim
that our speaking of the Word of God is God's Word as spoken by him.
Moreover it is in Kohlbrügge's doctrine of grace that Barth sees the real
answer to the tendency of the whole of the nineteenth century, both in
its liberal and in its conservative wings, to confuse the Word with our
faith or our formulations of it.[1] God's grace, which makes Christians
Christians is free, and—everything depends on this—it remains free,
and can never be thought of as coming under the claim or the control or
the possession of man. Both as justification and as sanctification, both
as objective and subjective, grace remains God's grace in all the freedom and sovereignty of God himself. When that is grasped, then a
proper understanding of the Word goes along with it, as the Word which
we can never master or convert into our own word or tell to ourselves,
as the Word which we must hear and ever hear anew in all its own
incontestable objectivity and freedom over against us. Because this Word
comes to us in the royal act of divine justification and forgiveness of
sinners, it resists all semi-Pelagianism, whether in its rationalist or its
pietist forms, as of the very sin it has come to forgive and judge in
forgiving; because it comes as absolute grace freely putting us in the
right with the Truth of God, it relativises all our formulations of the
truth, exposes their claim to adequacy or finality, and summons us to
unceasing acts of repentant rethinking and obedience in bringing our
mind into ever new conformity with self-revelation and communication
of God in his sovereign Word.

The fact that Barth had to struggle with errors on two different fronts
was in some ways grist for his dialectical thinking of these years, yet it
was dialectical thinking also that helped him both to take seriously the
objective nature of the Truth mediated in the Word and to be aware of
the dogmatism that forgets that the Word of God is Event and treats it
only as object. Even in theological articulation and formulation we are
attacked by the Word of God, for it objects to our desire to master it
and resists our intellectual schematisms, and breaks through the net of
our subjectivity that we throw around it, so that our understanding and
expression of it is essentially fragmentary and dialectical. *The Word of
God retains his own objectivity*, and therefore remains mystery, transcendent to us, exalted above us, even when he communicates himself
to us.

[1] *TC*, p. 215 f. Cf. Berkouwer, op. cit., pp. 46 ff.

Barth became increasingly aware also that even the dialectical method suffers from an inherent weakness, for by its very nature it cannot yield an utterance that carries a compelling meaning and cannot finally bear positive witness to the Truth. Even this dialectical way comes to an end when God himself speaks, for his Word is not broken or dialectical; rather is it the boundary or limit of all our attempts.[1] How can human utterance carry the self-utterance of God? After wrestling with this problem in a sustained discussion on the task of the ministry of the Word of God, Barth made the significant statement: 'It may be that the Word, the Word of God, which we ourselves shall never speak, has put on our weakness and unprofitableness so that *our* word *in* its very weakness and unprofitableness has become capable at least of becoming the frame, the earthen vessel of the Word of God.'[2] Then at once the question arises, if this is so, can theology, should theology, pass beyond prolegomena to Christology? This carries us to the third point we have to make here.

(c) God's Word is not only object of our knowing but Subject. As Word of *God* it is never object without being Subject.[3] God is the Lord who reveals himself to us by addressing us in his Word, but in such a way that his Word is always God speaking to us in Person in an ever-renewed encounter of speaking and hearing, of giving and receiving. That is what happens when we engage in exegesis and wrestle with the text in order to let ourselves hear God's Word speaking to us out of it. Our wrestling cannot make the text convey to us the Word of God— but that is the sovereign mystery, the downright miracle of God's grace: God himself speaks to us out of the Holy Scriptures and in such a way that he is both the Lord of the speaking and the Lord of the hearing.

In other words, *God's Word is identical with Jesus Christ*, and therefore it is in the power of Christ that the Word is heard as well as spoken. In Jesus Christ God relates himself immediately to us, when from our side we are separated from him, and establishes a two-way connexion between himself and us and us and himself. If Christ is the Word of God become Man, then he is not only the Word of God come to man, but as Man he bears, he is, the Word of God. In him our weakness and unprofitableness have been taken up, so that in him our human word in spite of its weakness and unprofitableness may be not only the frame

[1] *WW*, p. 209f, and *ChrD*, p. 460.   [2] *WW*, p. 216.
[3] *ChrD*, pp. 215ff, 149ff, etc. See James Brown, *Subject and Object in Modern Theology*, London 1955, pp. 140ff which gives a full account of Barth's later thinking on this in his *Church Dogmatics*.

and the earthen vessel of the Word, but the speaking of that Word.[1] Jesus Christ, then, the Word made flesh, is not only the Word as God utters it, but that same Word heard and uttered and lived out by Man. That is the Word we hear in the Holy Scriptures, the Word of God in human form, which can be uttered by human lips, so that by the grace and power of Christ our uttering of the Word of God may also be God's own speech to men. Therefore we may fulfil our task in preaching and in teaching, not only by saying that God has become Man, but by saying it as *God's* Word to man, believing that in our speaking in his Name, it is God himself who speaks it; it is ours to utter only as he puts it into our mouth and ours to utter it after him. It is because the Word of God is not only God in his self-revelation, but Man, man to whom the Word is communicated, that it can be received by man, known by him, uttered by him, and yet remain God's very Word. It is Word which as God and Man carries in itself and conveys in its self-communication the active possibility of true and faithful response to it. That is the direction in which Barth's theology moved as toward the end of this period he produced his first attempt at dogmatics, *Die Christliche Lehre im Entwurf. Bd. I. Die Lehre vom Worte Gottes, Prolegomena zur christlichen Dogmatik,* 1927.

3. Christian Dogmatics

Many of Barth's would-be friends were aghast at this turn of events, and began to accuse him of a lapse back into scholasticism.[2] They had welcomed his great prophetic protests, his attempt to break away through the bog which had sucked Christianity down into the depths of a romantic-idealistic bourgeois culture; although they looked upon him as a sort of pioneer extremist, they professed to welcome his contribution as 'a marginal gloss' or as 'a corrective', to use his own terms, to prevailing theological tendencies. But when Barth insisted on thinking through the new starting-point systematically and consistently, they drew back and started to attack him. But Barth was prepared for that, and sought to meet it all the way through the work by insisting that it was under the compulsion of sheer obedience to the truth of the Word of God that a careful, scientific attempt at consistent understanding of its own inner content had to be undertaken. 'As I look back upon the

---

[1] Cf. *Erklärung des Philipperbriefes,* 1927, p. 57 f (ET, 1961, p. 63f); *ChrD,* pp. 220 ff, 254 ff.

[2] Barth's letters to Thurneysen (*Gd-Md*) make it quite clear that genuine dogmatics became a burning interest of Barth right from the start of his Göttingen professorship.

road I have taken, I appear to be like someone groping his way up a
dark church tower who unwittingly laid hold of the bell-rope, instead
of the railing, and to his horror heard the great church-bell strike over
him but not only for him. He had not wished it and he could and would
not wish to repeat it. After meeting with such an experience he will
climb down as cautiously as possible.' Then, Barth added, if his previous
work had played and might still play the part of a corrective or marginal
gloss, that was not what he had set out to do, for he was simply one who
had put himself at the disposal of the teaching of God's Word.[1]

But Barth also saw that it was imperative to put off the prophet's
mantle that others had thrust upon his shoulders, for this prophetic
guise was leading to all sorts of exaggerated 'Barthianism' which he
deplored, which so clung to the protesting elements wrapped around
his early thought that they made it out to be the very kernel, and so
avoided facing up to the really fundamental questions that had to be
raised, and not least the hard work a new dogmatics would involve.
Barth refused to be treated as a sort of prophetic virtuoso playing about
dialectically with problematics of modern theology—he insisted on being
'an ordinary theologian'.[2] No doubt he did stand for a spiritual movement, but it had its own grounds in the Word of God, its own deep
resources, and those must be brought to light in an ordered *theology*.

Moreover, it had become perfectly clear to him that the dialectical
rejection of mysticism and dogmatism was not enough—the theology of
the Word required a positive doctrinal articulation adequate to the positive truth of the Word of God and yet appropriate to its nature as event
and grace. The way forward must come from a concentration upon
Christology, upon the Word made flesh, for therein there opened up the
possibility of a dogmatics genuinely bound up with a form taken from
the Word rather than from contemporary and temporal philosophies.[3]
The dialectical thinking had helped to open up that road, for in rejecting
mysticism, it rejected epistemological Apollinarianism—that is, a dis-
placing of the human subject by the divine Subject in our knowledge of
God's Word, and in rejecting dogmatism, it rejected epistemological
adoptionism—that is, the adopting or the objectifying of human forms
as the objects of theological veneration and knowledge.[4] But with the

[1] *ChrD, Vorwort*, p. ix.   [2] *ChrD*, p. ix.
[3] At the same time Barth was determined not to allow his Christological
approach to keep him from full and adequate treatment of the Fatherhood of
God, creation, providence, etc. Cf. the letter of March 20, 1924, *Gd-Md*, p. 106.
'Mit der Menschwerdung gilt es jedenfalls vorsichtig umzusehen, damit man
sich nicht in das exklusive "Jesus Christus"-Loch der Lutheraner verrennt.'
[4] Cf. *ZdZ*, 1930, pp. 378ff, and *ChrD*, pp. 294ff, 325f.

man's hearing is grounded beyond him in God's Word. That Word does not depend on man, for its actuality is altogether grounded in itself. Hence the meaning and possibility of dogmatics is not found in Christian faith but in the Word of God. The Word of God is not founded and maintained on Christian faith but the Christian faith is founded and maintained upon the Word of God. We know God only through God and in God, or in that we are known by him, and therefore we cannot offer any proof of our knowledge of God outside of our actual knowledge of him, that is, outside of our acknowledgment of his self-revelation. We cannot offer any evidence of our knowledge of God's Word, except in that we recognise that Word in its self-evidence to us and participate in its communication. But does that not mean that we both start from God as our presupposition and end with him as our conclusion, that we are really moving in circle?

Barth admits that, looked at from the point of view of logical form, that is a *petitio principii*. If this were the religio-psychological circle of theologians like Wobbermin (beginning and ending with man's self-understanding) that would be a damaging criticism, but the question must be asked whether in a genuine *theo*-logy we are not shut up to this kind of movement by the very nature of the subject-matter, that is, by the very nature of God himself? That is indeed the case, for in the knowledge of God we are concerned with One who is his own ground and his own evidence, and knowledge of this God can take place only as he breaks into the midst of our knowing in this world, to give us knowledge of himself from beyond any possibilitiy of our own. Scientific theology can operate only through the critical, backward inquiry of a thinking that takes its rise out of the prior act of God's self-revelation. It would not be scientific if it retreated from its own reality and reached for outside standards of logic or alien forms of description; it must operate solely from within the concrete situation set up between it and its object, and to follow through its thinking wholly under the control of that object, the Word of God. Apart from the incursion of God's Word into the movement of our thought, any so-called knowledge of God on our part would be empty and meaningless—we would be left within the vicious circle of our own subjectivity and vanity.[1]

In view of this, Dogmatics must be described as the methodical and interpretative reference of the human word in preaching back to the Word of God proclaimed in it. That takes place through a critical explication of the relation between the preached Word and the Revelation

[1] *ChrD*, pp. 105ff. See also *ZdZ*, 1929, 6, p. 561, and *CD* II.1, pp. 244ff.

attested in the Scriptures in order to test the agreement, the propriety and the adequacy of the preached Word to the material content and ground of Revelation. This reflexive movement places the human word of the Church under the judgment of the Word of God and so gives it orientation and direction. It is that critical testing and controlling of the proclamation of the Church by reference to the Word of God heard in the Holy Scriptures that gives to dogmatics its scientific character. By *dogma* is to be understood the fundamental agreement between Church proclamation and the Truth of God made known in his revelation. Dogma is in no sense to be taken as identical with the ultimate Truth of God but it is the essence of the agreement in the God/man, Revelation/Church relationship into which we must inquire, a relationship which arises from the act of the divine grace on the one side and from the responsible fulfilment of the Church's commission on the other side. Dogmatics is not to be understood, therefore, in the Roman sense, as the unfolding of revealed truths immanent in the historical life of the Church, but as the critical inquiry into dogma, and therefore a corrective and constructive inquiry into the relation between the dogmatic formulations of the Church and dogma.[1]

In so far as dogma is the relation of Revelation to the human word of the Church, it is God's eternal, unchangeable, infallible, definitive Truth, but in so far as it is the relation of the human word of the Church to Revelation, it is temporal, incomplete, changeable, fallible truth. On the one side dogma may be regarded as archetypal truth, but on the other side as only ectypal truth. Dogma thus provides dogmatics with its *scopus* by pointing to the ultimate Truth after which it inquires, and in relation to which all its dogmatic formulations are to be regarded only as fallible attempts to approach it, but made in the recognition that the ultimate Truth lies on the other side of the eschatological boundary and limit set to human activity on earth and in history. Thus dogma, referring to truth as we know it, is essentially an eschatological concept, and dogmatics is the activity of the pilgrim Church, the *theologia viatorum*. As such it must never seek to usurp God's point of view, or to identify its statements with God's Word. It can never be the last word. It must regard itself as summoned to perpetual inquiry in which the statements it attains in its struggle to be obedient to the Truth of Revelation are to be regarded as having the nature still of questions after the Truth, and as pointers and guides towards it for the use of the Church in the fulfilment of its commission to proclaim the Word of God to mankind.[2]

[1] *ChrD*, pp. 112ff.   [2] *ChrD*, pp. 121ff.

(2) Under the second heading of *The Revelation of God*, Barth goes on to inquire into the ultimate ground of our actual knowledge of God in the Church. If, under the actuality of the Word of God, the inquiry was one which moved from below upward into Revelation, that is, from the form which God's Word takes in human preaching to the Word of God itself attested in Revelation, then the inquiry in this second chapter is one which moves from above downward, from the constitutive Revelation of God to Holy Scripture and to the proclamation of the Church. The basic theme of this, the main section of the volume, is that Revelation is God himself, and therefore belief in Revelation is precisely coincident with belief in God, and belief in God is exactly belief in God in his Revelation. In that Revelation is God revealing himself, God in his Revelation, we are concerned immediately with God as Father, Son and Holy Spirit. In other words, immediately we are concerned with the God who speaks, the God who reveals himself as the Lord, we are concerned with the Trinity—with God who alone is the Revealer, who exclusively is Revelation, and is himself that which is Revealed. Or, to put it in still other words, this is the inquiry into the Subject, Object and Predicate of the statement *Deus dixit*, 'God has spoken.'[1]

Up to this point in his discussion, Barth has established three main things: (*a*) God stands over against man, the preacher of his Word, primarily as he who commissions him, who lays his Word upon human lips, without ceasing to utter his Word himself and to be the only One who speaks in and through his Word. (*b*) God stands over against man, the hearer of his Word, primarily as he who is the Answerer to the question of man's existence which can only have become a question because its answer had already been given. (*c*) God stands over against the knowing of man primarily as he who gives him knowledge of himself, so that only with this gift can man begin to know him at all. Now, Barth seeks to gather up all those three statements in the single statement that 'God reveals himself as Lord.' This statement is to be understood, he says, as an equation. God's revelation is the revelation of his Lordship, of his confrontation of man, his address to him, his control over him, and his undertaking for him. Man, as the receiver of Revelation, is never in any circumstances the lord. He is commissioned with the Word of God without being given any power over it, for he can only listen to it. The Word has already answered him before he has inquired of it, so that he can only think it *a posteriori*. In the Word man is known before he knows, so that he can *only* begin to know with its actions upon him.

[1] *ChrD*, p. 126f.

This word 'only' describes the limits within which man is placed as a receiver of Revelation.[1]

It is only in and with the act of God's Revelation upon him that man knows he has a Lord, before whom he is summoned to be the obedient servant—'Speak, Lord, for thy servant heareth'—and learns to live in gratitude and joy with God as his Lord. That is the meaning of Revelation, into which dogmatics inquires. But immediately it inquires into the activity of that Lordship and into the modes of that activity, it is concerned with the doctrine of the Trinity, for the Trinity is the doctrine of the living, active God, who reveals himself as Creator, Saviour and Redeemer. The Trinity sets forth the fact that, in all our knowledge of him, God is active and never passive. He is always the Lord, the Subject, whom we can never master or convert into a mere object of our knowledge, whom we cannot know at all except in so far as he gives himself freely to our knowing. The Trinity is the doctrine of the Mystery of God, that is, the living reality of God whose possibility resides wholly in himself, and whom we cannot know or understand except in and through and out of himself. It is to the Revelation of God in its concrete content that the doctrine of the Trinity points, and at the same time it sets a limit to our knowledge, for, since the Truth of God is grounded in itself, it cannot be measured by our thinking or formulations of it, but remains the transcendent ground of all our knowing and speaking of him.[2]

Hence, that *God reveals himself* is seen to be the root of the doctrine of the Trinity. Historically speaking, that means that the doctrine of the Trinity arises out of the concrete revelation of Jesus Christ as the Lord, so that the dogmatic inquiry into the ground of our knowledge of God leads into the heart of Christology, into the doctrine of the Revelation of the Father in the Son through the power of the Holy Spirit.[3] Thus, after expounding the basic contents of the doctrine of the Trinity, Barth goes on to inquire into the Incarnation of the Word as the objective possibility of Revelation, and into the outpouring of the Holy Spirit as the subjective possibility of Revelation. The question as to the ground of God's self-revelation must carry our thinking into the inner necessity and meaning of the Incarnation and into the conditions of the possibility of our reception of that Revelation through God's grace.[4]

Through the Incarnation we understand that the ground of Revelation lies in God alone, and that there is no other possibility of Revelation

---

[1] *ChrD*, p. 131 f.   [2] *ChrD*, p. 138 f, 170 f.
[3] *ChrD*, p. 141 f, 149 ff.   [4] *ChrD*, p. 214 f, 284 f.

concentration upon the Incarnation of the Word, upon Jesus Christ, God and Man in one Person, dialectical thinking had to fall away and positive Christological thinking had to take its place.[1] 'Dogmatic thinking is from end to end thinking κατὰ τὸν Χριστόν, or it is not dogmatic thinking at all.'[2]

Die Christliche Dogmatik was published deliberately as an *Entwurf*, that is, as a project or first sketch. It was meant to open up discussion through an attempt to get to grips with the problems of a real dogmatics cleared from their entanglement with all sorts of extraneous questions.[3] Dogmatics of this sort, dogmatics standing on its own feet, without support and confirmation from other sources, but within the framework of thinking grounded in revelation, was really unknown, and therefore the new dogmatics was admittedly a complete break with what had preceded it, e.g. the *Dogmatik* of Barth's own teacher, Herrmann.[4] The thinking of modern times with which it stood in some line was that of the Blumhardts, Dorner, Kierkegaard, Kohlbrügge, Kutter, Julius Müller, Overbeck and Vilmar, who are expressly mentioned in the preface.[5] But in spite of that connexion Barth insists that he is striking out on a lone road, for at least two hundred years this sort of task had not been taken seriously in Protestant dogmatics. Far from claiming to be the last word, his dogmatics was but the attempt of a beginner, and what he desired was that someone else would come along and do it better.[6]

The task which Barth set himself in this volume of prolegomena was not to supply *a priori* or in the abstract an epistemology, and then to order the contents of our knowledge of God on that basis, but rather to take a preliminary leap into the midst of the actual knowledge of God we have in the Church, and to consider in that way what theological thinking actually bound up with its subject-matter is.[7] Such *prolegomena* must take the form of a survey of the *legomena*, the doctrine of the Trinity, Christology, the doctrine of the Spirit, the doctrine of the Word, of faith, and of the Church, in order to discern their own proper form and structure, so that the explication of the material content of that knowledge may be undertaken only through forms lawful and relevant to it. It is an attempt to inquire from within actual knowledge after its own ground and presupposition, and through a clarification of the

---

[1] See 'Parergon', *Evangelische Theologie*, 1948-9, pp. 223f, 266, 272.
[2] *ChrD*, p. 437.
[3] *ChrD*, p. viif. See the letter to Thurneysen of 1924, *Gd-Md*, pp. 97ff.
[4] *ChrD*, p. vi. Cf. the letter of Feb. 15, 1925, *Gd-Md*, p. 131f; and *TC*, p. 238f.   [5] Ibid.
[6] *ChrD*, p. viii.   [7] *ChrD*, p. 16.

way in which it has arisen to bring it into orderly and careful articulation. Only in the actual course of such exposition and explanation would a proper, relevant and legitimate epistemology emerge. That is the essential way of science, and it is a *science* in that proper sense, relevant to the nature of its own object, that dogmatics claims to be.[1] Therefore it must never allow itself to be torn away from its object and erected into a system of ideas, claiming truth in itself as if it were ideology and not theology.

Die Christliche Dogmatik is divided into four chapters, 'The Actuality of the Word of God', 'The Revelation of God' (as Father, Son and Holy Spirit), which forms the central mass of the volume, 'The Holy Scripture', and 'The Proclamation of the Church'.

(1) Under the heading of *The Actuality of the Word of God* Barth takes his starting-point within the Church where God meets us in his Word, for what we are concerned with in theology is the speaking God, not a dumb God, whom we know only through a feeling of utter dependence, not a God we reach only after our own talking and argumentation, but the God who comes to us and speaks to us and asks of us the response of faith and prayer and worship.[2] It is in the Church that God's Word meets us, not in the form of an utterance straight from heaven but in the form of human proclamation, and therefore theology arises also within the Church where through the questioning and answering of critical self-reflection the Church tests its preaching and hearing by the standard of the Word of God. The Church's proclamation is, therefore, not only the starting-point but also the goal of dogmatic activity, for it is the purpose of dogmatics to serve the proclamation of the Word by clarifying it and protecting it from impurities and perversions.[3]

The break with the dogmatic tradition emanating from Schleiermacher is here very evident, that is, with a dogmatics of the religious man, which has its starting-point in the depths of his soul and not in the Word of God, the dogmatics of the man who does not need to hear the Word of God for he has heard it already within himself. That radical divergence from the tradition of Schleiermacher is apparent throughout the whole volume.[4] At this point Barth is concerned to make clear that

---

[1] *ChrD*, pp. 1ff and 10ff. Cf. also Heinrich Barth, 'Das Recht unserer theologischen Fakultät', *ZdZ*, 1928, pp. 477ff; and Heinrich Scholz's introduction to Schleiermacher's *Kurze Darstellung des theologischen Studiums*, pp. xxvff.
[2] Cf. here Barth's essay on Herrmann, in *TC*, pp. 238ff.
[3] *ChrD*, pp. 18-36.
[4] Cf. especially 306ff. But cf. Barth's fascinating discussion of Herrmann's dogmatic principles in which it becomes evident that it was in following out a truth he learned from Herrmann, but interpreting it quite differently from

the Word of God which is the subject-matter of dogmatic activity is not the word that man says to himself or the concretion of his own self-understanding. It is a genuinely objective Word from God which makes use of human speech as its means on earth, so that the human word in the Church's preaching is empowered and accompanied by that Word of God which assumes it into the movement of its own self-communication and authenticates itself in and through it.[1]

This is expounded by Barth in his doctrine of the three forms of the Word of God: behind the form in which it sounds forth to us in the Church's proclamation, there is the form which the Word has assumed in the Holy Scriptures in which the Word attests itself in the words of the prophets and apostles; and behind that is the Word uttered in the original and immediate self-revelation of God.[2] It is because of this condescension of the Word of God to become speech to man through the medium of human words, from men to men, that the Church, in obedience to the command of God and relying upon his promise, can dare to speak in his Name and to take his Word in exposition of Holy Scripture upon its lips, knowing that God himself will speak and through its faltering human utterance make himself known.[3] Dogmatics is not concerned with any one of these three forms in which the Word of God comes to us, but with the three forms in their unity and their threefoldness. It is concerned with the situation set up between the speaking God and the hearing man in which man is both questioned before God and is given the answer to that questioning, and therefore it is concerned to trace out the way of the knowledge of God actual in that situation, which it finds to be the way, not of man's cognition so much as recognition of God, not of knowledge so much as of acknowledgment of God, in making himself known to him.[4]

As one would expect, Barth insists that this God/man, God-speaking/ man-hearing, relationship is *irreversible*. We do not hear the Word of God except in the Church, in the midst of our fellow-men and women in historical relationships, but that does not allow us to pass from man to God, to argue from history to God's Word. This is one of the important points where we can see on Barth the influence of Overbeck's notion of *Urgeschichte*, although it is quite frankly changed in his usage and brought into line with the doctrine of the Word. *Urgeschichte* means for Barth that the Revelation of God enters into our actual history and

---

Herrmann, that he was led to break a way through the circular reasoning of Neo-Protestantism (*TC*, pp. 253 ff).
[1] See the letters of 18 and 28 May, 1924, *Gd-Md*, pp. 111 ff.
[2] *ChrD*, pp. 37 ff.   [3] *ChrD*, pp. 47 ff.   [4] *ChrD*, pp. 63 ff, and 82 ff.

meets us within it, God speaking in person in concrete particular ways, but in such a way that Revelation is not tied to history or resolved into it, for that would mean that Revelation, like all else that is placed under history, only comes in order to die and perish. Revelation is rather that which breaks into history and becomes historical without being resigned to the history of this passing world; and therefore it becomes historical in a way that breaks through the history of the fallen world, not because it is less real but because it is more real. That is the new kind of history that takes place in Christ, *Urgeschichte*, the original history of Revelation, history which is not merely historical event, but history invaded by the creative and redeeming Word of God, history which we can only grasp and understand by listening to the Word of God, by participating in its happening, and which we cannot understand by abstracting it from the speaking and revealing God who meets us in it. Rather is it from the point of view of *Urgeschichte* that we are to understand all history for then we can see beyond its uncertainties and relativities and contingencies and ambiguities to its true meaning and foundation in the God of history.[1]

The supreme instance, the concrete form of this Revelation history, is the Incarnation, and therefore the speaking of God in his Word cannot be explained except by direct understanding of the Word made flesh. It is in the light of the Incarnation that we see that God's Word is never to be thought of simply as timeless, self-eventuating event, but rather as concrete, particular event, within space and time, involving an *illic et tunc* of the speaking God and a *hic et nunc* of the hearing man. But because this Revelation is irreversible, it cannot be perceived through the inspection of history, even of New Testament history, far less the history of the Church throughout the centuries. That the Word of God in history does not and cannot mean that history is the Word of God, therefore neither the history of dogma, nor the investigation of the historical consciousness of the pious soul or of the Church, can take the place of proper Christian Dogmatics which has its material content and its creative norm in the Word of God alone.[2]

This approach of Barth, however, raises another important question: Whether after all his argument is not caught in a *petitio principii*?[3] We do not begin either from man or from God but from man and God posited together by God's grace in a relationship between God speaking and man hearing. That relationship, however, is an irreversible one, for

---

[1] *ChrD*, pp. 43ff, 80ff, 230ff, etc. [2] *ChrD*, p. 81.
[3] Cf. again Barth's essay on Herrmann, *TC*, p. 255f.

man's hearing is grounded beyond him in God's Word. That Word does not depend on man, for its actuality is altogether grounded in itself. Hence the meaning and possibility of dogmatics is not found in Christian faith but in the Word of God. The Word of God is not founded and maintained on Christian faith but the Christian faith is founded and maintained upon the Word of God. We know God only through God and in God, or in that we are known by him, and therefore we cannot offer any proof of our knowledge of God outside of our actual knowledge of him, that is, outside of our acknowledgment of his self-revelation. We cannot offer any evidence of our knowledge of God's Word, except in that we recognise that Word in its self-evidence to us and participate in its communication. But does that not mean that we both start from God as our presupposition and end with him as our conclusion, that we are really moving in circle?

Barth admits that, looked at from the point of view of logical form, that is a *petitio principii*. If this were the religio-psychological circle of theologians like Wobbermin (beginning and ending with man's self-understanding) that would be a damaging criticism, but the question must be asked whether in a genuine *theo*-logy we are not shut up to this kind of movement by the very nature of the subject-matter, that is, by the very nature of God himself? That is indeed the case, for in the knowledge of God we are concerned with One who is his own ground and his own evidence, and knowledge of this God can take place only as he breaks into the midst of our knowing in this world, to give us knowledge of himself from beyond any possibilitiy of our own. Scientific theology can operate only through the critical, backward inquiry of a thinking that takes its rise out of the prior act of God's self-revelation. It would not be scientific if it retreated from its own reality and reached for outside standards of logic or alien forms of description; it must operate solely from within the concrete situation set up between it and its object, and to follow through its thinking wholly under the control of that object, the Word of God. Apart from the incursion of God's Word into the movement of our thought, any so-called knowledge of God on our part would be empty and meaningless—we would be left within the vicious circle of our own subjectivity and vanity.[1]

In view of this, Dogmatics must be described as the methodical and interpretative reference of the human word in preaching back to the Word of God proclaimed in it. That takes place through a critical explication of the relation between the preached Word and the Revelation

[1] *ChrD*, pp. 105 ff. See also *ZdZ*, 1929, 6, p. 561, and *CD* II.1, pp. 244 ff.

attested in the Scriptures in order to test the agreement, the propriety and the adequacy of the preached Word to the material content and ground of Revelation. This reflexive movement places the human word of the Church under the judgment of the Word of God and so gives it orientation and direction. It is that critical testing and controlling of the proclamation of the Church by reference to the Word of God heard in the Holy Scriptures that gives to dogmatics its scientific character. By *dogma* is to be understood the fundamental agreement between Church proclamation and the Truth of God made known in his revelation. Dogma is in no sense to be taken as identical with the ultimate Truth of God but it is the essence of the agreement in the God/man, Revelation/ Church relationship into which we must inquire, a relationship which arises from the act of the divine grace on the one side and from the responsible fulfilment of the Church's commission on the other side. Dogmatics is not to be understood, therefore, in the Roman sense, as the unfolding of revealed truths immanent in the historical life of the Church, but as the critical inquiry into dogma, and therefore a corrective and constructive inquiry into the relation between the dogmatic formulations of the Church and dogma.[1]

In so far as dogma is the relation of Revelation to the human word of the Church, it is God's eternal, unchangeable, infallible, definitive Truth, but in so far as it is the relation of the human word of the Church to Revelation, it is temporal, incomplete, changeable, fallible truth. On the one side dogma may be regarded as archetypal truth, but on the other side as only ectypal truth. Dogma thus provides dogmatics with its *scopus* by pointing to the ultimate Truth after which it inquires, and in relation to which all its dogmatic formulations are to be regarded only as fallible attempts to approach it, but made in the recognition that the ultimate Truth lies on the other side of the eschatological boundary and limit set to human activity on earth and in history. Thus dogma, referring to truth as we know it, is essentially an eschatological concept, and dogmatics is the activity of the pilgrim Church, the *theologia viatorum*. As such it must never seek to usurp God's point of view, or to identify its statements with God's Word. It can never be the last word. It must regard itself as summoned to perpetual inquiry in which the statements it attains in its struggle to be obedient to the Truth of Revelation are to be regarded as having the nature still of questions after the Truth, and as pointers and guides towards it for the use of the Church in the fulfilment of its commission to proclaim the Word of God to mankind.[2]

[1] *ChrD*, pp. 112ff.   [2] *ChrD*, pp. 121ff.

(2) Under the second heading of *The Revelation of God*, Barth goes on to inquire into the ultimate ground of our actual knowledge of God in the Church. If, under the actuality of the Word of God, the inquiry was one which moved from below upward into Revelation, that is, from the form which God's Word takes in human preaching to the Word of God itself attested in Revelation, then the inquiry in this second chapter is one which moves from above downward, from the constitutive Revelation of God to Holy Scripture and to the proclamation of the Church. The basic theme of this, the main section of the volume, is that Revelation is God himself, and therefore belief in Revelation is precisely coincident with belief in God, and belief in God is exactly belief in God in his Revelation. In that Revelation is God revealing himself, God in his Revelation, we are concerned immediately with God as Father, Son and Holy Spirit. In other words, immediately we are concerned with the God who speaks, the God who reveals himself as the Lord, we are concerned with the Trinity—with God who alone is the Revealer, who exclusively is Revelation, and is himself that which is Revealed. Or, to put it in still other words, this is the inquiry into the Subject, Object and Predicate of the statement *Deus dixit*, 'God has spoken.'[1]

Up to this point in his discussion, Barth has established three main things: (*a*) God stands over against man, the preacher of his Word, primarily as he who commissions him, who lays his Word upon human lips, without ceasing to utter his Word himself and to be the only One who speaks in and through his Word. (*b*) God stands over against man, the hearer of his Word, primarily as he who is the Answerer to the question of man's existence which can only have become a question because its answer had already been given. (*c*) God stands over against the knowing of man primarily as he who gives him knowledge of himself, so that only with this gift can man begin to know him at all. Now, Barth seeks to gather up all those three statements in the single statement that 'God reveals himself as Lord.' This statement is to be understood, he says, as an equation. God's revelation is the revelation of his Lordship, of his confrontation of man, his address to him, his control over him, and his undertaking for him. Man, as the receiver of Revelation, is never in any circumstances the lord. He is commissioned with the Word of God without being given any power over it, for he can only listen to it. The Word has already answered him before he has inquired of it, so that he can only think it *a posteriori*. In the Word man is known before he knows, so that he can *only* begin to know with its actions upon him.

[1] *ChrD*, p. 126f.

This word 'only' describes the limits within which man is placed as a receiver of Revelation.[1]

It is only in and with the act of God's Revelation upon him that man knows he has a Lord, before whom he is summoned to be the obedient servant—'Speak, Lord, for thy servant heareth'—and learns to live in gratitude and joy with God as his Lord. That is the meaning of Revelation, into which dogmatics inquires. But immediately it inquires into the activity of that Lordship and into the modes of that activity, it is concerned with the doctrine of the Trinity, for the Trinity is the doctrine of the living, active God, who reveals himself as Creator, Saviour and Redeemer. The Trinity sets forth the fact that, in all our knowledge of him, God is active and never passive. He is always the Lord, the Subject, whom we can never master or convert into a mere object of our knowledge, whom we cannot know at all except in so far as he gives himself freely to our knowing. The Trinity is the doctrine of the Mystery of God, that is, the living reality of God whose possibility resides wholly in himself, and whom we cannot know or understand except in and through and out of himself. It is to the Revelation of God in its concrete content that the doctrine of the Trinity points, and at the same time it sets a limit to our knowledge, for, since the Truth of God is grounded in itself, it cannot be measured by our thinking or formulations of it, but remains the transcendent ground of all our knowing and speaking of him.[2]

Hence, that *God reveals himself* is seen to be the root of the doctrine of the Trinity. Historically speaking, that means that the doctrine of the Trinity arises out of the concrete revelation of Jesus Christ as the Lord, so that the dogmatic inquiry into the ground of our knowledge of God leads into the heart of Christology, into the doctrine of the Revelation of the Father in the Son through the power of the Holy Spirit.[3] Thus, after expounding the basic contents of the doctrine of the Trinity, Barth goes on to inquire into the Incarnation of the Word as the objective possibility of Revelation, and into the outpouring of the Holy Spirit as the subjective possibility of Revelation. The question as to the ground of God's self-revelation must carry our thinking into the inner necessity and meaning of the Incarnation and into the conditions of the possibility of our reception of that Revelation through God's grace.[4]

Through the Incarnation we understand that the ground of Revelation lies in God alone, and that there is no other possibility of Revelation

---

[1] *ChrD*, p. 131f.　　[2] *ChrD*, p. 138f, 170f.
[3] *ChrD*, p. 141f, 149ff.　　[4] *ChrD*, p. 214f, 284f.

than that which we see in the actuality of the Son or Word of God become man—man, that is to say, in the same sense as we all are men, as
flesh, or as the Bearer of our contradiction with God and with ourselves.
It is in Jesus Christ the incarnate Son that we have the Word of God in
its pure form. He is God meeting with us, speaking in Person. In him
the Word of God is made flesh of our flesh, and the Truth of God is
Actuality in our midst. There are two aspects of this one event. On the
one hand, we must think of it as the breaking-in of the transcendent
Truth of God into our historical existence, yet in such a way that God
remains God, and his Truth is transcendent to all the relativities and
ambiguities of history. This is in no sense a denial of history but rather
its affirmation, because it anchors history in pure history and roots it
again in the divine creative act. As we have seen, this is what Barth calls
Urgeschichte, genuine, actual, primal history that is the predicate of
God's action in Jesus Christ and which cannot be abstracted from the
fact of Christ, the miraculous ingression of God into our human and
historical existence. It is here in this union between the Revelation
which is God himself and our historical existence in the flesh that we
have the pure Word of God in a form which creates for us the objective
possibility of thinking it, understanding it, and receiving it. Here what
is utterly impossible for us becomes possible, the unknown becomes
known—in *Jesus*. And it is precisely here in Jesus, where we meet God
face to face, that we really know that, apart from this action of God
upon us in him, God remains for us unknowable, and utterly beyond
any human possibilities. It is thus the seriousness with which Barth
takes the humanity of Jesus that is the concrete ground for his rejection
of all natural theology, and all aprioristic notions of the knowability of
God, behind the back of Jesus Christ.[1]

The other aspect of this, however, must be made clear, for it is equally
important. This pure Word of God strikes us, meets us, encounters us,
in the midst of lostness, of our opposition to God, of our sin against
him, and in the midst of the contradiction in which we find ourselves to
ourselves. The Word is not broken or refracted by contradiction or sin
in itself, for in itself it is completely and unreservedly the Truth and
Revelation of God, but in Jesus Christ that Truth has entered into our
darkness and alienation in order to be there unreservedly and completely
Revelation of God. In Jesus Christ the Truth of God and Actuality meet
in the midst of our separation from God and hostility to him, so that he

---

[1] *ChrD*, pp. 225 ff, 230 ff and see pp. 136 ff. Cf. the discussion of the notion of
capax infiniti in the light of the Virgin Birth of Jesus, pp. 269, 272 ff.

is the fulfilment of God's Revelation moving through our conflict, rejection and judgment, into new creation. That is the life and passion of the Son or Word of God become man who submits himself to our existence in contradiction under the Law and takes upon himself our judgment, and is obedient even unto death. Thus, by overcoming our contradiction, he creates for us the objective possibility of receiving God's Word and appropriating God's grace in him. In him God's Word becomes reconciliation in the midst of our time and history, and in that it is the actuality of reconciliation, it is also the actuality of the divine revelation to man.[1]

It is in that unity of revelation and reconciliation that we see the absolute miracle of God in Jesus Christ. But again we can see this in its two-fold aspect. On the one hand, it is the ingression of God into our human existence, the assumption of our human nature, manifest in the Virgin Birth of Jesus—Revelation as the way from God to man; but on the other hand, it is also the raising up of our human nature from its corruption and lost condition into union with the divine life, manifest in the resurrection of Jesus. The whole life and existence of Jesus on earth bracketed between the birth and the resurrection is the actuality of God's revelation, in which God has given himself to man and reconciled man to himself, thus creating for man the objective possibility of Revelation. Jesus Christ is himself the absolutely new way God has provided for man from above; the way, the truth and the life of God among men, and therefore the way, the truth and the life of man with God. What is decisive here is the complete union of God and Man, the completeness of both the Deity and the Humanity of Jesus Christ. If he were not completely God he would not be identical with God's Revelation; if he were not completely Man he would not be to us the actuality of God's Revelation.[2]

From the Incarnation Barth addresses himself to the outpouring of the Holy Spirit as constituting the subjective possibility of Revelation. Here he is concerned to inquire into the conditions under which man can become a hearer and receiver of God's Word, while yet remaining creaturely man, and while yet in his distance and separation from God, without any capacity of his own for him. This is only possible on the ground of the Holy Spirit who is God come to us in his own reality and who makes knowledge of him possible by actualising within us a possibility from beyond ourselves altogether.[3]

The objective possibility of Revelation is given in Jesus Christ in

[1] *ChrD*, pp. 254 ff. [2] *ChrD*, pp. 272 ff. [3] *ChrD*, p. 284 f.

whom God communicates himself to man, reveals himself, opens up knowledge of himself for man—apart from the reality and actuality of that fact, there would be no possibility of Revelation for man at all. But the obverse of that is that God also comes to man, is personally present in him, opening up man from below, empowering him to receive what God gives and reveals, and so enabling him to participate in the opening up of knowledge of God from the side of God in Jesus Christ. It is by the pouring out of his Holy Spirit that God establishes a correlation or a correspondence between his self-revealing and man's receiving, within which alone knowledge of God can be actualised in man. Barth is concerned, however, to show that this does not take place on the ground of any inherent or latent possibilities immanent in man as such, but is in fact a supernatural and miraculous event in which man is given to know God from beyond any conceivable possibility from his side. To receive the Holy Spirit in this way is a recognition of the fact that we do not possess the Holy Spirit, and do not possess a possibility fo. God in ourselves. In other words, actual knowledge of God in the power of the Spirit opens our eyes to the fact of our own helplessness and incapacity over against God; it is something we can understand only from the positive knowledge we have through the Spirit.[1]

To put it in another way, this experience of the Holy Spirit carries with it an acknowledgment that the Holy Spirit is not the same as our spirit, for it is the experience of the transcendent Spirit of God come to us, and who carries us across the limitations of our own weakness into communion with the living God. This Spirit comes to us as Creator, Reconciler and Redeemer, i.e., in a creative and redemptive action in which the contradiction between man and God overcome in Jesus Christ is actualised as the victory of God within us.[2] The great sign of this Barth sees in Baptism, and to be sure, in infant Baptism, for it is there that we see so clearly that the subjective possibility of our knowledge of God is derived from beyond us in the objective act of the Spirit opening us up subjectively from below. That is what Barth speaks of here as *grace*, the pouring out of the Spirit upon man as an actuality for man from beyond him altogether. That is not to say that Baptism is itself grace or that actuality, but rather the sacrament or visible word which God has given to us to point us to the Word of God as made creatively actual by the power of the Spirit. Baptism—infant Baptism, water-Baptism, once for all administered—declares to him, Barth says, in a way drastically different from any in which he can tell himself, that grace

[1] *ChrD*, pp. 291 ff.   [2] See also *The Holy Ghost and the Christian Life.*

applies to him, and comes to him, and it assures him in the face of all his doubts that, in his battle of faith and obedience, he is not concerned with some Quixotic farce but with the Word of Truth.[1]

This doctrine of the subjective possibility of the Spirit Barth has to maintain on two fronts; against the Roman, Augustinian idea which thinks of a basic continuity between the spirit of man and the Spirit of God, and which is fundamentally a form of Semi-Pelagianism[2]; and especially against the teaching of Schleiermacher in his great reversal of the relation between the Spirit of God and the spirit of man which had the effect of blotting out the boundaries between them, and establishing a Protestant counterpart to Roman Semi-Pelagian pietism.[3] Far from being the subjective possibility of man for God, this interpretation of the Spirit within the depths of the human spirit is the most powerful expression of the contradiction of man with God and with himself. As against this teaching of Schleiermacher, so entrenched in Neo-Protestantism, Barth presses home the teaching that the work of the Holy Spirit upon us and in us cuts away from us the thought of any other possibility of man for God than that which we have in faith and obedience to God's Word in the communion of the Spirit.[4] Neither revelation nor the possibility of it is in any sense to be understood as a predicate of man, but solely as a predicate of God and as his gift in grace to man, to which he can only respond in faith and gratitude and by renunciation of any claim to such a possibility on his own.

What happens, then, in the pouring out of the Holy Spirit is that God assumes us within the circle of his own communion where we know God only in and through God, as we are known by him, and in which we share in God's knowledge of himself, of the Son by the Father and of the Father by the Son, through the Holy Spirit. It is within that circle of communion that we find that grace is both answer and question in the Gospel and man's response is both faith and obedience, and behind all stands the Yea and Amen of God. Man grasps God only as he is grasped by God, and lays hold of him only because God has first laid hold of man.[5]

(3) Under the heading of *The Holy Scripture* Barth comes from his inquiry into the ground of Revelation and its concrete content to its communication in human speech, that is, within the speech of man to man in history, and therefore within the transiency and fallibility of all

---

[1] *ChrD*, p. 299f.
[2] See again *The Holy Ghost and the Christian Life*, and *ChrD*, pp. 301 ff.
[3] *ChrD*, pp. 306 ff. [4] *ChrD*, pp. 311 ff. [5] *ChrD*, pp. 318 ff, 325 ff.

human speaking and acting. This is an inquiry into the nature of Holy Scripture as the original and legitimate witness to God's Revelation and the means which God in the free decision of his grace uses in order to speak to men in all ages his one divine Word. And therefore it is an inquiry into the Scripture-principle or the concrete norm which dogmatics employs in testing the language of the Church about God.[1]

The Bible is a historical datum and as such is open to historical investigation. When the Church and dogmatics speak of these Scriptures as *Holy* Scriptures they are making a judgment about them, however, which the historian *qua* historian is unable to make, for that is essentially a theological judgment. The historian as such can only discern in the Scriptures human documents and human words which lay no claim upon him for special consideration. But when the theologian makes his judgment regarding the Holy Scriptures, without disregarding or being able to disregard their historical nature, he regards and understands them not from out of themselves but from the *Urgeschichte* to which they bear witness, that is, from the fact of the original act of divine revelation in history which does not merely pass over into history as such but, while becoming historical event, is more than historical for it remains true to its own unique nature and majesty as Revelation of God transcendent to mere history.[2] As Barth has said earlier in the volume, Revelation is seen to be more than eternal history, for it is a point in temporal history, but it is more than temporal history for it is not bound to the irreversible sequence of temporal history—rather does it surround it as a circle round its centre and so encloses all history beyond, before and after. Thus all history is positively related to *Urgeschichte* as the circumference to the centre, as prophecy to fulfilment, as Advent to Christmas.[3]

In other words, when the Church acknowledges that the Scriptures are the Word of God, it reaches back behind their character as history to the object of the knowledge mediated through them. The Church finds in the Bible a primary datum, which is not to be separated from it nor to be confused with it, which is veiled in the Bible as much as it is unveiled through it, which is both hidden and revealed, namely the Word of God in its primary form, Revelation. In the Bible that Revelation has become history, but in such a way that, as history, it is the predicate of God himself, the history whose Subject is the living God who, as the Eternal, is the boundary of time. Here then the historian comes up against an event which is without any analogy in history, and which, as historian, he is unable to recognise, but which, if he recognises

---

[1] *ChrD*, pp. 334 ff.   [2] *ChrD*, p. 335 f.   [3] *ChrD*, p. 239.

it, he can recognise only as a member of the Christian Church, that is, through a theological judgment. That is a judgment, however, which can only be made within the actuality of the knowledge of God, within the theological ellipse set up when God's Word breaks into the movement of our thought and fills it with the content of God's self-revelation. That is the presupposition and ground of the Church's doctrine of Scripture, namely, the ground, object and content of the Word which the Church hears in Scripture. But if the Church acknowledges that it hears God's Word in Scripture, it is bound also to acknowledge that God has spoken in it, and to respect the Scripture as the holy medium or echo of God's Voice, and in that sense is itself the Word of God. Here, then, the form which the theological ellipse takes is that Scripture is recognised as God's Word by the fact that it *is* God's Word—for that is the *form* which God's Word has freely taken in giving us actual knowledge of God as the one Lord.

The Word of God comes to us in the Bible through the speech of sinful, fallible men to whom God has spoken and who bear witness to his speaking. We do not have here a direct speaking of God from heaven, but a speaking through a transient and imperfect human medium. No doubt the human word we hear in the Scriptures is not always appropriate or adequate to the Word which its authors have heard and to which they bear testimony, but nevertheless it is human word which God has freely chosen and decided to use as the form in which he speaks his Word to us. It is that objective side of the Scripture, the object of its testimony, that gives the Scripture its fundamental character as holy and inspired Word. There are differences between the Old Testament and the New Testament, between the middle of the Bible and the marginal areas, and there are significant differences in the witness between the prophets and apostles, Matthew and John, Romans and James, and so on, but all these differences are relative compared to their unity in the object, and it is that relation to their object which makes them what they are, *Holy* Scripture in which God speaks his Word and in which we hear his Word. Historically regarded, there may well be developments and changes in the religious experiences of the biblical writers, but that does not give us leave to speak about progressive revelation or a development of the Word of God, for the Word of God is God himself in his Revelation, and it is that one, complete Word which the Church hears in Old and New Testament, for the Holy Spirit utters that same Word, God himself, to the Church in all times and ages.[1]

[1] *ChrD*, p. 338 ff.

This does not mean that the Revelation of God can be read directly off the pages of the historical Scriptures, for the actuality of Revelation is only indirectly identical with the actuality of the Bible. Or, to use Barth's other way of speaking, although in the Scriptures the Word of God has become history, the history as such is not the Word of God. The Word does not have a history; it takes place historically and concretely, and we can hear it only through encounter with that historical happening of the Word, in which we come up against the Subject of that historical happening, God speaking in his Word. It is because we cannot speak of a direct identity of the Scripture as such with Revelation, although we cannot separate the Scripture from that Revelation, that our knowledge of the Bible as the Word of God is itself an event, an ever-new breaking-through to Revelation of faith and obedience.

It is important, then, to recognise that in the Bible there is this 'wall' between us and divine Revelation, namely, the man-conditioned and time-conditioned character of the witness. If we deny or ignore it, then we turn the Bible into an organ of direct and immediate oracular communication, and, in point of fact, deny Revelation itself, that is, deny God himself in his Revelation whom we hear and know only in decisive encounter and to whom we respond in faith and obedience.[1] Or, to put it in another way, the *Bible* is the *Word of God* to the Church in all ages because of the identity between them given by the action of the Holy Spirit in speaking the Word of God in the Bible, and in enabling the Church to hear that Word in the human words of the Bible. Hence the actuality of communication of God's Word to us in the Bible is grounded in, and included within, the actuality of Revelation itself.[2]

In the previous chapter Barth's inquiry took us into the doctrine of the Trinity as the ultimate ground of Revelation, for Revelation is God himself in his Revelation, but that Revelation was made objectively and subjectively possible for us in the Incarnation as the concrete way which Revelation took in coming to us, and in the pouring out of the Holy Spirit as the way which Revelation took in enabling us to receive that Revelation. Having established in this chapter that the actuality of the communication of God's Word to us in the Bible is grounded in the Actuality of Revelation itself, Barth goes on to inquire into the concrete way in which the communication of God's Word reaches us, and the concrete freedom which we have for that Word. There follows, then, a discussion of the objective and subjective conditions, the authority of

---

[1] *ChrD*, p. 344f. See also 'Das Schriftprinzip der reformierten Kirche', *ZdZ*, 3, pp. 119-140.   [2] *ChrD*, p. 358f.

the Church and the freedom of the conscience in which we hear the Word of God, corresponding to the objective possibility and subjective possibility of Revelation in the Incarnation and the gift of the Spirit.[1]

The first question that requires to be answered, then, is: How can and ought we to hear the Word of God speaking to us in the Scriptures? How does it actually happen, and how should it happen if it does not? What are the objective conditions under which the Word of God comes to us? Barth's answer is that it takes place and should take place within the authoritative sphere of the historical Church. We are not able, and ought not, to hear God speaking to us in the Scriptures otherwise than as objectively determined through the concrete authority of the Church, i.e., through the context and form in which the witness of the prophets and apostles comes to us *via* the Church, through the interpretation given to it by the representative teachers and doctrinal decisions of the Church, through the particular law under which the Church itself stands and hears the Word today. In other words, we actually hear the Word of God speaking through the Scriptures in such a way that our hearing is predisposed and determined and shaped through the previous hearing of the Church and through our place in the context of the Church as it hears that Word today. We must not think that we can or should isolate ourselves from it, just because in God's purpose the Word is communicated to us through the proclamation of the Church, and through proclamation that arises out of its hearing of that Word for itself and its interpretation of the Scriptures from generation to generation.

We have to reckon with the fact that the Scriptures are handed down to us over the chasm of the centuries, and therefore never directly, but only through the medium of a hearing and an interpreting that have gone on century after century. They come to us in and through the fellowship of the historical Church where God has placed us in order that we may let ourselves be addressed by one another in proclamation and in order that we may learn from one another in the hearing and understanding of the Word, but for that reason the Scriptures come to us also broken through the time-conditioned and transient forms of the past, and indeed of the present. Thus, on the one hand, the Word of God comes to us in the Scriptures in the form of the authority of human history, not as our own but as another law, as a ἕτερος νόμος, that is to say, the authority of the Church. Hence in acknowledging the Bible to be the Word of God we are also acknowledging the authority of the Church, and are summoned to honour our fathers and mothers in

[1] *ChrD*, pp. 362ff.

the faith who hand it down to us.[1] But the Church itself stands under the same law of hearing and interpreting, and its service of the Word from generation to generation is not fulfilled in any haphazard or arbitrary or merely temporary fashion, but in the continuous life of the people of God throughout history and in responsible fulfilment of its commission to proclaim and teach the Word of God.

On the other hand, because the Church is commissioned by the Word and lives through serving it, the Church lives through its obedience to the Word. Therefore, the authority of the Church is itself limited by the Word mediated through the Scriptures, and must be regarded as an indirect, relative and formal authority under the direct, absolute and material authority of the Word itself. And yet this is the true authority of the Church; its submission to the authority of the Word, and this is the authority to which we submit as we have our life through hearing the Word mediated to us by the Church.[2]

But now, Barth insists, we must go on to ask a second question: How can and ought we to be obedient to this authoritatively communicated Word in the Church? What are the subjective conditions under which obedience to it should take place? Barth's answer is that we are not able, and ought not, to hear the Word of God speaking to us in the Holy Scriptures otherwise than as subjectively determined through the concrete freedom of the conscience, i.e., in the independent and responsible act of each individual, in which he forms for himself his own representation of the witness of the prophets and apostles, grasps it within the possibilities of his own thinking and lets it speak to him in his own particular place in history. In other words, we hear and grasp the Word of God within the sphere of the Church and its fellowship—certainly within the sphere of the authority of the Church, but that is not to be understood as causality; rather is it the authority of the divine command and blessing, and therefore within the sphere of freedom where conscience answers to the divine command and is made free for it by the divine grace.[3]

We hear and grasp the Word of God, interpret and apply it only within the fellowship of others, within the sphere of reciprocal personal relationships, where there is both receptivity and spontaneity at work, that is in *conscientia*. On the one hand, that means that I am personally and individually responsible to the Word of God which I hear, to think and act in obedience to it. To do that responsibly I have to listen to the Word as communicated by others, follow their thinking and think with

[1] *ChrD*, pp. 365ff.   [2] *ChrD*, pp. 382ff.   [3] *ChrD*, pp. 388ff.

them, and in that context think it out for myself, and in obedience to the Truth of God to confess it and speak it to others.[1]

On the other hand, that means that I must fulfil my own responsibilities to the Word of God within the sphere of the freedom of others, so that my own freedom of conscience is bounded by theirs within the fellowship of the Church and under its authority to the Word of God. I cannot and ought not to hear and grasp the Word of God mediated to me through the Scriptures in isolation from the freedom of the membership of the whole Church, but only along with others as those who are summoned to hear and grasp and know along with me, that is, in the sphere of the *conscientes*, in the freedom of the Christian *conscientia*. This means, however, that the freedom of conscience within which I am to hear and grasp the Word is an indirect, relative and formal freedom, for direct, absolute and material freedom is to be ascribed only to the Scripture as to the Word of God.[2]

(4) Under the heading of *The Proclamation of the Church* Barth takes up the fourth part of his inquiry with which he ends his prolegomena, thus returning to the problem with which he began. Here the question is raised as to how far there is a communication of divine Revelation in the present, and how our speaking and hearing are related to it. Concretely, it is the question as to how far the proclamation of God's Word by the Church is to be regarded as the Word of God itself spoken and heard by men. That is the question that gives rise to dogmatics as the critical inquiry into the nature of the Church's speech about God, and hence in this final chapter Barth is concerned about the nature and function of dogmatics, its formal and material task in the service of the Church's proclamation of God's Word.[3]

The problem is set by the fact that God's Word is spoken by men in the form of their human word. On the one hand, we presuppose the fact that God commits himself with his Word to the Church and commands it to proclaim it in his Name. The Church could not think of doing that or dare to do it apart from the divine command and the promise and blessing which accompany it. On the other hand, we presuppose the fact that the Church undertakes this commission, seeking and daring to do the impossible thing, to speak God's own Eternal Word in its human words. There can be no question about the fact that that attempt must fail, for its human speaking is not only fraught with weakness but error —God alone is true, all men are liars. But the miracle of grace by which

---

[1] *ChrD*, pp. 393 ff. [2] *ChrD*, pp. 400 ff.
[3] *ChrD*, pp. 411 ff, 429 ff, and 447 ff.

the whole Church lives is that, in spite of the failure of the Church, and the impossibility of the task, God is pleased to use that weakness and failure in a victorious communication of his Word to men in the present, and so makes good where we do badly. There is thus a divine success actually hidden in human failure which by a sovereign act suborns human failure into its service.[1]

That does not mean that we can take human preaching of God's Word for God's Word *simpliciter*, or assume that the equation, *the preaching of the Church*, which it undertakes in obedience to God's command, *is the Word of God to men*, is self-explanatory, for what we are concerned with here is not a direct relation reposing upon any inherent identity between the word of man and the Word of God, but an indirect relation that depends entirely upon the decision of God's free grace, and which can therefore only be known and understood in faith. Moreover, because the grace of God abounds, that does not mean that we may continue in error, for preaching is an act of obedience in which we are not exempted from responsibility, and in particular from a self-critical examination of the nature and form and extent of our obedience. On the other hand, the realisation of our own weakness and failure, which we only reach in faith, lets us see that the actual communication of Revelation in the present must be *God's* affair, and therefore it is our task in the human speech of preaching, to make room for God's speaking. Or, to express it more concretely, our task is to see to it as far as we can that it is not ourselves that we are preaching, but that it is really to God's Word that we are pointing—that is the critical service which dogmatics renders to the Church, which Barth calls the task of *pure teaching* or doctrine in the service of the self-communication of Revelation in the present.[2]

That does not mean that dogmatics creates pure doctrine, but that it is an inquiry, again in utter reliance upon the grace of God, into the purity of doctrine, into the correctness of the Church's teaching and into its agreement with the Word of God which allows God's Word to sound through Christian preaching and to declare itself directly and authoritatively. Pure teaching is possible in so far as Christian preaching is measured, or critically cleansed, by the standard of biblical Revelation. Fundamentally, that task has to be undertaken by the whole membership of the Church as a movement of repentant self-examination before the bar of the Word of God, but dogmatics serves that activity in the Church by putting at its disposal the rigorous and disciplined inquiry which is its function as a science.[3]

---

[1] *ChrD*, p. 412.   [2] *ChrD*, p. 418f, 426.   [3] *ChrD*, pp. 423f, 431f.

Dogmatics begins from the fact, then, that the religious speech of the Church about God suffers from an ambiguity that requires clarification, in order that, as far as possible, God may be heard unambiguously. This does not mean that it is the task of dogmatics to bring to clarity the religious self-consciousness of the Church or of the preacher—that was the way of the *Glaubenslehre* of Schleiermacher which is here rejected—for the ambiguity which faces us is not that which is set up in the tension between an honest and dishonest, a genuine and a false, or a profound and a superficial piety, but the tension between that piety itself, with all its inner tensions or lack of them, and the Word of God. A piety that is not dishonest, or hypocritical, or superficial, may after all be actually heathen. Dogmatics has to test the piety of the Church, therefore, and all its religious speech about God, through an examination of its necessity, meaning, norm and goal, and in particular through measuring it by the standard of the Revelation attested in the Scriptures which the Church claims to expound.[1]

Dogmatics makes it hard for the preacher, but at the same time does him honour, in refusing to leave him to himself. It confronts him in his own thinking and in his own pious speech about God, with the critical standard of the Word of God, by challenging him to test the relation between his preaching and divine revelation through listening again to the Word of God attested in Holy Scripture, and so challenges him to new preaching and teaching under the direction of that Word. That must not be taken to mean that dogmatics claims to tell the preacher what to preach or how to preach, for that the preacher can only learn in direct hearing of the Word of God in exegesis, but dogmatics seeks to help the preacher through setting before him a sort of paradigm of Christian thinking and speaking in the light of which he may be able to correct his understanding of revelation, test his obedience to it and find his way to new preaching and teaching in accordance with it.[2]

In the course of this activity a responsible dogmatics operates with what Barth calls a 'formal principle' and a 'material principle', by which he refers to the scientific task of theology in employing a dogmatic norm, and in elucidating the nature of dogmatic thinking, as they arise out of its proper subject-matter.

Its formal principle dogmatics understands to be the Word of God. Dogmatics must itself listen to the Word of God and submit to it as the norm of all its thinking and speaking, if it is to serve the Church, and the clarification and purification of its preaching and teaching. For the ful-

---

[1] *ChrD*, pp. 428, 429ff. [2] *ChrD*, pp. 431ff.

filment of this formal function, Barth mentions three things as requirements for dogmatics. In the first place, it must assimilate its demonstra-
tions and statements to the biblical mode of thinking and speaking. By
that Barth does not refer to a superficial alignment of theology with
biblical attitudes and statements, but a penetration into the basic outlook
and inner thought-form of the prophetic and apostolic witness. That is
not easy to attain. It will involve strenuous thinking and hard exercise
in exegesis and humble learning—and is therefore the opposite of all
easy dogmatism or biblicism: 'Lord I believe, help my unbelief.' We
must become accustomed to breathing the air of Revelation and thinking
and speaking as naturally within it, as a new-born child takes to breathing and drinking. That is true biblicism, to get within the inner form of
the biblical Revelation and to let it shape the form of all our thinking
and speaking of God.[1]

In the second place, Barth points to the need for dogmatics to operate
within what he calls 'a confessional-theological school'. Again, that is
not to be understood as a return to confessionalism, but rather as the
requirement to think dogmatically not in some empty space, but within
the definite context of our place in history where the Word of God has
been handed on to us by our fathers and on the concrete ground where
knowledge of God has become actual for us within the *Una Sancta*. In
the third place, Barth adds that dogmatics must operate within the
sphere of the Church's authority, within the sphere where we are under
authority to one another in the Word of God, and where the Church has
a commission to fulfil in responsible preaching and teaching, and in self-
testing and correction. Dogmatics may not be romantic, nor may it
attempt to engage in timeless thinking and speaking, nor pass by the
actual space where the Bible and dogma are handled to some higher
world beyond. Nor, of course, is dogmatics some private occupation, or
some academic game to be played by the clever and the interested.[2] All
this means that dogmatics, with all the freedom which human thinking
involves, takes place within the heteronomy of God, and within the
concrete determinations taken and prescribed by God's Word in its
operation among men, and not within some sphere where man is left to
his own pious reflection and speaking and to the circle of his own self-
correction alone. Dogmatics cannot be pursued therefore as a study in
itself or *in abstracto*, for the object of its study, the self-revelation of God
in Jesus Christ, is only to be found within the sphere of actual faith and
obedience where that revelation is heard and received—in the Church.

[1] *ChrD*, p. 437f.   [2] *ChrD*, pp. 440f, 444f.

In short, dogmatic thinking is thinking that is really in accordance with Jesus Christ, on the ground and within the community where he makes himself accessible to us.[1]

From the formal principle, Barth then turns to discuss the material principle of dogmatics. Dogmatics is concerned, as we have seen, with the effort to relate the word of the sermon back critically to Revelation attested in the Scriptures. We are not engaged here in another effort, but with the other side of the same movement in which Revelation is regarded, not only as the norm affecting dogmatic thinking formally from without, but as the *object* affecting it materially from within.

Barth prefers to speak here of 'object' rather than 'content', and so differentiates his understanding of the material principle from that of Lutheran dogmatics which understands by it a motif (or several motifs) selected from the material content of dogmatics, placed at its head as the fundamental statement (or the epitome) of the proper and central content of biblical Revelation, and employed as the principle of a dogmatic system. Barth points in this connexion to the doctrine of justification in older Lutheran dogmatics, and to the realisation of the Kingdom of God through Jesus Christ, as in the dogmatics of Nitzsch, etc. But by what right, he asks, is one motif selected from the other contents of dogmatics? Does this not mean that the biblical Revelation is no more than the means of regulating an insight which we already have and bring to it? Where does it come from? It will be difficult, he says, to avoid the answer that it derives from religious experience, but what religious experience has to say is what needs to be tested and weighed in dogmatics first of all.[2]

The term 'content', however, is ambiguous in this connexion. On the one hand, it may denote the material content of preaching, all of which needs to be critically tested and none of which can be erected into a criterion for the testing of the rest of it. On the other hand, it may denote the material content of the biblical Revelation, the Word of God. It would be better, says Barth, not to speak of this as the 'content' of dogmatic thinking, for dogmatics has no mastery over the Word of God, but is rather mastered by it. 'Content' in this sense Barth calls 'the object' of dogmatics, that which objectively encounters it and remains objective to it, and is identified as such with the norm of dogmatic thinking. Thus the formal principle and the material principle of dogmatics are one and the same, for they derive from one and the same source in the sovereign Word of God.

[1] *ChrD*, pp. 436 and 446.   [2] *ChrD*, p. 449 f.

The formal determination of dogmatic thinking arises out of its submission to the Word of God as its norm—that can be described as the 'heteronomy' of dogmatics; likewise the material determination of dogmatic thinking arises out of its attachment to the Word of God as its object—that can be described as the 'autonomy' of dogmatics. But actually both this heteronomy and this autonomy are really to be regarded as 'theonomy', for the thinking that takes place within the authority of the Church and within the freedom of conscience is all under the Lordship of God.[1]

In other words, when dogmatic thinking tests the speech of the Church about God, there takes place a critical activity in which the thinking of the Church is freed from every other 'law' and subordinated to one Law, the Lordship of the Word of God. It is precisely in this self-submission to its own proper object, that dogmatic thinking becomes emancipated from every 'system' of thought and is genuinely free to think on its own ground, in the autonomy given to it by its own object. By committing itself to the Word of God dogmatic thinking breaks loose from the control of all external presuppositions and becomes really free to think positively about the Word of God. That is the material mode of dogmatic thinking deriving from, and building on, its own proper object.

If this is so, then properly understood the material principle of dogmatics destroys at its very root 'a dogmatic system'. If 'system' there is here, it is the ordered thinking that arises through thinking consistently from a centre, but because dogmatics does not employ any systematic principle, or seek to erect any independent system, it is better not to speak of a system at all. All that can arise here are *loci*.[2]

Now, the object of dogmatic thinking is *God speaking* in and through the prophetic witness. Because we are obliged to respect the nature of that object, that is, its objectivity, the 'God speaks' must never be converted into an 'I speak', and therefore the thinking that dogmatics engages in, face to face with it, must be an *open structure*, for the conversation with God can never be closed, far less foreclosed, by man. Thus theological inquiry must be a perpetual inquiry. 'Not as though I had already attained, either were already at my goal, but I follow after, if only I may apprehend that for which I was apprehended by Christ Jesus' (Phil. 3.12). Theological inquiry is never at its goal; it never reaches the point where its thinking is absolutely determined by its object, for it must constantly acknowledge the inadequacy of its con-

---

[1] *ChrD*, pp. 446, 448, 451.   [2] *ChrD*, p. 451f.

I

formity to it. It remains human thinking, human activity, that for all its obedience is only relatively determined by its object. The acknowledgment of that relativity is once more an acknowledgment that its thinking can never take the form of a closed system, for it must ever be open toward its object.[1]

If dogmatics involves a material mode of thinking corresponding to the nature of its object, God speaking to us and asking of us response to him, then that must involve a thinking in faith and obedience. That is, the kind of thinking that takes place face to face with an object that is *indissolubly Subject*, i.e., within a relationship in which he is the Lord and I am the servant, in which he is accessible to me only in his Lordship over me, and in which he enables me by his Spirit to respond to him beyond any power that I have in myself. That is the kind of thinking that takes place within faith and obedience, the knowledge and activity in which, by the grace of God and through the miracle of the Holy Spirit, I am participant in Revelation. Our own thinking is always the thinking of an object and never of God, but through the power of the Spirit my thinking becomes thinking of God as Subject, a thinking from within the communion which he sets us between himself and me, in which my thinking is taken into command and, in spite of its weakness, is enabled to be real thinking of him.

Here dogmatic thinking takes the form of question and answer, and answer and question, in accordance with the speaking of God to me and his asking of me inquiry of him and response to him. Here his Word breaks into my monologue and turns it into dialogue, into dialectical thinking in which two partners are locked in conversation, in which the answer to the Word is never final but always in the form of an inquiry back to the Word again. That is the significance, Barth says, of the coupling of terms he has been concerned with all through the discussion: faith and obedience, heteronomy and autonomy or authority and freedom, the speaking of the Holy Spirit to us and in us, the Incarnation of the Word and the pouring out of the Holy Spirit, reconciliation and sin, *Urgeschichte* and *Geschichte* in Revelation, God's Word and man's word in the Bible, and in the sermon as well. The original exemplar of that, from which all these derive, which necessarily makes all dogmatics dialectical, is *God* and *Man in the Person of the Redeemer, Jesus Christ*. He who would eliminate that word 'and' and speak instead of 'God-man', or who would make out of Jesus Christ one name, Jesus-Christ, would be no dialectical theologian. That is the true centre of all our dogmatic

[1] *ChrD*, p. 452f.

thinking, in Jesus Christ: in him Word of God and word of man can neither be separated from one another nor be confused with one another. That is the central fact which sets aside Ebionitism on the one side and Docetism on the other, the two basic attempts of man to turn this into one word that can be uttered by man. Thus we can see at the very centre that it is the nature of the object of dogmatic thinking, God speaking to us in Jesus Christ, which gives to that thinking a material structure in accordance with it. The whole round of dogmatics manifests this material structure through relation to this centre in Jesus Christ.[1]

As such, dogmatic thinking, reposing upon its object, is responsible thinking, bound up with our very existence before God. It is the function of the Church, for the Church proclaims the Word of God and therefore requires the service of dogmatic science. He who would enter this service learns from the Church that he stands before God and belongs to God, and that he must take God as seriously as his own existence—not just any God, but the God of the Church, the God who has revealed himself. Only in this way does he engage in this function of the Church. Although it is a science and an art, the very object of dogmatics will not let it be anything else but a service, and that is a service determined by definite question to be answered.

That is the autonomous activity of dogmatics, but clearly it is a relative autonomy, an autonomy that is qualified by the autonomy of the Holy Spirit, and is therefore a theonomy. It is we who think in dogmatics, we who ought to think, but we ought also to know, that when and so far as we think the truth, it is God alone who really thinks the truth. Only in this act of deep humility and courage, of reverence and joy may we think the truth.[2] The relation of the *Dogmatiker* to his object is to be described in the words of the Psalm: 'Praise the Lord, O my soul, and all that is within me, praise his holy name.'

*

Looking back over this period of Barth's development from his early dialectical thinking to a theology of the Word, to a positive Christian dogmatics centred in Jesus Christ, we can see that the polemical engagements on the right and on the left, the audacious thoughts and language of the *Romans*, the restless, tireless questioning of everything down to the bed-rock, all converged toward breaking a way through the whole history of modern Protestantism in order to let Jesus Christ speak for

[1] *ChrD*, p. 457 f.   [2] *ChrD*, p. 462 f.

himself as Lord God. So it happened. Barth reached the point where he allowed Christ to speak to him out of the Bible by speaking against Barth's own self and against man's desire to make out of Jesus a modern idol. At last he had broken clean through the subjectivism of romantic religion and idealist philosophy to the Word of God, or rather the Word of God had broken through to him. And because it was a Word that had already been uttered by God in human form, within the frame of human life and action and speech, the theologian was summoned and enabled to think it and speak it after him.

From henceforth his theology becomes unambiguously *Theology of the Word*. Henceforth the concrete Word of God speaking to him out of the Scriptures becomes the object of theological knowledge and activity, the way that that Word took in coming to man in the Incarnation yields the way in which his theological knowledge of God, Father, Son and Holy Spirit, is to take, and the form which that Word assumed in Jesus Christ yields the inner logic whereby that theological knowledge is to be articulated. But the working out of this is still obstructed and obscured by Barth's inheritance of language and thought forms which had been shaped in the mould of pantheistic and existentialist philosophy and religion. For example, the notion of an *existential-consciousness*, as he calls it, plays, if not a fundamental, at least not a little role in the detailed exposition (omitted from the foregoing account) of the God/man relationship set up by the Word and the Spirit. The danger of this came home to Barth through wide-spread debates with Lutherans and Romans in the nineteen-twenties and early nineteen-thirties. This is where the greatness of Barth is very apparent. He debated with his opponents, giving back in masterly discussion more than they gave him. He answered their questions by other questions, with great and kind humour (and sometimes a little wrath), exposing their misunderstanding, but all the time he let himself be criticised and questioned by the Word of God, and allowed the debates in which he was plunged to expose to him his own mistakes, which he was not slow to acknowledge, and then there came the third great stage in the development of Barth's theology, in which, as Barth himself put it, *he emerged out of his egg-shells*.

V

TRANSITION TO *CHURCH DOGMATICS*

THE really decisive transition in Barth's thinking took place about 1930. In March of 1929 he delivered several formidable lectures in Dortmund under the title *Schicksal und Idee in der Theologie*[1] in which he sought to clarify the relation of theology to philosophy and to think his way through to a thoroughly consistent *theology* untainted by *ideology*. It was in the following year that he held his seminar on Anselm's *Cur Deus Homo* in Bonn, and published, along with his brother Heinrich, a book on the Holy Spirit, *Zur Lehre vom Heiligen Geist*. The results of the study he carried through on Anselm were published in the following year under the title *Fides Quaerens Intellectum*. These are all works of great significance, for they show us the transition from the *Christliche Dogmatik im Entwurf* of 1927 to the *Kirchliche Dogmatik* of 1932.[2]

1. Re-examination of Christian Dogmatics

Die Christliche Dogmatik im Entwurf brought to a head the development of Barth's theology in its second stage. It was an introductory volume to a new dogmatics, setting forth the doctrine of the Word of God, and concerned with the working out of a theology within the sphere of the biblical Revelation and within its fundamental form of thinking. As we have seen, it was meant to be very strictly a theology of the Word of God, rooted in the prophetic-apostolic witness, developing out of exegesis, and working within the context of the questions and answers that arise within the faith and function of the Church.[3] It was an attempt at a positive theology genuinely concerned with its own proper task rather than with the subsidiary task of carrying out a discussion with the age, and therefore it was to be pursued like a positive science, convinced of its right to study its own given subject-matter, and to pursue its own cause without subservience to any *Weltanschauung*, refusing to be obstructed by critical or sceptical questions directed to it from grounds

---

[1] Published first in *ZdZ*, 1929, pp. 309-348, and republished in *FuA*, pp. 54-92.
[2] See 'Parergon', *Evangelische Theologie*, 1948-9, p. 272, and *CD* I.1, p. vi.
[3] *ChrD*, pp. 435 ff and 462.

outside its own chosen field, and developing its own proper determinate method, rejecting any and every method imported from beyond its boundaries as illegitimate, and therefore rejecting the need to submit to criteria deriving from other exact sciences or from philosophy. If justification was needed, it must be provided through an exhibition of its own theological existence and its own internal rationality, letting its relevance to the world of thought and culture appear *a posteriori*.

The new dogmatics, however, met with an opposition from his colleagues which Barth himself has described as general and vehement. That was to be expected of the Germany of the nineteen-twenties where psychological and numinous interpretations of the Christian faith, and phenomenological and existentialist philosophies were in the fashion, all working in some way or other within the nineteenth-century assumption of a religious *a priori* or some prior understanding of existence. Barth reacted to his critics with considerable self-criticism, for he was not slow to see that much of their criticism was justified. But what surprised many of them was that he reacted positively where they were most critical, and negatively to the points which some of them singled out for appreciation. The reviews and debates that followed the *Christliche Dogmatik* made it only too clear to Barth that he himself was still too entangled in the philosophical presuppositions from which he had tried to emancipate himself, and that he must carry through once again a complete rewriting of his work such as he had to do with his *Römerbrief* twelve years previously.[1]

The two chief questions he had to face and clear up, for they affected everything else, were the relation of theology to culture and the nature of theological method.

The general question of the relation of theology to culture he had inherited from Schleiermacher, and, as we have seen, he had been wrestling with it all through his theological career, in order to break through the frame of modernity into full theological freedom and to find a new basis and starting-point for a positive dogmatics. 'The Church and Culture' had been the subject of an address in 1926,[2] in which, in spite of his fundamental disagreement with Schleiermacher,[3] he sought to set forth a more positive account of the relation of Church to culture, yet without falling into the error of justifying the ideals of culture on the

---

[1] *CD* I.1, Foreword, p. vii.   [2] *TC*, pp. 334ff.
[3] See the review of Brunner's *Schleiermacherbuch, Die Mystik und das Wort*, in *ZdZ*, 1925, pp. 38-61, and *TC*, pp. 136ff, 159ff, in which it is apparent that though his own critique of Schleiermacher was more fundamental than Brunner's, it was also more appreciative of Schleiermacher's intention.

ground of divine laws alleged to impregnate nature and society. 'The Church will not see the dawn of the Kingdom of God in any work of human culture, but still will keep an open door for the signs which announce themselves, perhaps in a great many works of human culture, that the Kingdom of God is coming near.'[1] There is indeed a continuity of creation reposing upon the faithfulness of God in all his ways and works, manifest in his creative and healing will in Jesus Christ; and hence we must affirm the continuity of human nature and life, in spite of man's fall into the abyss of sin, with God's creation, but for that very reason we cannot seek to ground that continuity in man himself and so to produce an ideological basis for the assimilation of theology and culture.

Barth sought to set this forth through a consideration of what he called the *realms* of *creation, grace* and *glory.* Because the Gospel does not reject the purpose of creation but rather affirms it and looks at it in the light of its goal in the final purpose of God, the Church can offer definite contributions towards the task of culture in seeking wholeness, unity and completeness. But because the Church cannot consent to the sanctification of actual culture as such, its contributions create certain problems for civilisation.[2]

The Church lives under grace, and therefore within its claim upon the whole of its existence, creating genuine ethical disturbance and contributing to the ethical conscience of society. It does that by proclaiming the Kingdom of God's peace and justice and love, and the positive promises of God for humanity which are latent in creation itself. Grace denies that we can achieve that on our own, but it does place us under the constraint of obedience, and demands that everywhere we shall be concerned for sheer *humanity.* Thus the Church in a real sense affirms the law of nature lying behind all culture which derives from God's Word and preaches obedience to it.[3]

On the other hand, the Church serves the order of glory as well as of grace, and in that service it proclaims the limits and boundaries set by God to all creaturely and human achievement precisely by proclaiming a future divine fulfilment when he will make all things new. Because that goal is not only proclaimed but belongs to the life of the Church, the Church cannot but stand apart from culture, in an eschatological reserve vis-à-vis all worldliness, and therefore must be critical of its own profaneness and aware of its own ambiguities—it must learn to interpret its life against the stream of the culture in which it swims. It must proclaim

---

[1] *TC*, p. 344.   [2] *TC*, pp. 341 ff.   [3] *TC*, pp. 344 ff.

the divine No against all human attempts to erect towers of Babel or to identify the Kingdom of God with the achievements of society and civilisation—it must point to and live on the boundary of eternity, where the new world of God's redemption is always on the point of breaking in, and therefore proclaim to all the Word of grace and reconciliation with the coming Lord.[1]

Behind this attempt to set forth a more positive account of the relation of Church and culture lies Barth's old conviction regarding the universal range of the Kingdom of God, the cosmic relevance of his Word, the solidarity of the Church with the world under grace, and therefore the judgment of grace, and also his sense of responsibility for modernity. But how could he think out the relation of the Church to culture *dialectically*, without compromising with the presuppositions of the pre-vailing culture, for, as Barth himself admitted, behind the negative contrapositions of dialectical thinking there lie assertions that are ambig-uous in the highest degree?[2] How could he have a theology that took seriously the human pole in the God/man, Creator/creature dialectic without letting it pass over into an ideology, a theology of man that did not pass over into an independent anthropology or become little more than an ideological expression and justification of man's cultural back-ground? It was that ambiguity that came to light as the *Christliche Dogmatik* lay before Barth in print, and the reviews began to come in.

The confusion and misunderstanding had to be cleared away, and so Barth set himself to cut the strings of compromise, by making unambig-uously clear that the Church cannot address itself to culture on its own ground, nor on the ground of any supposed divine laws embedded in the structures of the natural order. He must assert as never before the radical judgment of grace upon every movement from the side of natural knowledge or philosophy toward divine Revelation, and so clear away anything that might obscure the depth of the gulf between the sin of the world and the holiness of God, or undermine the absoluteness of grace in the positive but irreversible connexion it establishes between Revela-tion and human reason. It was, apparently, the clash between Gogarten and himself, that helped to open Barth's eyes to the depth and subtlety of the problem and the menace that lurked in any mistake at this funda-mental point.[3] Gogarten's view of the relation between the Church and

---

[1] *TC*, pp. 347ff.   [2] *WW*, p. 209f.
[3] F. Gogarten, 'Karl Barth's Dogmatik', *Theologische Rundschau*, 1929, p. 70f, and Barth's reply, *CD* I.1, pp. 141f, 194f. See also Barth's *Fragen an das Christen-tum*, 1931 (republished in *FuA*, pp. 93ff) and *Theologische Existenz heute*, 1933, and compare Gogarten, *Gericht oder Skepsis*. Barth's early uneasiness with

(German) nature and culture, Barth felt, could only lead the Church back into relativism, secularism and paganism, and therefore against every ambiguous doctrine of *gratia non tollit naturam*,[1] it must be made abundantly clear that while God in his grace has not come to destroy human nature but to recreate it, his Revelation does not speak to man on his own ground. What was at stake here was not only the integrity of theology but the very existence of the Church.

Events were moving fast in Germany at this time toward the 'National-Socialist' revolution, and Barth's clear-sighted understanding of the literature that was being poured out, without and within the Church, roused him to mighty prophetic protests. When the upheaval came and once again, as in 1914, leading theologians like Gogarten revealed the failv ᵕ of their ethics, and therefore of their fundamental hold upon the Gospel, by lending their support to the so-called 'German-Christian' movement, and when this time the Church found itself struggling for its very life, Barth stood out as the great theological leader ᴐf the Christian faith.[2] When the foundations were shaken, it was theological integrity that counted. Hence, as F. W. Camfield has expressed it: 'Was it not now crystal clear that any theology which looked to sources of revelation outside of God's Word in Jesus Christ was a servant of the false gods? And when the dragooning of the Church by the Government began, Barth discovered that the one way of offering effective resistance was to hold fast to the one ground of Christian security, the Word of God in Jesus Christ as attested by the Scriptures. There has rarely been in the whole history of the Church a theologian so amply vindicated by history as Karl Barth.'[3] This was the position taken by the *Confessing Church* of Germany in *The Declaration of Barmen* in May, 1934, in its stand against the 'German-Christians' and 'National-Socialism'.[4]

It is in this context that one must understand the sharp controversy between Barth and Brunner that broke out a little later, when to Brunner's teaching about *Nature and Grace* Barth published his startling

---

Gogarten's theology, and increasingly critical attitude to both Gogarten and Bultmann, whom he likened to one another, are very clearly revealed in the letters of 1921 to 1925, *Gd-Md*.

[1] The notorious sentence from St Thomas Aquinas, *Summa Theologica*, I.q. 1.8 ad 2; q.2.2 ad 1; q.2.2, q.188 c.fi.; 'Grace does not destroy nature but perfects and completes it' or 'supplies its defect', which was widely used in the nineteen-thirties by Catholics and Protestants in Germany to justify a concordat between the Christian Church and historical German nature ('blood and soil') and national consciousness.

[2] See especially *Theologische Existenz heute*, 1933, in which Barth warned the German Church of the grave menace to the very basis of its existence in God's Revelation.   [3] F. W. Camfield, *Reformation Old and New*, p. 22.

[4] See 'Karl Barth zum Kirchenkampf', *TEh*, NF. 49, 1956.

Nein. At this very crucial point and on this fundamental issue Brunner's ambiguous teaching was, Barth felt, a disservice to the Church, for it lent support, even if it was against his own intention, to the mounting menace of naturalism and paganism in Germany. And yet the controversy was, in its way, a lapse into the old dialectic in which the negatives on both sides carried latent ambiguous assertions. The negative title of Barth's pamphlet certainly betrayed his real intention which was not to operate through a denial of the competence of man's reason—that is why even a 'negative point of contact' with the natural man is out of place—but rather to operate solely through the positive message of the Gospel. To use Camfield's exposition again, 'Barth will have us follow the positive way of revelation itself; confine ourselves to the way of God to man as it stands in the witness of the Scriptures to Jesus Christ; take our bearings from that movement which is not a movement *of* the world, but a movement *to* the world, and draw out all our insights and understandings concerning the relation of God to the world and of the world to God from thence; thus, not to argue about natural theology and set out to refute it, but turn our backs upon it and take another way; not to discuss the point of contact between revelation and the natural reason, but perceive the connexion which revelation itself establishes with reason; not labour after the interpretation of man as an historical being, but discern how revelation makes him a truly historical being. He will have us free our mind from all anxieties about ourselves and our rights, and make our thinking an act of pure obedience in the confidence that, in our obedience, we shall find the rightful demands of our reason met and satisfied.'[1]

Looking back from his later teaching, we can see that the weakness of Barth's attempt to clarify the relation of theology to culture in the late twenties and early thirties was that it lacked as yet the full Christological basis which he has now attained. He was not in a position then, as he is now, to speak positively rather than only dialectically of 'Humanism',[2] and of 'the Humanity of God',[3] that is God's sovereign togetherness with man, and even of a 'theological culture'[4] flowing from it, for although he could affirm in 1926, for example, that the Word of God over against culture is substantially Word of grace, and Word of reconciliation,[5] he was unable to work it out and to show that what he claimed,

[1] Op. cit. p. 23.
[2] Cf. 'Humanismus', *Theologische Studien*, 28, 1950. See also 'Die Wirklichkeit des Neuen Menschen', *Theol. Studien*, 27.
[3] *GGG*, pp. 31 ff.
[4] *GGG*, p. 44 f.
[5] See the chapter on 'Church and Culture' § 4, in *Theology and Church* (*TC*, pp. 341 ff).

namely a positive and constructive connexion between the Word of God and human reason, between the Grace of God and human life, between Church and State, could be fully substantiated. That had to wait for the full development of the *Kirchliche Dogmatik* to which he now turned, the first part-volume of which he published in 1932.[1] Meantime there can be little doubt that Barth was right in taking the sharp, difficult line of cutting his theological basis clean away from all compromising entanglement with the presuppositions of the cultural context within which as a theologian he had to live and think, and therefore within which he had to employ as tools the forms of speech and thought that lay to hand.

So much for the general question raised by the debate over the *Christliche Dogmatik*. Now we have to turn to the acute question of *theological method*, and in particular to the problem of the relation of Barth's dogmatics to existentialism and the prior understanding of man bound up with a general anthropology. Barth realised that in spite of all his efforts the *Christliche Dogmatik* was seriously compromised in that direction. To fulfil his task more adequately he had to take extensive soundings and lay broader foundations, listen carefully to the voices of the Bible, the Fathers and the theologians, but above all to carry out a comprehensive clarification through wrestling with the basic text of the Bible. That meant eventually a very great enlargement of the original volume on prolegomena into the two half-volumes of the *Church Dogmatics* I, in which he thought through his problems in the deepest historical dimension, and within the sphere of the Church where theology is bound to the Word of God and we must join 'with all saints' in learning to hear that Word aright and give it rational articulation.

In carrying this out, Barth swept aside all remnants of the language of idealist philosophy, even of Kierkegaard and particularly of the existentialist misunderstanding of Kierkegaard; he threw out the old dialectic between eternity and time and all talk about timeless crisis, and interpreted the Word of God in the most concrete and positive way, strictly in terms of the person of Jesus Christ, the Incarnate Son of God, who is true God and true Man in one Person, and even more strictly in terms of the Holy Trinity as the ground and basis of everything. In the course of this Barth had to renounce his previous errors and introduce deep

---

[1] Barth's positive answer to the relation of Church (*justification*) and State (*justice*) was adumbrated in his important writing *Rechtfertigung und Recht* (ET *Church and State*, 1939) before its elaboration in the volumes of *Church Dogmatics* III.

modifications in his understanding of the material content and method of his theology.[1]

The first thing he had to depart from was a dangerous use at certain points of existentialist philosophy. To his horror, Barth found that what he had written of the need to pass over 'from the thought of one who deals with things from without to the thought of one who, by his existence, participates in things' was interpreted by Siegfried[2] as follows: 'Upon this foundation (meaning the existential thinking introduced) he proposes to build up his dogmatics.'[3] According to Barth, that had not been his intention, but clearly he had given some ground for it, there and elsewhere, and admitted that he had fallen into the very error he had warned against—of a wrong use of philosophy, that is, where theological statements are proved by reference to similar ones with a philosophical content, entailing the substitution of a philosophical theme for a theological one. Barth maintains that it is legitimate for dogmatics, as for every other science, to make use of philosophical terminology for the exposition of its theme, if it is done with a specifically theological intention, and the transferred sense in which the philosophical terms are used is made clear.[4] In other words, theology may, and indeed cannot help but, avail itself of forms of thought and speech derived from some philosophy, but they must be subordinated to the specifically theological form of thinking which it derives from its own proper object—or its own material content. There is always a risk involved, and therefore it is part of the critical task of dogmatic science to test the forms theology uses to ensure that they are adequate to their proper object, which it can only carry out by new exacting reflection upon the Word of God. That is to say, what is required of dogmatics is *a deeper penetration into the objectivity of the Word of God*. This is precisely what Barth has set himself to carry through in all the volumes of the *Kirchliche Dogmatik*, for that is the ultimate answer of theology to every external challenge from the side of philosophy.[5]

The second error which Barth had to eradicate from his first attempt at dogmatics was the tendency to set the doctrine of the Word of God in

---

[1] Cf. J. McConnachie, *The Barthian Theology*, p. 46f, and H. U. von Balthasar, *Karl Barth, Darstellung und Deutung seiner Theologie*, 'Wendung zur Analogie', pp. 92-123.

[2] Th. Siegfried, *Das Wort und die Existenz*, I, 1930, p. 35f.

[3] *CD* I.1, p. 141f.

[4] See especially 'Schicksal und Idee in der Theologie', *passim* (*FuA*, pp. 54-92). See also *ChrD*, p. 403.

[5] Apart from Barth's discussion of this in the first volume of the *Church Dogmatics*, both parts, see particularly vol. II.1 for a sustained discussion of objectivity, ch. V on 'The Knowledge of God'.

the framework of an anthropology, as if the starting-point of theology were in a determination of the being of man, even of religious man, considered in himself, apart from God.[1] Psychologically, or existentialistically, this meant using some prior self-interpretation of man's existence as a basic tool and norm for theological thinking. Epistemologically, it meant that theology must first develop its theory of knowledge and then, in the light of that, go on to examine and explicate its subject-matter. Both of these derive ultimately from Cartesian and Kantian teaching, and belong to the fundamentally subjectivist tradition of modern Protestant philosophy. What is at stake here is not only the problem of theological integrity, but the question of the scientific method proper to dogmatics.

This was the error of which Barth himself was admittedly guilty when in the *Christliche Dogmatik*[2] he wrote: 'God's Word is not only speech but address. We cannot hurry hither or thither, either into heaven or into the abyss, in order to lay hold of it and read it; rather it is "in our mouth and in our heart", for it has come to us. That is to say, the hearing man is included in the concept of the Word of God just as much as the speaking God. He is "co-posited" in it like Schleiermacher's God in the feeling of absolute dependence. One does not speak of the Word of God if one does not speak of it at the same time as being received through man. Or more concretely, one does not speak of the Word of God unless one speaks of the man who receives it, of the human *I* which here, finally and ultimately comes up against the *Thou*, which is its origin and in fellowship with which alone it can exist as *I*. That is why the Word of God is a concept which is only accessible to an existentialist thinking.' Barth tells us that he was amazed to find that he had written this,[3]—but it is only one of many similar statements—and admits that in trying to derive the nature of the Word of God at all from the analysis of the concrete situation of the hearer, he was misled by a false tendency derived from phenomenological and existentialist thinking. To put forward, as he was doing, an anthropology, even a Church anthropology, as the ground of knowledge for decisive statements about the Word of God, was to show reverence to false gods.[4]

Man is indeed 'co-posited' in the address of the Word of God, but certainly not like Schleiermacher's God in the feeling of absolute dependence. He is put there by the sheer act of God's grace, that is, factually and not in an essentially necessary way; he is put there by the

---

[1] *CD* I.1, pp. 38ff, 141ff, and 213ff.   [2] *ChrD*, p. 111.
[3] *CD* I.1, p. 159.   [4] *CD* I.1, p. 142f.

concrete act of God in addressing man, but that cannot be converted into a general truth in which 'man' belongs necessarily and essentially to the concept 'Word of God'.[1] But Barth's full answer to this question, which is given in the profound discussions of the second half of this volume,[2] is that Jesus Christ is the 'Man' who is included in the Word, for he is the Word made flesh; he is himself the Word of God addressed to man and also Man hearing and receiving that Word adequately and appropriately and perfectly. Therefore he, Jesus, is both the objective and the subjective possibility of its revelation to us and of our receiving of it, for through reconciliation and union with him in the power of the Spirit we are enabled to hear and understand the Word, as we are quite unable to do on our own.[3]

This represents a development of the teaching already contained in *Die Christliche Dogmatik*, that the Word of God is *God* and *Man*; Word of God to man, and at the same time that Word assuming human form as word of man in answer to God. But it involves a radical stress upon the concrete particularity and uniqueness of the Word as *Man*, as well as God, in Jesus Christ, and the vicarious nature of his unique Humanity which is the true ground of our humanity and in which we are given to share through the communion of the Holy Spirit. In this way Barth destroyed in his own thinking the last remnants of an *analogia entis* in its existentialist form, and established his characteristic doctrine of *analogia gratiae*, an analogous relation set up by the grace of God between man and God in and through Jesus Christ, in which knowledge of God takes place within a genuine relation of creaturely correspondence, reflection, and conformity to God himself in his self-communication and self-revelation. It is to this creative relation of grace grounded in the union of God and Man in Jesus Christ that the *I-Thou* relation in created human nature, between man and wife above all, is itself related. To the *co-humanity* of grace in Christ there corresponds a *co-humanity* of love and obedience in man. That is the great final change that comes over Barth's thinking, from dialectical to analogical (i.e. Christological) thinking.

This means that the final and ultimate answer to the problem of an independent anthropology, or the propriety of a prior understanding of man for theological method, is to be found in Christology. Therefore, Barth rejects the development of a theological method in abstraction from its actual content and insists that dogmatics must keep itself to *a*

---

[1] *CD* I.1, p. 159f.   [2] *CD* I.2, pp. 1ff, and 25ff.
[3] *CD* II.1, sections 25 and 26.

posteriori reflection upon its own subject-matter as the scientific procedure required of it by the Word of God. To express it in other terms, Barth rejects as fundamentally false any procedure which seeks to move from an independently, and therefore arbitrarily, constructed possibility, to its reality, and insists on a procedure which works out the possibility only on the basis of its reality.[1] It is because Jesus Christ is the Word of God, he to whom the Scriptures bear witness, that theology must focus its attention upon him speaking to it out of the Scriptures, in order to let him, as its proper object, give to it its essential forms and determine for it its necessary methods. Christology, therefore, has for Barth a supreme *critical* significance, for it is through Christology that theology is enabled to break through subjectivism, in its romantic-idealist or its existentialist forms, to the sheer reality of God. And it is through radically Christo-centric thinking that pure *theo*logy can arise and be preserved from all corruption from the side of anthropocentric thinking, and therefore from all ideological distortions arising out of man's self-centred reflection of the structures of his own existence in the history of society and of the world. It is because Christological thinking carries within it a thinking from out of the concrete act of God's grace in atonement, that it provides theology with its critical criterion by means of which it can distinguish objective theological thinking from all mythological objectification of man's subjective states and experiences.[2]

Reflecting upon the recrudescence of existentialism after the second world war, and looking back to the discussions of those days twenty years earlier, Barth has had this to say. 'For its introduction into theology, I myself must bear a good deal of unwitting responsibility, for I paid tribute to it in my commentary on the Epistle to the Romans (1921) and even in my well-known false start, the *Christliche Dogmatik im Entwurf* (1927). In the light of these works, and in respect of certain features of my theological thinking in its later development, I must admit that I have learned something from what Kierkegaard and his modern followers teach. As far as theology is a matter of criticism, polemics, destructive argument, demythologising, etc.—and there must always be a place for these things in theology—existentialism has doubtless proved a useful instrument (although not even in this respect would I consider it the only or most effective one). It is thus understandable

---

[1] *ChrD*, p. 252f; *CD* I.2, p. 8.
[2] This critical significance of Christology for Barth's thought is very clearly perceived and expounded by Charles West, *Communism and the Theologians*, pp. 215f and 223f.

that especially many of the cleverer students often snatch at it with a certain ecstasy and use it with a certain frenzy. But I cannot see that where it has been expressly applied—for after all negation is no supreme art nor the overthrow of all kinds of false idols a superlative task—it has produced positive results worth mentioning, and for the moment I do not see how it can. With all due thanks to those who wish to instruct us about what must not be said in theology, I am far better pleased with the man who is at pains to show us what one may say.'[1]

The more positive emphasis, and the more reconciling tone and humour of that statement is typical of the later Barth, but behind it lies the great structure of a positive theology which could not have been built had he not years earlier had the courage and the austerity to take the stand he did against Gogarten and Bultmann and even, sadly, against Brunner. And as it has turned out, it is Barth himself who has laid the deep, broad foundations for a 'theological culture', rather than they.

In addition to the errors Barth had to correct in the *Christliche Dogmatik*, he had also to introduce certain fundamental modifications which affected the presentation of the whole of his theology of the Word substantially. These modifications all concern the immense emphasis laid upon the Word of God as sheer *Act* of God or eschatological *Event*. We have already seen that, from the side of Barth himself, that was meant to express and guard the downright objectivity of the Word of God, but as we have also seen, it carried with it a sharp dialectical way of thinking. That was the difficulty, for it provoked an existentialism and hindered the development of a full Christology. So long as the emphasis in Revelation lay upon the pure *Act* or *Event*, an existentialism of some kind was bound to arise if only to anchor the event down to earth or to clothe it with flesh, but this meant the projection of the human decision into the essential nature of Revelation, and could only lead to some form of co-redemption. That in turn could only be held in check by a severe and critical form of dialectical thinking backed up by forensic justification. In that case there could be no advance on Barth's part from the position adopted in the *Römerbrief*.

On the other hand, the emphasis upon pure Act or Event, with its attendant dialecticism, could only carry with it what Gogarten had called a 'timeless theology'.[2] If the Word had only tangential relation to history

---

[1] *CD* III.4, Preface, p. ixf.
[2] See *Theologische Rundschau*, 1929, p. 70f, *Gericht oder Skepsis*, and earlier works, *Glaube und Wirklichkeit*, and *Ich Glaube an den Dreieinigen Gott*, and now the later work, *Entmythologisierung und Kirche* (ET *Demythologising and History*, London 1955).

or to humanity, then theology could only conceive of the Incarnation, the Crucifixion, the Resurrection, the Ascension and the Parousia as refracted, and it might well be necessary, forms of consciousness answering to some timeless 'reality'. Thus these doctrines could have no objective ground in reality and could only have form as the necessary determination of our thinking or willing. In other words, the whole false problem of mythology would be forced back into theology.[1] Gogarten saw that what was needed was an ontology of history of some kind, but his answer to that was to seek for it in the historical nature of man, which, as Barth saw, could only lead, and did lead, back into paganism.[2] But the debates on this question showed Barth that he must penetrate much more deeply into the nature of the Word of God, and from his emphasis upon the pure *Act* of the Word, go on to emphasise also the *Being* in the Act. If theology was to hold its own ground and be determined by its own subject-matter, then it must really come to grips with the *Reality* in the event of Revelation, that is, with the actual *Being* of God come to man as Word in Jesus Christ.

There are two related questions here requiring clarification, both of which had already been raised by Barth in his debate with Harnack[3] and received discussion in the *Christliche Dogmatik*.

The first concerns the nature of Revelation. In Revelation, Barth insists, God comes himself and communicates himself to men, for the Word he speaks is grounded in his own Person. The content of Revelation is God, for what God gives is identical with the Giver. Hence when man believes in God he believes by believing Revelation, and when he believes Revelation he believes God himself, for Revelation is God. This relation of Revelation to God himself, the divine *I am*, the divine *Subject*, to the *Lordship* of God, was already set forth in the *Christliche Dogmatik*, and it was shown to involve the doctrine of the Trinity—the *ratio* of the Trinity is the *ratio* of God's Revelation.[4] But it was only when he re-wrote it in the *Kirchliche Dogmatik* that Barth managed to think it through sufficiently in relation to the *Being* of God, of his *being* Father, Son and Holy Spirit.[5]

His studies in the history of dogma once more came to his help, for he saw more clearly that this was the great question lying behind the struggles of the Church in the fourth and fifth centuries, when it had to clarify its mind on the doctrine of the Trinity, in acknowledgment of the essential deity of Jesus Christ and of the Holy Spirit. That meant

---

[1] *CD* I.1, pp. 375 ff. [2] Camfield, op. cit. p. 25 f.
[3] *FuA*, pp. 22 ff. [4] *ChrD*, p. 150. [5] *CD* I.1, ch. 11, § 8.

that the doctrine of Revelation and the doctrine of the Trinity were inseparable, for precisely in Revelation we have to do with the *Being* of God as Father, Son and Holy Spirit. That was now Barth's concern. It is in the doctrine of the Trinity, therefore, that he must go on to penetrate more deeply into the nature of the Word of God as grounded in his Being, through knowledge of the *Being of God in his Act*.[1]

Again, Barth's studies in the theology of the Reformation (not least the *Institutes* of Calvin and the *Heidelberg Catechism*, but also the works of the dogmaticians) convinced him that the same question was at stake in the struggle of the Reformers over justification by grace and the nature of Revelation. In grace the Gift which God bestows is identical with himself the Giver—concretely, this meant Jesus Christ, for he is the Deed of God identical with himself, and in him God gives none other than himself to men for their salvation and justification. Hence the Reformation is to be understood as the struggle to reaffirm in its fulness the Nicene doctrine that God is himself the content of his revelation.[1] It is therefore through the doctrine of Christ that we penetrate right into the nature of the Word of God, for it is on the ground of Christology that we contend for the full doctrine of God himself in his Triune Being. Once more this had to be worked out fully in the *Church Dogmatics*, but already in 1930 in the little work on *The Holy Ghost and the Christian Life* Barth cleared the ground in a debate with Roman Augustinianism for the biblical and Nicene understanding of Grace as identical with the Giver, and as rooted in the Church's understanding of Father, Son and Holy Spirit. God's revelation is God himself, the one, ever-present, eternal, living God, the Holy Trinity.

The other question is related to this; the concreteness of God's revelation in the historical actuality of Jesus Christ. It was at this point, as we have seen, that Barth had to contend with a basic error in Neo-Protestantism, which resurrected the Platonic and idealistic notions which the Church had fought hard in the early centuries to put behind it in its struggles with Gnostics, Origenists, and monophysites, namely, its horror of corporeality, its horror of the Being of God in space and time.[3] The hour had come for Barth to think that through in his doctrine of the Word, to penetrate into an understanding of the fact that God himself, in his own Divine Being, is present with us here in the historical actuality of Jesus Christ, and therefore to derive from that Being and

---

[1] For the full exposition of this in the doctrine of God, see *CD* II.1, ch. VI, § 28.   [2] Cf. *ChrD*, pp. 197f, 210ff, etc. and *God in Action*, p. 14f.
[3] *FuA*, pp. 22f, 26f; *CD* I.2, pp. 128-31; and *ChrD*, p. 168f.

Reality in the historical Event the essential form theology requires for its operation both in inquiry and in doctrinal construction. So long as that was not done, it was not possible for Barth to advance far into a full or adequate interpretation of the doctrine of Christ, that is, of two natures in one Person—thinking that remained dialectical must ultimately inhibit understanding of the Being of Jesus Christ. But, on the other hand, so long as Christology lay undeveloped, it was not possible to make further progress in understanding the Being and Act of the Word, or the Reality in the Event of Revelation, for without full consideration of the Incarnation of the Word in Jesus Christ, such a discussion could only hang in the air.[1]

It is obvious that any advance along these lines must raise a whole host of questions, philosophical and epistemological, as well as purely theological questions, which must be faced squarely if advance is to be assured. Theology does not carry out its activity in some room which it occupies all on its own but in the same room occupied by philosophy. There is, therefore, a philosophical angle, or at least there could be a philosophical counterpart, to almost everything that theology has to say. Certainly theology has its own peculiar nature, its own inner necessities and concerns, but because it shares with philosophy the same room, it cannot develop those concerns without thinking through its problems in relation to those of philosophy. That does not mean that theology must confound its problems with those of philosophy or transcend them in some synthesis, for it must be true to its own inner necessities, but it does mean that it has to reckon with problems of thought posed to it by philosophy, just because theology, like philosophy, has to do with *human thinking*. Theological problems and philosophical problems overlap, and it is in that overlap that theology must watch itself very carefully to make sure that, through the activity of human thinking, some *ideology* is not after all set up in place of *theology*.

That was the temptation which Barth had detected in himself in the *Christliche Dogmatik*, and therefore, as he turned to think through and develop the theological issues that arose out of it, he was determined also to clarify the relationship between theology and philosophy, through facing the fundamental questions posed from the side of philosophy, in a self-critical re-examination of theological activity. That is the importance of his Dortmund lectures on *Schicksal und Idee in der Theologie*.

---

[1] Cf. D. Bonhoeffer's *Habilitationsschrift* of 1931, *Akt und Sein*, in which he goes beyond Barth's early emphasis on God's *Act* to his *Being* and *Act*, offering criticism of Barth at the very point, however, when he had already advanced to his doctrine of God's *Being* in his *Act*. See *Akt und Sein*, pp. 60ff.

2. The Problem of Philosophy

Once more we may turn back for a moment to the discussion between Barth and Harnack. Harnack opened with fifteen questions to 'the despisers of scientific theology' and defined scientific theology as concerned with historical knowledge and critical reflection.[1] Barth replied that he, to whom the questions had obviously been directed, far from despising scientific activity in theology, was concerned to be properly scientific in that he was determined in all historical knowledge and critical reflection to respect the nature of the subject-matter of theology, which was not faith nor experience but the object of faith, God in his revelation. The scientific character of theology was bound up with its recognition that the *object* of its knowledge was, originally, and always would be, *Subject*. This object was given to theology in the proclamation of the Word and in the apprehension of faith, and it was the task of theology, by making use of historical knowledge and critical reflection, to develop its understanding of it, but always in accordance with the nature of the object, that is, of God in his revelation.[2] Harnack's final reply was that, as there is only one scientific method, so there is only one scientific task, pure knowledge of the object, but, he added, the concept of Revelation is not a scientific concept.[3]

In that discussion, Harnack had failed to see that, while scientific activity is concerned with the pure knowledge of its object, for that very reason the nature of the object must be allowed to prescribe the specific mode of rational activity to be adopted in knowing it, and therefore genuine scientific activity requires that its method be modified in accordance with the particular subject-matter concerned. In the knowledge of God, we are concerned with an incomparable object (the Lord God), and therefore it cannot be scientific to carry over from our knowledge of other objects the specific form of rationality or the specific method of knowledge science has had to develop in accordance with their (creaturely) nature.

That is the epistemological and methodological question that agitated Barth in the years 1929 and 1930. It is a question that moves constantly between two poles, the given *object* (its nature and reality), and *thought* about the object (its mode and its truth), and therefore it is a question that will tend to be given either a more realist or a more idealist answer

---

[1] *FuA*, p. 7f. See also the *Briefwechsel* between Harnack and Erik Peterson in 1928 in which Harnack accused Barth of 'scientific and religious naïveté', republished by E. Peterson in *Theologische Traktate*, 1950, p. 296.
[2] *FuA*, pp. 9ff and 18ff.   [3] *FuA*, p. 30f.

in accordance with where the emphasis is laid, upon the object itself or upon thought about it. That is the basic area where the problems of theology and philosophy overlap, and clarification is needed, the area which has seen so many tensions and conflicts in the history of thought, as between nature and spirit, the particular and the universal, being and thought, realism and nominalism, etc. That is the area that Barth intended to cover by the use of *Schicksal und Idee* in the title of his Dortmund lectures.[1]

In these lectures Barth takes his stand within the Church as the realm within which knowledge of God arises, and defines theology as the science of God as the object of the Church's proclamation. It is a science pursued within the Church (even though that may be formally carried out in Universities) and one in which investigation of the truth about God is ordered in accordance with its subject-matter. It is not the investigation of the Truth of God as such, for God himself remains the presupposition, the limiting conception on the boundary of theology, as indeed of every other science, who as such cannot be brought within human knowledge or human science as an object. Theological science is, however, the investigation and exposition of the Truth of God as it is proclaimed and ought to be proclaimed in the Church, that is, not of a God whom we have first to seek, but who has given himself and continues to give himself to us to find, who has revealed himself and continues to reveal himself to us in his Word. Theology, then, has God not only for its object, but for its object only so far as it has him as Subject, so far, that is, as its investigating and expounding of his Truth have no other source than the knowledge which he gives us of himself. But the Church, in which all this takes place, is a realm of human life in which proclamation of God's Word is a human endeavour, and therefore the theology that takes place within it is an undertaking of human science, employing as its instrument human thought and speech, with their definite laws, and possibilities and limits, which other sciences use.[2] Theology operates, therefore, with the same tools, as well as in the same field, as philosophy, but it fulfils its task in developing the understanding of its object in its own way, through its acknowledgment of divine revelation, and therefore in a way that philosophy does not and cannot undertake. Nevertheless, just because theology is a human undertaking, in spite of its divine origin and its divine object, it cannot make that understanding directly recognisable or unambiguously clear, not to speak of offering a demonstration of it. Theology is never in a position

[1] *FuA*, pp. 54ff. [2] *FuA*, p. 55f.

to control the object of its knowledge, nor is it able to master, as it would like, the instruments it employs. Rather must it rely unceasingly upon the grace of God who alone can justify its knowledge of him, for in giving himself to us as the object of our knowledge, he is to be understood, derived, substantiated only out of himself.

This does not absolve theology from rigorous control of its thinking and speaking or from the discipline of constant self-critical revision, for it operates under the total claim of its incomparable object who remains Lord over it and requires of it unceasing vigilance and faithfulness in obedient conformity to his self-revelation. Thus the measure of its acknowledgment of the lordship of its object is the measure of its readiness to submit to searching tests and exacting criticism in order to meet the most stringent demand from the side of the object for objectivity on the part of theology.[1]

Such theology, however, operates under the constant pressure of temptation, just because it occupies the same room or field as philosophy. Theology is not free thought, but is thought bound to its object, thought that does not move in any direction that it chooses but in a direction chosen for it by the activity of the object in his sovereign self-giving and self-revelation. Theology is thinking bound to God who communicates himself in his Word to the Church to be recognised and known as God. The self-giving, self-communicating, the speaking on the part of God calls for a corresponding activity on the part of theology in receiving, appropriating and hearing. Its knowledge is gained by way of obedience; it is thought out, not from a centre in itself, but from a centre beyond itself, in God, or rather, it is not knowledge that is first thought *out*, but knowledge that is thought *in* because it is derived from hearing.[2]

Over against this, philosophy appears so much better, freer, more universal, for it is not bound to a concrete object in the same way as theology, nor is it under constraint to the Word of God or restricted to the Church, but is in a position to speak freely in the name of every man. Over against the philosopher, the theologian is tempted to ask what the philosopher will think of him. Will he accept the theologian's commitment to revelation? Will he respect the fact that his statements are made only in acknowledgment of God's Word? And so the theologian is tempted to be a kind of philosopher himself, who makes his statements, not on the ground of what is said to him or of what he hears in God's Word, but on the ground of what he can think out and say for himself

---

[1] This was more fully expounded later in *CD* II.1, pp. 204ff.
[2] *FuA*, p. 58f.

or tell to himself—that is, without reference to the Bible and the Church, without laborious exegesis of the Scriptures and careful listening to God's Word. What is more, instead of seeking for an explanation of his knowledge of God from within its own actuality, and instead of testing the reality of that knowledge on the basis of which it actually arose, he steps away to some place outside the knowledge of God to test it by some general criterion or abstract possibility of knowledge; instead of looking outside of himself to God alone, to uphold and justify and validate his understanding in seeking understanding of him, he looks within himself to find justification and verification in the inner power of the reason and in the movement of his own thought; and so instead of beginning with God he seeks to end with him as the reality reached at the end of his reflection upon the world or as the goal of his thinking.

That temptation is particularly easy for the theologian to fall into, for his thinking has not only to travel along the way from God to man, but also to travel along the way from man to God, and therefore his theology must not only begin with God but also find in God its goal. What he hears, and *thinks in*, he must also *think out* to the end. It is because theology is such a human undertaking, indeed all too human in its thinking and speaking, that the theologian must constantly be on his guard lest the God at the goal of his theological knowledge should simply turn out to be but the result of his human thinking, the conclusion to his own argument—a 'god' that he has thought out for himself.

In order to test theological thinking, to see whether it has betrayed itself into some form of philosophy or ideology, Barth proposes to examine it at the two poles between which theological and philosophical thinking constantly move, the given object and thought about the object. The discussion Barth offers is of such importance, both for its own sake and for our understanding of his thought, that we must give full consideration to it.

A. *The Problem of Realism*

When we say that God is the object of theological knowledge, we assume that he is the *given Reality*, so that our statement is a typically realist statement.[1] But how are we to understand it? Our primary know-

---

[1] The word Barth uses throughout this discussion is *Wirklichkeit* which he prefers to render *Aktualität* rather than *Realität* because of the relation between *Aktualität* and *Akt*, actuality and act, which it involves. In English, however, *reality* is sometimes a better rendering of Barth's thought, if we remember that it is a living, active Reality with which we are concerned. We shall render it mostly by actuality, but sometimes by reality as the context may demand.

ledge is one of experience, concerned with the actualities of our existence.
Doubtless man's first naïve steps in reflection on his relation to God
arise here and lead toward thinking of him as the fate or unavoidable
actuality with which his life is bound up.[1] Then when he seeks critical
clarification and deepening of his experiential knowledge he is faced
with the question of truth. Is God to be understood simply as the unavoidable actuality determining his existence—as his fate? Or is man to
seek his fate, or destiny in God? Where, who, or what is God? When
theological knowledge undertakes this task, it cannot escape the critical
questions as to objectivity, givenness, or reality posed by philosophy
with which it shares the same field of discourse, and so the problem of
realism is a very serious and inescapable problem for theology.[2]

Classical realism, as represented, for example, by Thomas Aquinas,
was given its particular form through the doctrine of *analogia entis*. The
statement 'God is' does not only mean that God participates in being,
but that he is himself Being, the source and perfection of all being. But
that statement has its counterpart in another to the effect that all being
as such participates in God, in the very great unlikeness of the creature
to the Creator, but also in very great likeness due to its participation in
being. The realist takes his stand upon a basic conviction—so fundamental, that it cannot be grounded on anything else, and is simply to be
accepted—that in the given realities of his experience he encounters the
likeness of God. But here there takes place an easy passage from the
conviction that God *can*, as it were, be read off what is given to experience, for it is in the likeness of God, to the conviction that he *must* be
read off what is so given; in the actualities of his experience he is necessarily up against God. Thus God is ontologically and noetically man's
unavoidable fate.

We, and the things outside of us, then, stand in relation to God simply
in virtue of the fact that we *exist*. 'We' and 'the things outside of us'—
realism has here a double aspect corresponding to our inward and outward experience, or to a subjective and an objective givenness. According to the doctrine of *analogia entis*, both *I who know* and the thing
outside of me as *the known* must be like and unlike God, if it is to be
to me the likeness of God, and *I* am to know *God* in it. But in knowledge
of God how am I to relate *I who know* and *the object known* to one
another? In the classical realism of St Thomas both sides are strongly

---

[1] This is the notion of *Schicksal*, fate, which is deeply embedded in German
thought and is particularly bound up with historical determination, or destiny.
Cf. the statement of Herrmann, 'what Schleiermacher calls God, is *das Schicksal*'
—cited by Barth in *TC*, p. 245.   [2] *FuA*, pp. 62 ff.

emphasised, the outward and inward experience, the objective and subjective givenness of God, and he takes pains to keep them in balance over against one another. It is possible, however, for greater emphasis to be laid on one side or the other, without abandonment of the fundamental position of realism, for the stress on one side always demands a return to the other as its complement.[1]

All theologies of experience involve a movement to and fro between the idea of an inner, subjective, and of an outer, objective givenness of God. In illustration of that Barth points to the inner bond between pietism and rationalism, the one appealing to a subjective experience of God in the world within, and the other to an objective experience of God in the world without, as its theological criterion; to the different emphases in the younger and the older Schleiermacher, and to the alternating emphases in the development of Neo-Protestant theology after him, between faith and history, history and faith. Is it not possible that the tension between subjective and objective here is only a sort of family quarrel, and that the 'God' of the 'subjectivists' and the 'objectivists' alike is to be identified with the unavoidable necessities of their experience, i.e. with fate?

Hence the problem inevitably arises: How are we to distinguish what is genuinely objective from our own subjective states? That is a question that evangelical theology must take no less seriously whenever it insists that God is the object of theological knowledge. We cannot be content with an objectless knowledge, and it would surely be a deplorable expedient to fall back upon faith only as the object, instead of God. We cannot avoid speaking of the *being* of God, and taking in a realist sense the statement that *God is*. The problem is not lessened but sharpened for us when we remember that we are not concerned with some 'God in himself' but with God in his revelation, or with God as he is revealed through his Word and known by the Church, i.e. within the sphere of human encounter where God's Word is preached and heard.

'The Word was made flesh and dwelt among us.'[2] That means that the Word of God, God himself, entered into the mode of being of nature and history in which we share, and so into our own mode of being. It is there that we meet with the divine self-giving or revelation, i.e. with Jesus Christ as God the Word addressed to us, and with the Holy Spirit as God both illuminating that Word for us and enlightening us to understand it. That takes place within the sphere of our actuality and being, where revelation can be the object of our experience; that is to say, it

---

[1] *FuA*, p. 63 f.   [2] John 1.14.

takes place within the relationship, so basic to Christian ethics, between the *I* and the *Thou*, in which we are to think of the *Thou* as the given reality for the *I*, and yet of the *Thou* or 'my neighbour' as the likeness of God, in which I encounter him: 'Inasmuch as ye have done it unto one of the least of these my brethren, ye have done it unto me.'[1] God encounters me in the likeness of my *neighbour*, of another *Thou* over against me, within the objective/subjective relationship of the *Thou* and the *I*. He comes to me in it as Jesus Christ the Word addressed *to me*, and as the Holy Spirit enabling me to understand him and respond *to him*.

In this case, do we not have in *Jesus Christ* and the *Holy Spirit*, or in the *Thou* and the *I*, the two poles of thought in theological realism, that is, the outward and inward givenness of God, and the outward and inward experience of him? What is God's revelation but the divine self-giving within that objective-subjective likeness of himself where we may experience him, where he both gives himself to us and lets himself be found of us, outwardly and inwardly? Hence does not Revelation mean that God meets us as the unavoidable actuality of our existence, that he becomes, as it were, our fate? It is here, then, in this understanding of God as *Actuality* that we discern the justifiable and inalienable concern of every genuine theology in *realism*.[2]

Now, if we are to think of Revelation as the *Actuality* of God for us in the midst of our actuality, and of God as *acting* upon us there and confronting us with his *being* in that *act*, then it is understandable if we should want to test the actuality of God by the standard of our own actuality with which we are so familiar. What would God be if he were not actual, in the same sense in which we experience ourselves or the world as actuality, as act, as being, indeed as unavoidable fate—although we would hasten to add that he is actual in a pre-eminent way? God is thus not another actuality but *the* Actuality or Reality through which and in which our own actuality and that of the world is actuality—the *causa prima, ens realissimum*, and *actus purus*, the One Actuality that lies behind and is present in every other actuality. It is as such, *in similitudine*, within the subject/object, I/Thou relationships of our actuality that God is the object of our outer and inner experience. Taken in that way, the conception of God proves to be a serious conception corresponding to our actual experience. It must give expression to actuality, to the *one* Actuality that transcends and includes within itself, that lies hidden, and yet not altogether hidden, behind every other actuality. It

---

[1] Matt. 25.40.   [2] *FuA*, p. 65f.

must justify itself as the conception of an experienced reality. How else would theology, operating in the same field as philosophy and of all human thinking, have it to be true? How else could theology properly and adequately fulfil its function except as *realist theology*? Ought not *realist* to be equivalent to *Christian* on the ground that Christ and the Holy Spirit import the *Actuality* of God in the world and for us?[1]

If realism goes, then Christianity goes along with it. He who is not aware of that, or who is not open to its relevance cannot be regarded as an informed or a serious participator in theological activity. But when we remember that theology has to think and speak of God on the ground of his own Word, we must be watchful lest in its need for realism in its thinking and in its commitment to some specific form of the human logos, it should unwittingly think and speak about something altogether different from what, as theology of the Word of God, it ought. We cannot take it for granted that the realist thinking in which theology is engaged is identical with or is even in agreement with thinking that is governed by the Word of God, its proper object.[2]

Thus, theology has certain questions which it must put to itself and to realism, on the answer to which will depend, not whether, but *how far* its thinking and speaking may be realist. But all these questions converge in one question, directed at the fundamental assumption that lies at the basis of realism, namely the naïve conviction that within certain limits man *can* find God within the givenness of the subject-object relationship, and that the *similitudo dei* between the knower and the known *must* take place. Are we in a position, face to face with the God of Revelation, to take up this realist assumption into theology? Is that conviction really grounded in God's revelation? Is Revelation simply to be the supernatural ratification and confirmation of that naïve presupposition of a capacity and necessity for God that is somehow posited with our existence as such? That was in fact the line taken up by Thomas Aquinas on the ground that grace does not destroy nature but upholds and perfects it, as well as on the ground of an analogy between the being of the creature and the supreme Being of the Creator. Because, even at the lowest level, man participates in the *lumen divinum* or the uncreated light of the Supreme Being, experience of God is for Aquinas the only possibility available to man even in virtue of Revelation. Beings as such, and we men simply in virtue of our being, participate in the likeness of God. Hence experience of God is held to be an ontological possibility and necessity for us. Protestant realists have not taken over this unusually acute and consistently thought-out position of St Thomas, or have only made partial use of it. But is their conviction as to the possibility of man's experience of God any the less—the conviction in which they credit man, or at any rate Christian man, with being perfectly capable of God?

Such an assumption calls, not so much for a negation as a question-mark, or an exclamation mark, for when a man actually hears the Word of God he takes up a very different position. He knows that the Word of God which he hears does not import for man a ratification or confirmation of some naïve conviction as to his own capacity for God; rather does it interrupt such a conviction. It says something *new* to him and does not just reinforce and clarify what he knows anyhow and can learn otherwise. That is what always happens when the Word of God comes to man; it communicates to him new knowledge, like light in the darkness; it comes to him always in his sin as grace that both forgives and judges him. If he hears something that he already knows, then it is something other than the Word of God, for what is the use of the Word of God if it only tells him what he already knows?[1]

That is the primary and basic question we have to direct to all theological realists, whether they have taken into consideration the fact that the grace of God *contradicts* sinners. It is on this ground that grace opposes the sinner, that is, on the ground of the contradiction between God in his revelation and us in our sin, that we can distinguish the objectively given reality of God and of his Word from our own subjective states or the other objectivities which we encounter in our experience of the world around us. It is only under this proviso that we may engage in realist thinking and speaking in a theology of the Word of God—that is to say, only on condition that we take in deadly earnest the nature of the Actuality of God as *Act*. St Thomas certainly laid great emphasis upon the *actus purus* of God but in quite a different way from what is meant here—rather must we predicate the knowability of God of God himself, that is to say, derive it from his divine freedom to let himself be known, and known compellingly, by man, and not predicate it of our own free will in any sense. Man's capacity for God is not something that belongs to him as such for his creaturely will is not only weak in itself and weaker still through sin, but perverted and just as incapable of knowing God as of obeying him. Hence the *similitudo dei* or the likeness of God in us required for knowledge of him, is something new given from heaven in the very act of knowing God.[2]

[1] *FuA*, p. 69.   [2] *FuA*, p. 70.

Going on from that basic question, Barth asks further questions as to the possibility of our *inner* and *outer* experience of God. We cannot, of course, call in question an inner experience of God for that would be to call in question the Holy Spirit and the possibility of his witness in the heart, and therefore the possibility of seeking and finding God within us. But we must ask the realists whether by inner experience of God they really mean the Holy Spirit, whether they have considered the fact that he is no less God than the Father and the Son and that, therefore, he is to be understood only out of God himself and not out of us? What we must be concerned to do here is to distinguish the objective act of the Holy Spirit upon us and in us from what is merely our own inner experience or state. We must be assured that we are not just prisoners of the circle of our own subjectivity, and that it is not just our own heart that we have set on God's throne. It is perhaps at this point that we are subjected to the sharpest test as to whether we are really engaged in theological activity, or simply in realist philosophising.[1]

Rather different is the question we have to direct to our outer experience of God. To call this in question would be to call Jesus Christ in question, which we cannot do. But we must ask whether *Christ* is actually meant when realists speak about God as the object of their experience or knowledge and, if so, whether they are taking seriously his deity. It is more than suspicious when Christ is interpreted as one in a series of historical entities, or God's Revelation is understood only within the framework of some general history, for then man is quite clearly ascribed the power to determine what Revelation might be, and so a criterion is put into his hand which enables him to recognise Christ as Christ only on the ground of his own judgment. If that is the way of it, Barth says, then we must add here too that this is not theological thinking so much as some kind of realist philosophising about God as history.

If, in regard to our inner experience of God, we had to inquire into the distinction or necessary distance between the objective reality and our experience of it, here we have to inquire into the unavoidable character of the experience, and its claim to be experience of God and therefore its right to theological consideration. We may put the question rather sharply by asking whether the experience of which theological realists speak is of a God who is just there (*eines daseienden*), a sort of unavoidable fate, or of a God who comes (*eines kommenden Gottes*).[2] If

---

[1] Op. cit. p. 70f. This is the burden also of Barth's little work on the Holy Spirit mentioned above.

[2] Cf. Bonhoeffer's criticism of Barth here: 'Gott bleibt immer der Herr,

this experience yields a notion of a God who is unavoidably there rather than one who comes to us, would it not be better to call him *Nature*? And would it not be better to speak of the theology of this God as 'demonology' rather than 'theology', for such a God, *deus sive natura*, is not the God who is revealed in the Word of God?

B. *The Problem of Idealism*

If the question as to *actuality* gives rise to realism, the complementary question as to *truth* gives rise to idealism.[1] It is the question that seeks to penetrate behind the given, the objectifiable, the finite, behind all actuality to its ultimate legitimation and substantiation, to the infinite presupposition of what is given, objectifiable, finite, to the all-inclusive *Idea*. Idealistic thinking has a refracted, humble side and a strong, arrogant side. On the one hand, it takes its rise, negatively, from doubt regarding the naïve realist conviction, and is the fundamental inquiry into the reliability of the correlation (so self-evident to the realist), between object and subject, subject and object. It is the question as to the source of the givenness of this correlation, and to the limits of the knowledge that takes place within it. On the other hand, in the course of this inquiry, thinking takes the field, positively, as the criterion of actuality, and so discovers itself in its precedence and superiority over against pure being. Idealism (whether in its Platonic, Nominalist, Cartesian or Kantian forms) is the self-reflection of spirit over against nature; it is the discovery of the correlation between thinking and truth, the discovery of the creative logos as the source of the givenness of the correlation between subject and object.

Why should we not find theology taking this road? Barth asks. Is there any philosophical idealism without the problem of theology? Is it not rather the idea of God that leads to the second step in reflection, idealist reflection? Certainly there has never been a serious theology that could escape the problem of idealism. Even a realist theology, as we have seen, cannot be a theology at all without a powerful ingredient of idealism. That is evident also in the attempt to speak of the given reality on the ground of the analogy of being or likeness of God. We recall St Thomas' use of the *via negativa* to reach the concept of pure Being or Act by way of abstraction from all the properties of being given to us in our experience. Whenever there is serious thinking about

---

immer Subjekt, so dass, wer ihn als Gegenstand zu haben meint, nicht mehr *ihn* hat; er ist der "kommende", nie der "daseiende" Gott' *Akt und Sein*, p. 61.
  [1] *FuA*, p. 72 f.

the idea of God, a distinction must be drawn between the givenness of God and the givenness of all other being, a distinction so fundamental that the Being of God in relation to all other being is treated as 'not-given' and 'non-being'. We recall also the realism of Schleiermacher, pivoted more upon the subject than the object, in which there was a similar critical or negative knowledge of God, that is, not of One who is given to our experience, but of One upon whom we are nevertheless conscious of being absolutely dependent.[1]

Wherever this inquiry into the hiddenness and otherness of God over against all that is given in our experience, wherever the concern of mysticism, the immediate knowledge of God has a primary place, there we have idealist theology. This essential relation between idealist and mystical thinking, Barth points out, shows that idealist theology is not necessarily to be traced back to some system of philosophical idealism. Just as we cannot dismiss theological realism as disguised philosophy, so we must give theological idealism its due. One can be a theological realist or idealist without being involved, even by the way, with their philosophical counterparts, and therefore it is a disgusting device in theological discussion to try to dismiss one's opponent merely by reference to his realist or idealist instigators.[2]

Barth asks, therefore, whether the idealist principle of a distinction between 'the not-given' and 'the given' is not necessary for our understanding of the difference between God's revelation and all else that goes by the name of revelation. Are we not concerned after all in theology with *understanding*, with giving an account of God in the form of human thought, in the form of an activity of the human spirit in abstraction from, and in interpretation of, the given? Is not all theology as necessarily idealist as it is realist—necessarily so, in the sense that the act of reflecting upon the given actuality of God always involves a transcending of that actuality to its truth that is not given, or an understanding of 'the given' in the light of 'the not-given' that lies behind it? That does not mean that idealism requires to be objectless, for a genuine idealism does not look completely away from what is given to experience (objectively or subjectively), but joyfully acknowledges that all creaturely being is supported by the Creator Logos in God.

It is for this reason that the idealist will not make an idol out of the infinite or use the absolute to slay everything that is relative. He will affirm both mysticism and culture. He will not only be concerned with God in himself as the Idea, and the Truth, but will seek out ideas and

[1] P. 73f.   [2] P. 75.

truths and principles, theoretical and practical conceptions, and refer them to their source in God. Moreover, he will take the problem of the *Thou* and of fellowship with him not less seriously because his methodological starting-point is from the *I* in its isolation from the *Thou*. Genuine idealism describes a hyperbola which moves away from actuality into the realm of truth which does not self-evidently coincide with it, but then it moves back into actuality now understood as the realm of truths. It is because genuine idealism does not exclude but, in its own way, includes, the given, that a Christian, theological idealism, as critical understanding of the given, is possible for Revelation. Criticism here does not mean negation, but refraction and therefore a strengthening of the knowledge of the given; refraction through questioning of its realist assumption, and strengthening through the establishment of its genuine connexion with the given.[1]

Earlier, Barth says, we noted the provisions under which realism has its proper place in theology; God is not fate. God is not nature. Nor is God history. God is not just there. The Word became flesh, but the flesh is not therefore in itself the Word; only because and in so far as the *Word* became flesh, and in that irreversible relationship, can it be spoken of in that way. It cannot be said, however, that this delimitation in the presuppositions of theological realism can be unambiguously backed up. That is precisely where the relevance of idealism to theology comes in; it is the uncovering of the hiddenness of God even in his revelation. That is why it recalls that 'God is Truth' over against the cry of the realists that 'God is Actuality'. It does not deny the actuality, but it wishes to understand the Truth through it, in order that the Truth may illuminate it, apart from which it would not be God's Actuality. That is why idealism takes the trouble to criticise objective as well as subjective experience, and why, to the displeasure of the realist, it speaks of the signitive or symbolic character of the objective and subjective givenness of God. That is why it emphasises likeness to God, and the greater unlikeness.

How genuine and necessary an element in theology this is we can see in Augustine, the greatest of all theological idealists. Idealism is the necessary antidote in theology to any tendency toward demonology; it heeds the transcendence of God over the given, remembers the inadequacy of all human thinking and speaking of God and is on guard against the displacement of the proper object of theological knowledge by other objects. A theology thoroughly purified of idealism cannot be anything else than a pagan monstrosity. Classical realism is the best witness for

[1] P. 76.

the fact that a second step had to follow in theology, the critique advanced by idealism.[1]

But here too Barth has his questions to ask. The Christianity of idealism is not without its dangers, indeed it is on the whole in *greater danger* just because it has to take that second audacious step in deeper reflection upon God. The overthrowing of 'demonology' in theology can mean only too easily the setting up of an 'ideology', and it is much more difficult to distinguish genuine theology from 'ideology' than from 'demonology'. Hence we must look for criteria to enable us to judge the proper place of idealism in theology.

Above all we must reach agreement with the idealist that his hyperbola, his reference of actuality back to its source in the Truth, is not meant to be just a generally accessible way to God open at all times to everybody. It might well be the pride of the idealist that, with his reference to the timeless and universally accessible truth of the reason, he has an advantage over the contingent, particular, historical truths of the realist. That would certainly make him very suspicious to theology. Over against all undisciplined hunger for generally accessible truth, he must agree with the realist that by 'accessibility' is to be understood the possibility, not of our access to God, but of his access to us, if the foundation of theology in God's revelation is not to be denied. He must also condemn himself along with the realist to finding this access of God's truth to us wholly restricted to a single, particular event. He must concede that he possesses no criterion at all by means of which he is able to dig out the truth in the actuality, but that this criterion must be given in and with Revelation itself, if his hyperbola is not to be an empty game. Thus he must not regard Revelation as a general possibility of man, but as a particular possibility of God. As a Christian theologian he must regard it as the possibility of God given in Christ, that is, given by Christ in the witness of the Bible and the Church. He may not appeal to the human reason or to the phenomena of nature and history, in general and in themselves, as organs or witnesses or symbols of Revelation, but he must know that his critical activity in analysis and synthesis only has meaning where the Word of God, which is bound neither to our reason nor to the phenomena of the world, gives it this meaning.[2]

A second agreement that is to be reached with the idealist theologian is to the effect that even if his hyperbola or backward reference has to do with God's revelation, it cannot import anything more than a retracing of God's actual truth or true actuality by means of human conceptions or of a dialectical correlation of what is given and not given of God in his revelation. It cannot be a direct representation or presentation of, and so a substitute for, God's own Word.

Hence we must ask idealist theology whether it does not, against its own ultimate intention, exchange the divine Logos for a human logos. That question must be pressed, for example, against the theology of Albrecht Ritschl, which reposes altogether upon a rather primitively conceived contradiction between spirit and nature, and in which it seems to be quite forgotten that the world of spirit, just as much as the world of nature, is *world*, and that the world of spirit in itself is not at all the way to God. The fact that Schleiermacher was aware that that is to be sought above this intra-mundane contradiction is by itself evidence of his towering superiority over that other theological master of the previous century—which must not be forgotten even if we cannot say that this insight bore much fruit in his theology.[1]

Again, we have to ask the idealist theologian whether he agrees with us that the world of God beyond (*das Jenseits Gottes*) to which he points us, is not just 'the other side' (*das Jenseits*) of our own creaturely and fallen spirit, not just the relative invisibility of our own spiritual life, but 'the other side' of the Creator of the heaven and the earth of nature and of spirit, of all things visible and invisible; and that we must therefore remain content adequately to repeat and reproduce his Word; that our task, preserving the limits of humanity, as is the intention of a genuine idealism, can only be that of serving the Word, pointing to it and bearing witness to it by means of the dialectic of human conceptions. Theology is certainly a spiritual work (*Geistesarbeit*) but it is just as little 'human science' (*Geisteswissenschaft*) as it is natural science. It is science of the Word of God who dwells in unapproachable Light.

We do not fulfil the task of theological science through any art of our own, but solely in virtue of the fact that the Word of God has come to us and laid its claim upon us. The theologian does not attempt to repeat the work of the Word, or to displace it, nor does he think he can utter the Word of God himself. He can only re-echo it without the slightest suggestion that what he does is a creative act, or that the meaning intended is to be found in the dialectic of theology itself. Only under these conditions can the idealist also be a theologian.

The third question Barth presses upon the idealist is whether he is ready to agree that the establishment of the truth in our knowledge of

[1] P. 79.

God is *God's act*, not God's and ours, but God's act alone. The knowledge of God in his Word is the knowledge of faith. But faith understands its knowledge, not as man's own act, nor as the act of God and man, but as the exclusive act of God, as the informing of man by the Word of God. This will be the most difficult test which we cannot spare the idealist—the question whether he is willing entirely and finally to give up any notion of a 'tension' between the divine and the human act in theological inquiry, and so to concede that knowledge of God is by way of *ac*knowledgment.[1]

To speak here of a tension or of a 'togetherness of God and man' is to confuse this knowledge with some other kind of knowledge. For all other knowledge a 'tension' or 'togetherness' is significant, for it is the familiar antithesis between spontaneity and receptivity. Of course we cannot help but make use of that in our knowledge of God just because it belongs to human thinking. When the Reformers, for example, spoke of faith as merely 'passive' they did not mean by that that the spontaneous but not the receptive function of the reason is shut out. Wherever there is receptivity there is also spontaneity. In faith and in theological knowledge it is the whole reason that is involved, without any interruption of its functioning, with its receptive and spontaneous activity, but it is that *whole reason* directed and determined and ordered *from above it* by that which does not partake of its antithesis. That is the peculiar feature of theological knowledge compared to other knowledge, for in it the whole reason as reason is passively related to what is above it, and *obedient* to it.

To drag what is above it down into the antithesis between spontaneity and receptivity would be meaningless, for that antithesis has its place where we are concerned with *things*. That is the realm of everlasting tensions where reversibility obtains, where 'above' can mean 'below' and 'below' 'above', as the change-over from Hegelian idealism into the materialism of the second half of the nineteenth century has shown. Hence God must not be sought within the reason, nor may he be interchanged with the creaturely spirit, for it only knows itself within that antithesis, that is, in its own antithesis to something outside of it which may indeed involve tension but not a more or less one-sided superiority. That is why the equation *deus sive ratio* is just as intolerable for theology as the equation *deus sive natura*. Faith believes in neither of these opposite and obviously reciprocal limitations, in no such absolute which is only absolute in a reversible relation with the relative that confronts it.

[1] P. 80.

Faith believes in the Creator of all things and therefore has no other object but the Lord of the 'objects' *natura* and *ratio*, who gave them their origin and set them over against one another.[1]

If faith is indeed the knowledge of the Creator then it cannot understand itself as acting creatively, but only as acting obediently. It is knowledge of the truth solely in virtue of the fact that the truth is *spoken* to us to which we respond in pure obedience. That can take place only if God is *God* and not our *idea* of God, and if this God has spoken to us. All human speaking of this God that takes the form of objective knowledge, in the same field of discourse as philosophy and using the same dialectic, can only be an expression of this obedience to a divine imperative, and cannot seek to convert it into a reciprocity between God's activity and our own.[2]

c. *Theology and Philosophy*

Theology is at work with philosophy in the same field. It has its concrete concern to take up, but because it is at work with philosophy it cannot avoid the problem of philosophy in the development of its own theological problem. It too has to reckon with both poles of human thought, truth and actuality, and therefore cannot but think in dialectical togetherness of God's givenness and not-givenness.

As we have already seen, Barth points out, there is a one-sided realist and a one-sided idealist theology, a dangerous approximation to pure realism in which there is a confounding of theology with natural science, and a dangerous approximation to pure idealism in which there is a confounding of theology with humanistic science. The one results in demonology, the other in ideology. We also noted the corrective that arises with equal force from both sides, thrown up from the very subject-matter itself, the concern of each to assume that of the other into its own activity and somehow to bring the counter-thesis under its own denominator.[3]

Theology thus shares in the same kind of dialectical movement that goes on in philosophy, but what is to guarantee that Christian theology really attends to its own concern in all this and is not just some kind of philosophy? Whether it is good theology or not does not depend on a dialectical correction between realism and idealism operating within it, for that goes on in philosophy too, but depends on the way in which this dialectic is appropriated and used in theology. In philosophy an attempt is made to look through and beyond the dualism of the two ultimate

---

[1] P. 81.   [2] P. 82.   [3] P. 82.

poles of thought and to overcome them, i.e. an attempt to transcend the antithesis through a synthesis.

What philosophy does not try to do this in some way, no matter how cautiously? The one lays claim to *being*, the other to *logos*, as the comprehensive and reconciling principle; the one points to truth as the predicate of actuality, the other to actuality as the predicate of truth. But should the theologian think that this is the way in which to carry out his task, what philosophy is there which may not claim at bottom to be theology, its value depending on the caution and correctness with which it succeeded in making either its first or its second fundamental proposition valid as a comprehensive and reconciling third, and so achieving a synthesis? One thinks here of Aquinas on the realist and of Hegel on the idealist side. But it is not as simple as that.[1]

The art of operating with a synthesis is philosophy's right and it is not to be disputed by theology at all, but the question is rather this: Whether philosophy—even if it is a little less daring than that of Aquinas or Hegel, and even if it follows the calm detachment (or perhaps we should say, restrained enthusiasm) of a Kant—does not really intend to have the last word, or at least to think it can say one final concluding word? Good for philosophy if it is aware that as philosophy, as interpretation of the actuality and truth of man, it can appear on the frontier of the idea of God only as a question; good for it if it is aware that the theological problem of positive speech about God is not to be confounded with its own, and at least recognises its peculiar nature even if it is not in a position to justify it. Good for philosophy if it does not appear as disguised theology, as *Ersatz*-theology, or as theosophy, if it does not allow its synthesis to be confused with the idea of God. If that is the case, then, at any rate from the side of theology, there cannot be any complaint against its dialectic.[2]

On the other hand, when theology makes use of dialectic it must mean something very different, if it is not to jettison its own special concern. Whether it is slanted in a realist or an idealist direction, theology cannot erect either pole of its thought into a comprehensive principle. Why is that? Because theology can never be anthropology, the interpretation of the actuality and truth of man, for it is the interpretation of the *Word of God* spoken *to* the actuality and truth of man.

Theology does concern itself with the dialectical correlation of the antithesis of human thought, not because it thinks that, as a science of man reflecting upon human existence, it can give some answer to a con-

[1] P. 83.   [2] P. 84f.

tradiction or enigma in human existence revealed by the contradiction in human thought, but because theology derives from the Word of God which set that contradiction in the world of human thought and existence. Now the Word of God does not itself partake of that contradiction for in it, only in the Word, are the antitheses overcome. Therefore a theology that derives from the Word comes from the very place which philosophy would like to reach in its attempt to speak an ultimate word beyond the antitheses of human thought. In contrast to philosophy, then, theology is a form of thinking which takes its rise from a centre in the ultimate Word of God and moves from God to man, but for that very reason, it must reject any form of thinking which claims that, by reflecting upon the actuality and truth of man, it can reach up to an ultimate word worthy of the name of God. In other words, a theology that interprets the Word of God addressed to man cannot allow itself to be displaced by an anthropology that tries to solve the riddle of human existence through man's self-understanding.

What, then, is the relation between theology and philosophy? Between theology and a philosophy that remains strictly philosophy, there can be and will be, not only a benevolent neutrality, not only peace, but, at least for theology, the most instructive co-operation. But between theology and a philosophy which insists on being a theosophy there can only be war to the knife. And the reason for that is that theology must expose as utterly illusory any attempt by way of man's self-reflection to find the ultimate Word of God.[1]

Theologically speaking, what we are concerned with here is *sin*—that is, with the attempt of fallen man to thrust himself in between himself and God, and to make his own word out to be the ultimate Word of God. Thus the negative thesis which we have to maintain here is that the reconciling principle or synthesis which *we* establish or affirm, point to, or aim at, is *not* God. It might be remarked by the way, says Barth, that so far no philosophy has really succeeded in making such a reconciling principle conceptually illuminating, but our theological thesis must not be allowed to rest on the ultimate failure of the synthetic art of philosophy. The question that theology must ask is this: Whether the believing man, to whom God is revealed through his Word, can for one moment ascribe to himself, apart from the Word, any faith or knowledge of God? Must he not rather deny that he has any capacity for such knowledge, and admit that, in so far as he has confused God with Fate or the Idea, he has been following idols, arbitrarily deified 'forces, principalities and

[1] P. 85f.

powers'? Must he not agree that, compared with faith through the Word and in the Word, this natural religion of redemption, far from being a useful first step or preparation, is but as darkness compared to light or as death compared to life? Is it not true that such a 'natural' and a revealed knowledge of God can only develop harmoniously together where theology denies itself, and rejects its nature as a theology of Revelation? In other words, are we not really concerned here with a subtle form of Semi-Pelagianism?[1]

Surely Luther was right, Barth says, when he insisted that all attempts to apprehend God by the power of our own thought (*apprehendere deum in sua majestate judicio rationis*) is the last in the series of man's own works, and is quite inconsistent with the doctrine of justification. And is not even the 'wholly other' of Rudolf Otto in the last analysis but the image of man himself, the keystone in the arch of his own construction, and therefore not really a 'wholly other', but the last in the series of his own works? Hence, just when man thinks he has found in this 'wholly other' his God and has spoken his last word, he is clearly left alone with himself, shut up in the prison of his distance, estrangement and enmity to God. The dialectically-won god and his worship is just as perilous as any other kind of Pelagianism. It *is* perilous to interpose oneself between one's self and God, to wish to speak a human word at the very point where everything depends upon letting God's Word be spoken. That is the reason why theology must have nothing to do with the attempt to grasp at the One above and beyond the antitheses in man's thought and existence.[2]

On the other hand, *theology* must let itself be questioned in the same way in which it insists on questioning philosophy, for theology cannot avoid constructing on its part a *conception of God*. That is to say, theology, when it speaks of God, must not only take the road from God to man, but must also go in the opposite direction, and take the road from man to God travelled by philosophy. In so doing, it must run the risk of being misunderstood, of pursuing a philosophy and, still worse, of unwittingly becoming a theosophy. We have already seen how far theology must take the way of realism and of idealism, and so engage in the same dialectic as philosophy. But how far does theology, or can theology, travel this road with impunity?

We must recognise the fact that at any moment a theological dialectic may well become a sort of Trojan horse. As Luther himself showed, one can only fight against Erasmus with Erasmian weapons, that is, with

<hr />

[1] P. 86f.　　[2] P. 87.

theological dialectic. But who is to protect us from becoming little Erasmians ourselves? What is to protect us against the possibility of our best conception of God becoming, not only in the eyes of others but in our own eyes, only an *idea-god*, a construction of our own that sins against the article on justification?[1]

The fact that theology is under this constant threat ought to make us very hesitant to accuse others of theosophy. How do we know, especially vis-à-vis the great philosophers, whether their activity is really a chasing after the ghost of that *deus nudus* reachable *judicio rationis*, whether their thinking is only a going from here to God, and not as much as, and more than, ours, a coming from God to here? Are we aware how easily we, ourselves, may be caught not coming from God, from there to here? If we realise how easily we may fail, then we will not reject the possibility that, in philosophical speculation, in spite of the questionableness of its proceeding, something of the knowledge of God through his Word may be pressing through.

The truth is that theological actuality, our own and others', must always be as mixed and ambiguous as actuality is generally. That ought to make it clear to us that it is only in the Word of God that we know of an identity between truth and actuality, and know not to confound our own actuality with the truth, or that of others with untruth. We must question one another very energetically. Have we 'considered the great weight of sin'? Have we given sufficient thought to the fact that the reconciling principle is strictly and exclusively God's and not ours, that our dialectic may well point to it and presuppose it, but can never demonstrate it, not to speak of erecting it? Do we know that faith, through which alone we can know and speak of God, is not a daring human venture but sheer obedience? We shall ask one another these questions the more energetically we ourselves are questioned, and the more thoroughly we resolve to let ourselves be questioned. It will never do for us to reach out for a final judgment about others, or to engage in theological dogmatism, or to want a history of theology in which some are truly sheep and others are but goats.[2]

In view of these questions, Barth turns to consider the *criterion* that may be used in testing a particular theology to see whether it has only an idea-god or whether it really has the living God for its object. There cannot, of course, be any appeal to an external criterion, that is, to one outside the realm of faith or of the subject-matter of theology, for a true theological criterion must be appropriate to the nature of the object of

[1] P. 88. [2] P. 89f.

theology, and indeed derived from it. For such a criterion, Barth points to the idea of *divine election*. Election (i.e. in its epistemological reference) stands for the fact that theological thinking does not move in a direction of its own choosing but in one chosen for it, that it has its basis and necessity outside of itself, in God; that God, in fact, is the *absolute prius* of all our cognition of him.

Barth approaches this first from the practical side, where the critical question is whether theology is aware of its own relativity and has therefore the necessary patience vis-à-vis other theologies. A true theology derives from the Word of God which freely bestows itself upon us in grace, and by the same grace enables us to receive it. Therefore, we can never presume upon our hearing of it or erect our understanding of it into some standpoint of our own over against others. Humility before the truth and patience with others will thus be a practical test, for humility reveals whether theology finds its truth in itself or really in God alone, and patience reveals whether theology is seeking to establish its own right over against others or looks to God alone for its justification.[1]

The doctrine behind that is the free election of God. Election means that God chooses to give himself as the object of our knowing, but not as an object that we can master or dialectically encompass and control. A genuinely theological dialectic, therefore, will be one that is always open to the freedom and grace of God, a dialectic that will only serve the freedom of God's Word in its decision to communicate itself to us. God's Word thus means election, God's good-pleasure to reveal himself to us in a movement of grace, in which he does not bind himself to us but does bind us to him. A true theology of the Word will only act under the constraint of the divine decision and will not be one that depends upon the decision of man, and therefore it will never seek to convert the knowledge of God into an undertaking of its own. A true theology will act only in response to election, that is, in the recognition that it does not know God by virtue of its own ideas and concepts or by the inner power of its own dialectic, and therefore in acknowledgment that its own thought is inadequate to its object and its own ideas and concepts are unfitted to express and convey knowledge of him. But to act in response to election means also to act in joyful recognition of the fact that God has chosen to be served by theology, questionable instrument that it is, for it has pleased him as the One who transcends the contradiction of my existence and my thought, to come as Revealer and Reconciler, to take my place,

[1] P. 90.

and so to actualise knowledge of him from my side. Thus, theology does not happen on its own account; it takes place only because God, who will not be limited by our incapacities and inadequacies, gives himself to our knowing and makes himself the object of our actual knowledge.[1]

How can my conception of God in itself point to God? It has pleased God to make it point to him and so to use it. How can I establish a congruence between my thinking of him and his Reality? How can I make the actuality of my knowledge agree with the Truth of God? He only can do that, and that is what he is pleased to do in his grace—therefore even for theology there is a justification by grace alone. It is by obedience, then, through its faithfulness to justification or to election that a theology of the Word of God is distinguished from every ideology that seeks for its justification or its raison d'être within its own self-sufficiency.

As a second criterion for a theology of the Word, Barth points to *predestination*—but this is not really another criterion so much as the material form which the first must take in theological thinking. In other words, the critical test Barth proposes to apply to theology is: How far does it give central expression to predestination in its idea of God? How far is the material content of theology built round the absolute *prius* of God's grace? How far does it really repose on the ultimate objectivity of God himself? Unless predestination is set at the very summit of all our thinking, then that thinking has no ultimate meaning beyond itself in God, but can only run to ground upon itself. If we do not realise that the best thought of God we can produce may point not to God but to the devil, if we imagine that we can grasp God through some extremely acute and pious correlation of the concepts of Being and Thought, or Fate and Idea, if we attempt to work out our knowledge into a self-contained system, if we think we have grasped the Spirit by our word, and the Word by our spirit, if we make out of predestination a harmless little comment on the appropriation of salvation, then our thinking may well be suspect of being but human speculation about God, that is, an act of self-justification on our part setting aside the free, undeserved grace of God.

True theology begins where Christ himself began, in the womb of the Virgin—that is to say, in the concreteness in which the Word of God has come to us; in truth, because it is God's Word, in actuality, because it has become flesh, true God and true Man, and therefore the one, divine, constraining, justifying, sanctifying Word. That

[1] P. 91.

would indeed be theology of the Word, where it is altogether Christology.[1]

*

In order to point up the significance and relevance of this discussion for the development and clarification of Barth's theology, we may do well to pause for a little to consider several of the questions raised.

(a) Theology is the interpretation of the Word of God that has moved into the realm of human thought and speech occupied by science and philosophy. Theological thinking, therefore, takes place within the subject-object polarity of human thought, and so within the tensions that arise between realism and idealism, being and thought, history and idea, nature and spirit, etc. Theology cannot help but take part in that dialectic, and it cannot but use it in articulation of its understanding of God's Word. *Philosophia ancilla theologiae.*[2] Indeed, it is glad to do so, for philosophical discussion has much to offer theology, but—and this is where the difficulty arises—theology must learn how to use that in a scientific way, in the same way that other exact sciences use it, by letting it serve its own fundamental concern in accordance with the nature of its own object and the kind of thinking which the nature of that object requires of us.

We may note only two points that engagement in philosophical discussion contributes to Barth's own theological position. The dialectic between realism and idealism has undoubtedly helped him to grasp more profoundly the objectivity of the Word, and contributed to his movement into a fundamentally realist theology, but it has also shown him that, unless a realist theology has a real dash of idealism, its professed realism may only be the obverse of a fatal idealism. The primary contribution of idealist thinking to Barth is the critical refraction it introduces into the relation between subject and object, and its unavoidable question as to the adequacy of our thought-forms to their proper object. That is to say, idealistic critique prevents realism from confounding its own objective statements with the objective realities themselves, and therefore holds it in a steady realist determination to its object. *Mutatis mutandis,* that applies to dogmatic thinking, for this critical questioning, this humility before the object, this readiness to be called in question by the object, to meet objections from the side of the object, belongs to the scientific objectivity of dogmatics.

[1] P. 92.
[2] Cf. Barth's letter to Thurneysen of Feb. 15, 1925, *Gd-Md*, p. 132.

But philosophical dialectic is almost universally committed to the search for unity or synthesis—and this is the second point we note in Barth's appreciation of, and learning from, philosophy. Barth refuses to dispute philosophy's right to do that, for it cannot rest content with antinomy, or with a dialectical balancing of antitheses. It belongs to the nature of the human spirit to reach out toward a unitary understanding of existence—that is indeed part of its fundamental rationality. But when all is said and done, theology cannot concede that it is legitimate for philosophy to claim for its synthesis that it is the ultimate answer that rises above all antinomy and is to be identified with what the theologians call God. When theology, as interpretation of the Word of God, moves into this field, and finds that God's place has been usurped by a movement of thought from man, then there cannot but be conflict. By its very nature theology must renounce all philosophical prejudgments bearing upon its own object.

The contribution of philosophy to theology here is that it provides the foil whereby theology understands the Word of God to be the co-ordinating and reconciling Word of God's grace which he addresses to our intra-mundane contradictions and throws over them in order to point them to the only source of ultimate unity—in God, and in so doing, philosophy helps theology to see its responsibility for culture, for all scientific and all philosophical activity, and to see that it must take seriously all that human reflection upon nature and man yields by way of knowledge. But, on the other hand, theology has a critical duty to perform to philosophy (and in performing this, reaches greater understanding of its own nature), namely, in rejecting every identification of a philosophical synthesis with God, for in so doing it helps philosophy toward the self-criticism it needs to prevent it from turning into a theosophy, which would be both bogus philosophy and bogus theology. In such a diacritical relation between philosophy and theology each can contribute to the clarification and cleansing of the other.

(b) This carries us to our next consideration. Philosophical dialectic between realism and idealism is concerned with the relation between what is given and what is not given. In that dialectic, theology sees that there is room for a greater stress upon one side or the other of that tension, varying with different fields of reflection, but including that of theology itself. But theology also sees that a one-sided realism or a one-sided idealism can be a menacing error. A wholly realist theology would involve the identification of God with what is given to thought in its experience of this world, and so God would be identified with being as such, or with nature, or it might well be with history, particularly if this realist 'God' were thought of also as Act or Event. On the other hand, a wholly idealist theology would involve identification of God with what is not given, with what is reached, therefore, by way of abstraction from all experience in this world, and so God would be identified with Idea or Spirit as such or, if this idealist 'God' were also Act or Event, with dialectic or the co-ordinating principle that transcends all experience. In one case its temptation would be toward 'demonology' or the deification of nature, which has its mediaeval and its Neo-Protestant form, and in the other case its temptation would be toward 'ideology' or the deification of the reason, which also has its mediaeval and its Neo-Protestant form.

Thus the engagement of theology in this philosophical dialectic will help it to be aware of these temptations to the right and the left, but for that very reason theology must be aware of the subtle temptation to identify its own content with that to which the philosophical dialectic points on either side—that is, it must be aware of identifying God both with the philosophical notion of the given or objectifiable, and with the philosophical notion of the not-given or the unobjectifiable. It is only when genuine and serious engagement with philosophical thinking reveals to theology the fact that theological thinking and philosophical thinking move in opposite directions, and necessarily move in opposite directions,[1] that it will see that this confusion cannot be made without falsification of the fundamental basis of both theology and philosophy. This forces theology to think out radically from its material content the relation between the order of being and the order of knowing, in order to ensure that its 'God' is not, after all, only the conclusion of its argumentation; and to think out the relation between the ultimate objectivity of God himself and the objectivities of this world within which he gives us knowledge of himself, for the polarity between the given and the not-given of God is other than the polarity between the given and the not-given in our intra-mundane experience. It is just because the polarity of the given and not-given of God intersects the polarity of the given and not-given in our intra-mundane experience that it is so easy to confuse the one with the other and to fall into a subtle form of demonology (*deus sive natura*) or of ideology (*deus sive ratio*).

(*c*) Although the discussion of theology with philosophy makes theo-

---

[1] See Barth's essay 'Philosophie und Theologie', in the *Festschrift* for his philosopher brother, Heinrich, *Philosophie und Christliche Existenz*, ed. G. Huler, Basel and Stuttgart 1960, pp. 93-106.

logy aware of its own problems through seeing that philosophy wrestles
with a parallel set of problems, it does not, or should not, lead theology
to take itself out of the realm of human thinking occupied by philosophy
and science—even if it could do that—but helps every theology that
takes its task seriously to see that it must articulate its understanding
within the forms of thought and speech of the age, for that is part of
theological responsibility for the very humanity which is addressed by
the Word of God.

Because in theology faith seeks understanding, and understanding
seeks articulation within the same realm of thought as philosophy, it
makes use of the tools of thought and speech which it finds to hand, and
so seeks to shape articulation of its understanding within the form of
thinking shared by modern man, but—and this is its scientific as well as
its theological compulsion—to subordinate that form of thinking to its
own material content, or rather to its proper object. Scientifically, of
course, there is no such thing as a form of thinking detached from or in
abstraction from the subject-matter being investigated, so that what we
are concerned with here is rather what von Balthasar has called 'style'.[1]
For example, classical Thomism was theology expressing itself in the
style of the Mediaeval Age, but the same thing must be said of the contemporary form of Augustinianism. Thus in the mediaeval style there
operated the basic tension between realism and idealism, but the critical
question must be asked, whether the form that mediaeval realism took
did not lapse into the error of *deus sive natura*, and the form that mediaeval idealism took did not lapse into the error of *deus sive ratio*, and
whether the rise of nominalism is to be understood, not only as an
attempt within the mediaeval tension to break through to a new style,
but *actually* as a sharper dialectic between naturalism and terminism,
demonology and ideology? In other words, does the insistent problem
of nominalism in mediaeval theology not reveal that, while the theology
of the Church sought to articulate its doctrine within the thought-forms
of inherited philosophy, in point of fact it did not achieve an adequate
subordination of those thought-forms to its proper object, so that their
adequacy had constantly to be called into question, and, therefore, must
we not also ask whether, after all, a philosophical system was not
allowed to triumph over theology and to distort its understanding and
articulation? Is the distinction between mediaeval and Reformation
theology only a question of style or did the change in style have to do
also with a new attempt to break through the framework of a masterful

[1] *Karl Barth*, pp. 201 ff.

philosophy in order to bring thought into profounder conformity to its object, and so to achieve deeper objectivity through a movement that allowed the nature of the object to call into question all presuppositions in the forms of thought and speech we bring to its understanding and articulation?

There can be no doubt that at the Reformation there was an immense change in style from mediaeval to modern thinking. That is most obvious in the change to a more dynamic from a more static use of terms such as being, essence, substance, matter, form, idea, etc., and particularly in a new predominance of kinematic terms like time, motion, process, event, history, force, energy, etc. Modern thought has a more open and fluid form. But is that only a change in style? Does it not also represent a deep change in the doctrine of God from a basically Latin to a more Hebraic conception of the living, active God—which carries with it the immediate relevance of the last things, the ultimate realities of God, to temporal and historical existence? Does not this change in the doctrine of God belong to and contribute to the upheaval, the reconstruction, the movement, and the advance that have characterised all the science and life of modernity?

It is within this change in style and way of thinking that modern theology has had to seek understanding and reach articulation. But there is little doubt that, in this change, there has been a persistent tendency toward a deep rift in which event breaks loose from being, existence from essence, idea from reality, etc. And therefore the critical question must be asked: Whether the modern forms of nominalism are not seeking to perform in the other direction the service of their mediaeval counterparts, namely, in revealing that, while the theology of Protestantism has sought to reach understanding and articulation within the modern way of thinking, in point of fact it has not achieved an adequate subordination of these thought-forms to its proper object? Hence modern theology has to face the same question put to mediaeval theology: Whether a philosophical system has not been allowed to triumph over modern theology and to distort its understanding and articulation? Thus theology is challenged once again to carry through a basic reorientation in which the form of its thought may be brought into closer conformity with its object.

Is it not in this context that we are to see the relevance and importance of Barth's theology, and in particular this discussion between theology and philosophy? It seems evident that Barth's theological critique of Neo-Protestant and of Roman theology alike has a certain parallel to the critique of metaphysics mounted by modern analytical philosophy, but in sharp distinction to it, Barth has a positive contribution to make—and this is his main task—in dogmatic thinking, which carries with it a more positive appreciation of both older theology and older metaphysics than many of his theological and philosophical contemporaries will allow.[1] But if this is so, then the immense significance of Barth's theology is that in it we have a Herculean undertaking *to expound within the more dynamic and critico-idealist style of modernity a fundamentally realist theology.* That is why we have in him such a combination of the positive doctrines of the ancient Catholic faith with the dynamic biblical orientation of the Reformation, which makes him equally critical of mediaeval and modern, Roman and Neo-Protestant theologies, and in many respects equally sympathetic because appreciative of their intentions, which is most apparent in his admiration, in spite of all criticism, for both Aquinas and Schleiermacher.

(*d*) We cannot pass by a fourth consideration, raised by Barth himself, in that he will not avoid directing to himself the critical question he puts to both Roman and Neo-Protestant theology: Whether in his own undertaking his theology may not turn out in the end to be but the expression of some philosophical way of thinking rather than an expression of his understanding of the Word of God in the style of modernity? For Barth that question, which runs all through the commentary on Romans, is the radical epistemological relevance of justification by grace alone. He faces it therefore as a question that arises out of the very ground of his thought in the Word of God, as a question directed to him from the side of the object, as a question that challenges him to greater and deeper objectivity, that is, to utter obedience to the Incarnation of the Word of Jesus Christ.

Barth is aware of the fact that the supreme danger for theology today, and not least for his own, is that of ideology rather than demonology. That danger does not grow less the more complete his own thought becomes, for even though he resolutely rejects the employment of any systematic principle such as we see in the philosophico-theological *summae* of mediaeval theology, or in the dogmatics of Neo-Hegelians like Lüdemann, Barth's thinking is unavoidably systematic through his rigorous insistence in bringing his thoughts at every point into conformity to Jesus Christ in the centre.[2] Might it not be that this centre is being used as the masterful *Idea,* and that the whole construc-

---

[1] But cf. the views of Barth's friend Heinrich Scholz: *Abriss der Geschichte der Logik,* 1931; *Metaphysik als strenge Wissenschaft,* 1941; and the posthumous *Mathesis Universalis,* 1961.　　　　　　[2] Cf. Berkouwer, op. cit., *passim.*

tion of the *Church Dogmatics* is in spite of itself a massive ideology? We can put the question in another way, one in which Barth himself does not raise it: May it not be the case that what Barth has done is to achieve a mighty synthesis that reaches behind the antithesis of Roman realism and Protestant idealism to a higher unity, and that in his astonishing doctrine of election he has grasped at a comprehensive and reconciling principle that carries him above and beyond the deep contradictions in theological existence revealed by the Roman-Protestant dialectic? And therefore may not his theology turn out in the end to be but a disguised form of that *speculatio divinae majestatis*, that *apprehendere Deum in sua majestate judicio rationis* against which Luther warned us?

In reply to these questions, however, two things must be said:

(1) Barth is the most courageous of all theologians in applying to himself the critique of justification by Christ alone, and is therefore ready at every point to acknowledge the utter inadequacy of his own conceptual formulations and to admit that they have meaning only as they break off and point beyond them to One whom they themselves cannot describe or define.[1] That is to say, he adopts a form of thinking which is the strongest safeguard against all ideology, for it is a form of thinking that, from first to last, is under the criticism of the object. Ideology is a form of thinking that claims to have truth in itself, in its own statements or motions of thought, in its own dialectic and self-sufficiency. But theology, as Barth sees it, is a form of thinking that renounces all such claims, for as a form of thinking that has its source and its goal beyond itself, in God's Word, it can only submit to the claims of its object upon it and point away to the Truth beyond itself. Theology does not carry its own co-ordinating principle in itself—indeed it has none of its own; it can only let itself fall under the grace of God, and if it attains any co-ordination, that can only come from the good pleasure of God in throwing his reconciling grace round it and in making it serve him in spite of its unprofitableness and questionable nature.

(2) The function of theology, therefore, as Barth sees it is that of *service* to God's Word, i.e. service of Jesus Christ. It is theology that will only *serve* the concrete active form of the Truth in the Incarnation of the Word, so that every point must be brought into relation with that Truth in severe critical testing. Theology of this kind that insists on

---

[1] Cf. the remark of Heinrich Scholz (*Ant.*, p. 868, in 'Gott ist grösser als unsere Gedanken'): 'Es gibt keine Theologie, die fester auf dem Grunde dieses Fundamentalsatzes steht als die Theologie von Karl Barth.'

following the Word of God, that serves its interpretation, that derives from it the rational forms by which its own material is to be understood and ordered, is not one that will seek articulation through conceptual forms borrowed from other spheres of knowledge or other scientific pursuits. Theology that will only be a theology of Revelation, that lives through maintaining a critical front against every *Weltanschauung*, that operates with no *praeambula fidei*, no framework of prior understanding, that renounces every form of natural theology, is not something that can be accommodated to culture, or assimilated to the spirit of the age, or fall under the domination of a way of thinking rising out of the existence of the natural man, but one that can only challenge human culture to unceasing reconstruction, and be the greatest enemy of all ideological distortion of the Christian faith.

By its very nature, then, Barth's theology is one that carries within it a corrective against becoming an ideology itself—and yet that corrective is not something that it has in itself, for it is nothing else than the fact that the object of this theology is *Jesus Christ, the Lord*. It is from the side of this object that our humanity, and all that goes with it in its deformed condition by way of wishful thinking or *hybris* or self-interposition, comes under attack from pure humanity; and it is from the side of this object that all our human attempts to construct a way from man, to carry him over and beyond all that is relative and incomplete, to God, come under attack from God himself; it is from the side of this object, the crucified and risen Lord, that human ways of thinking are both judged and resurrected, crucified and remade. That is the critical significance of Christology for Barth's theology in his struggle to bring knowledge of God to rational articulation within the style and thinking of our day, yet in such a way as to free it from all entanglement and distortion from ideology.

Writing of this, Charles West has said: 'Karl Barth has made his case, as far as human words can make it. He has produced a theology so completely dominated by its object, Jesus Christ, God and man, that whatever other criticisms may be brought over against it, it cannot be accused of being one more reflection of and cover for human interests. Starting with the paradox in the Chalcedonian creed, Barth develops all his thinking in rigorous response to Christ alone, regardless of the claims which reason, ideals, principles or any other inner consistency or drive of human life make in their own right upon him. No one is more conscious than he of the danger of ideology which lurks on every side of this enterprise. No one is more concerned to make his thought in no sense an explanatory system, but a reference to the mystery of Christ in whom the fullness of human life is bound up; in no sense a law for human life, but a pointing to the act of God's grace which calls forth free human response and decision.

'But Barth does more. Precisely his most original presentations on the themes of the Christian faith give us, sometimes for the first time in history, a clear understanding of the way in which Christ himself can be the reality which breaks through all human ideology. That was indeed the major task he set himself. He fulfilled it in a series of bold theological ventures, so radical towards customary habits of human thought, that generations to come will be called upon to test and interpret them.'[1]

The immense contribution of Barth to the history of theology can be stated in another way. Catholic theology particularly in the West achieved a masterly expression within the framework of a fundamentally ancient way of thinking, in its Aristotelian form (Aquinas). The Reformation broke through that frame of thinking and released upon the world again an essentially biblical and dynamic way of thinking. In its secularised form this led in due course to the brilliant achievements of modern European culture, and then Protestant theology attained masterly expression within this framework of a fundamentally modern way of thinking (Schleiermacher). But in both the mediaeval and the Neo-Protestant theologies the frame of thought within which the positive doctrines of the Catholic and Evangelical faith were cast and articulated remained the ultimate master. Karl Barth has attempted, in a thoroughgoing critique of both, and in a profound dimension of historical understanding, to give fresh articulation to the Christian faith as a theology of the Word of God which breaks through the frame of every form of human thinking while employing all that ancient and modern thought can offer by way of tools and instruments of thought and speech. It would be impossible to claim for his achievement a *theologia perennis*, but it is certainly true that it will take many generations, if not centuries, to evaluate his service adequately.

In the foregoing discussion we have tried to assess Barth's theology from the point of view of its relation to philosophy, but it is questionable whether theology, as he pursues it, can be compared properly with philosophy. As it has turned out, does it not bear a closer comparison with an *exact science*, such as physics, which restricts its activities to the limits laid down by the nature of its concrete object, and develops a method in accordance with the nature of its object, bracketing it off

[1] Charles West, op. cit. p. 234 f.

from every world-view (either as an *a priori* condition or as an *a posteriori* product), and involving an open mind about what may lie beyond the limits of its own area of knowledge?[1] In other words, if we regard Barth's theology from the point of view of method, then the comparison with philosophy is not very felicitous.

It is to this question of method (*ratio*) that we must now turn, for it is at this point that Barth took his final step into the kind of thinking that characterises the whole of his *Church Dogmatics*.

3. Theology in its own Right

In order to discern properly the transition in Barth's thinking to scientific Church dogmatics, we must look at it from a somewhat different angle, but to get our orientation here, it may be best yet again to return to the *Briefwechsel* with Harnack.[2]

In that discussion, it became clear that Harnack worked with a deep cleavage between proclamation and theology, inner religious experience and history. On the one hand, he stood in the line of pietism and the subjective religious tradition of Neo-Protestantism, but on the other he adhered to the rationalistic idea of the Enlightenment that there is only one scientific method which theology shares with every other science, and in which its task is to master the object of its knowledge.

Harnack's position became even more clear in another *Briefwechsel* which he had with Erik Peterson in 1928.[3] In it he admitted that there were two strains in the Reformation, one which was more 'catholic', the objective strain, and the other a subjective strain which has since been steadily developed within Protestantism. It is to this second strain that Harnack admitted he himself belonged, which he spoke of as including Anabaptism, Enlightenment, and Schleiermacher, and described as 'the rationalising, subjective-religious line of Protestantism'.[4] The task of theology in this event was to bring the basic ideas of the Gospel into clear light through the employment of historical reflection and ethical and philosophical consideration, but he admitted frankly, that in the proper sense a Protestant theology cannot exist.[5]

---

[1] See *CD* III.2, p. 12f. Barth's language appears to have been influenced by Husserl. It is worth noting that Husserl's term for an exact science like physics was 'dogmatic science' as dealing with *actuality* (*Wirklichkeit*) in contrast to 'philosophic science' as dealing with *possibility*. See *Ideas* (ET, London and New York 1931), pp. 95ff, 214f. [2] *FuA*, pp. 7-31.

[3] This was published by Peterson in 1950 in *Theologische Traktate*, pp. 295-321.

[4] Op. cit. p. 303f.

[5] See Peterson's epilogue to the discussion, pp. 306ff, and 310.

In other words, Harnack was a typical representative of Neo-Protestant subjective-idealistic theology which held the essence of Protestantism to lie in inward spiritual religion and limited its essential scientific task to the clarification of religious phenomena through the history of ideas and the history of religion. Harnack was immensely upset by the 'Barthian' movement for it had hindered the consistent development of Neo-Protestantism and meant, he claimed, 'a lapse back into biblicism' which he admitted was in line with the catholic strain of old Protestantism but which he deplored as a return to the dogmatic authority of Scripture. It is instructive to note that both Harnack and Peterson shared a view of science as operating with external objectivities, which Harnack found in history and Peterson found in the dogmatic decisions of the Roman Church, whereas for Barth both of these were false objectivities and substitutes for the genuine objectivity of God in his Word.[1]

The real crux of the problem lies here; for Neo-Protestantism the object of religious knowledge is not rational in its own right, and therefore comes to expression only in symbolic form, so that the task of theology is to penetrate into the essence of this and to give it rational interpretation through employment of conceptual forms drawn from ethics and philosophy.[2] In so far as religious experience is a historical datum it is amenable to scientific investigation and reflection, but then it must be re-edited and reinterpreted according to the prevailing forms and norms of science in order to be made understandable by modern man.[3]

For Barth, however, this was fundamentally irrational, as could be seen in Rudolph Otto's work *The Idea of the Holy* which Barth had read with astonishment when still a pastor at Safenwil. From the very start Barth's thinking had taken the opposite course, through his preoccupation with the Word of God which he held to be fundamentally and inherently rational. That does not mean that the Word of God, or therefore the object of theology, is to be identified with rational propositions, or propositional ideas, for the Word of God is God *himself* in his

---

[1] See Barth's discussion of Peterson's lecture 'Was ist Theologie?', 1926 (republished in *Theologische Traktate*, pp. 11-43) in *TC*, pp. 286-306.

[2] Cf. the basic view of Paul Tillich, as expressed, for example, in *The Dynamics of Faith*.

[3] Nothing could be more instructive of Bultmann's relation to the thought of Harnack than his republication of *Das Wesen des Christentums*, in 1950, fifty years after Harnack first delivered the lectures in Berlin. In his second letter to Peterson, Harnack had pointed to those lectures as an indication of the only scientific method known to him of giving expression to the essence of Christianity. Bultmann's programme of demythologising the Gospel is surely a remarkable variation upon the same theme.

Revelation, but it does mean that in the Word we are confronted with an Object which is Subject, that is, with One who is *both Person and Message*. Revelation is not just the communication of life, but the impartation of rational truth which we are given in and through the Word made flesh and which is inseparable from the Person of the Word. Hence, Christian Theology cannot tolerate the idea that faith is not rational in its own right and that it is the task of theology to give it rational interpretation through employing conceptual forms drawn from elsewhere. Because the Word of God is itself rational event, theology is rational in its own right, through the rationality of its own proper object, for in its proper object it has to do with the one Truth of God himself.

This is the angle at which we must now study the movement of Barth's thought, his final reaction to the basic irrationalism and romanticism of Neo-Protestantism as well as the wordless mysticism that lies behind Romanism, and a penetration into an understanding of the inner rational nature of the object of theological knowledge and therefore into the method of theological procedure appropriate to that object. In short, it is the problem of *ratio*, in both senses of the word, *rationality* and *method*, i.e., the problem of scientific theology or dogmatics.[1]

That is the question that Barth faced in his study of Anselm in the summer of 1930. There can be little doubt that the writing, and publication (in the following year) of his study *Fides Quaerens Intellectum* represents the decisive turning-point in his thinking, for it marks the final point in his advance from dialectical thinking to Church dogmatics.

His love for Anselm, as he says in the Preface,[2] went much further back—it is to be found even in his Safenwil period. The significant thing is that he should have turned to it right at this juncture, in the summer Semester of 1930.[3] It certainly had a very far-reaching effect upon Barth's thought, for the writing of the *Church Dogmatics*, into which he threw himself immediately afterwards,[4] registers its impact at the im-

---

[1] Cf. H. Scholz's Introduction to Schleiermacher's *Kurze Darstellung des theologischen Studiums*, p. xxxf.   [2] Preface to the first edition: ET, p. 7.

[3] Barth also recalls in the same preface his discussions in Bonn that summer with Heinrich Scholz (Professor für Logik und Grundlagenforschung in Münster since 1928), who had a keen interest in the mathematical and logical aspects of scientific method. Cf. his article in *ZdZ*, 1931, 'Wie ist eine evangelische Theologie als Wissenschaft möglich?' (pp. 8–53); *Geschichte der Logik*, 1931; *Logistik*, 1933; *Metaphysik als strenge Wissenschaft*, 1941; *Vorlesungen über die Grundzüge der mathematischen Logik*, 2 Bde 1948, 1949; and his brief contribution to *Antwort* (pp. 865-69). Cf. too Barth's *CD* I.1, pp. 7f, 18f. The same influence is apparent in a recent work of Heinrich Vogel, *Grundfragen des Studiums der Theologie*, 1957 (ET by J. P. Smith, *Consider Your Calling*, 1962).

[4] See the preface to the second edition of *Fides Quaerens Intellectum*, p. 11f; '*Parergon*', *Evangelische Theologie*, 1948-9, p. 272; and *CD* II.1, p. 4.

portant points where the connexion between the subject-matter and the form and method is concerned.[1] It was in the writing of this brilliant and extremely important little work that Barth's understanding of the fundamental nature of theological method clarified and crystallized. In it he sought to grapple with the problem of scientific and exact statement in theology, and hence of the inner relation between faith and reason and of the objective, inner necessity or logic that must inform the whole structure of theology.

Without entering into a discussion of the whole work, we may content ourselves with noting some of the primary considerations that emerge from this investigation and affect the whole course of Barth's dogmatic thinking.

(1) The first thing to be noted is the fact that faith by its essential nature seeks understanding—*fides quaerens intellectum*. That was the original title of Anselm's *Proslogion* which Barth took over as the title of his work, for in its way it sums up everything that is involved here. God in whom we believe is of such a nature that we cannot believe in him without his becoming the Author of a true knowledge of him on our part. Hence, at its very root, faith entails a movement of the understanding. It is the task of theology to follow that movement through, to draw out the *quaerere intellectum* immanent in faith, advancing from implicit understanding to explicit understanding.[2]

This faith is not something vague and formless but specific, for it arises from a very definite happening to us, something new encountering us from God, namely, the Word of God. God remains unknown to us directly or indirectly. He is so unique and incomparable that we cannot infer him. We are quite unable even to conceive of him or his existence except on the basis of the Word which we hear about him, a Word that comes from him: the word of Christ. Faith is not faith if it is not the receiving of that Word by way of knowledge and affirmation. Hence the act of faith is never illogical or irrational but is essentially cognitive and conceptual.[3] Moreover, that Word of Christ reaches us through preaching and becomes the object of faith through hearing, and for that reason the Word of Christ, and so our understanding of it, can legitimately be represented by particular human words and expressions. Yet faith, as Anselm insists, is not a believing what is preached (although it includes

---

[1] *CD*, especially I.1, Intro. and Ch. 1; I.2, §§13, 16, 23, 24; II.1, Chs. 25-8.
[2] *FQI*, p. 15 f.
[3] *Fides esse nequit sine conceptione*, p. 19, 22. To say that faith is essentially cognitive and conceptual does not mean that it is simply intellectual, for faith involves trust and operates through love, as Anselm insists no less than Augustine.

that) but a believing in the reality of the Truth mediated to us through preaching. It is only for this kind of faith that real understanding is possible, because for it the reality of Christ, the Truth of God and the Author of our knowledge, is given to us as the object of understanding. In him both the beginning and the end of understanding are given to faith. Therefore, theological inquiry is a feasible task, not a moving from the unknown to the known, but a moving from what is given to our knowledge into clearer knowledge of it. This is what Anselm described by his famous *credo ut intelligam*, in which the *credo* cannot be separated from its task, *ut intelligam*, and the act of *intelligere* does not take place in abstraction from the *credere*.[1]

In this event theology may be spoken of as the activity of the reason within the knowledge bestowed on man by God, operating within the limits of noetic investigation required by the nature of the given object. Theology does not start from premises outside of faith and then move to faith, but begins with faith, that is, with God as he gives himself through his Word to be the object of our knowledge and trust, and moves from that beginning into deeper and clearer knowledge through understanding of the inner and necessary relation between the knowledge of faith and the inherent rationality of that which is believed, the very Truth and the Being of God himself.

Before we consider that further, we must note something else cognate to this, which is of considerable importance for Barth's thinking.

(2) Here we have that penetration to deeper, concrete objectivity which we noted was demanded of Barth, face to face with the Word of God, in clarification of his *Christliche Dogmatik*. At the same time, Barth's old sense of the exalted, ultimate objectivity of God is reinforced by Anselm's thinking of God as *quo maius cogitari nequit*. By that designation of God, Anselm wanted to keep before him the fact that in our knowledge of God we are concerned with One who is exalted absolutely above and beyond us. Before God we do not stand as one being before another being, but as a creature before his Creator, before the ultimate Objectivity which we cannot in any way transcend in our thought, and must never think of transcending.[2] This designation of God as 'something beyond which nothing greater can be conceived' is not just a logical abstraction but a form of thinking imposed upon us by the self-revelation of God which will not allow us to imagine anything greater than God, for any conception of a 'God' we could form on our own in this way would thereby cease to be a conception of the true God. Under-

[1] Pp. 22f, 26f, 102f, etc.   [2] Pp. 130f, 152f.

standing God as greater than anything we can conceive is inseparable from a knowledge of the object of faith, and therefore that object would disappear for our knowledge if we displaced this 'God' by one of our own imagination, even if that 'God' were reached by a *via negativa*. God is the very One who reveals himself in such a way as to command us not to imagine a greater than him.[1]

This is important for Barth, for it means that the acknowledgment that all our theological statements of God are inadequate and fall short of what he is, is not simply the result of a critical idealism, but the direct consequence of revelation and faith. It is by their essential nature that theological statements point beyond themselves to him who transcends them, for they are statements which we make as our minds are subdued by the object, the Lord our God, before whose face our thinking is true only in so far as it is true in God himself. Thus the proper attitude required of us before God, even in making theological statements, is reverence, worship and humility.[2] That fact is brought with great force by Anselm's habit of speaking about God while speaking to him—reverent theological statements never lose their basic second-personal character even when they are cast into third-personal form. Theological thinking and speaking is always an activity in the hearing and presence of God.[3]

True theological thinking, therefore, is thinking that really allows God to be God, precisely by the proper limitation of itself before him; it is thinking that is determined to be faithful to its transcendent, incomparable object, thinking that respects the utter objectivity of God. In so far as it is appropriate to its object, this kind of thinking does not ask for a 'greater' beyond the Creator, for that would be to ascend to a point where the creature cannot stand, and to ask for a standard of the Truth higher than the ultimate Truth itself, which would be an absurdity. Thinking that operates with true or good understanding is one that realises that it is not possible to think beyond God, or to think from a point where one can look down on God and oneself, but a thinking that from the start moves to him. To know God in accordance with the Being of God himself is to stand under the compulsion of his Being, as an obedient creature before the Creator, who lets God be to him the One who, in his sheer objectivity as God, prescribes for man the manner and the limits of his knowing of God.[4]

The objectivity with which we are concerned here in our knowledge

---

[1] Pp. 102 f, 107, 130 f, 152 f.   [2] Pp. 153 f, 158.
[3] Pp. 101 f, 150 f, 158 f, etc.   [4] Pp. 152 f, 169 f.

of God is not a static objectivity, for the given object is God's self-giving. Therefore the capacity of man for divine objectivity, for understanding of God in his objectivity, is not one that the reason can acquire and possess on its own, but only one that must ever be bestowed upon it through the self-objectification of God for man. It is in this activity of God who lets us know him in accordance with his self-revealing that we have to discern the ground of the possibility that our expressions of God may be true even when they are applied to God who cannot be expressed.[1] When God gives himself to us to be known, we are able to know him through divine action, in grace and illumination.[2] Theology, then, is an act of devout obedience responding to a decision that comes from the divine object; it is a knowledge operating by way of obedient acknowledgment and recognition of the Lord's communication of himself to us.

In other words, in our knowing of God, the decision that is required of us, if we are really to know him, is one that derives from and reposes upon an objective decision in God, who in Christ both gives himself to us, and enables us to know and have faith in him, and to love him.[3] Hence the mode of theological inquiry which is appropriate to the nature of the object is one of love and prayer in response to God's love and address to us, in which we love him above all else and seek him in love for his own Truth, in which we direct to God our inquiry in prayer and cast ourselves upon him in reliance and trust. In the fulfilment of our theological thinking, we rejoice thankfully in the fact that God himself makes our thoughts and expressions of him which we undertake in obedience to his Word, capable and adequate beyond any capacity of their own, for he it is who validates them by supplying himself as their object and thereby conferring upon them their truth.[4]

(3) True knowledge of the object in its objectivity involves penetration into its inner rationality. This is the function of theological understanding or *intelligere* which, as Anselm explained it, is the act of reading (*legere*) the text (as Barth calls it) embedded within (*intus*) the object.[5] God reveals himself to us by his Word in the Holy Scriptures, but our task in reading the outward text is to get at its inner meaning and basis, to read it at the deeper level of the solid truth on which the text rests. By a special act of the understanding that goes beyond mere reading, we penetrate into the objective *ratio* of the Word which enlightens and informs us.[6]

---

[1] Pp. 29f, 34, 37, etc.   [2] Pp. 71, 170f.   [3] Pp. 21, 37, 150ff, 170f.
[4] Pp. 35f, 39f, 158f, etc.   [5] Pp. 40f.   [6] Pp. 41f, 71.

According to Barth, Anselm is to be interpreted as using *ratio* in a three-fold sense. It refers both to the means we employ and the end of our quest in seeking understanding, that is, not only to the capacity to form concepts and judgments but to the rationality of the object of our faith, but behind all that it refers to the transcendent rationality of God himself which determines everything else. *Ratio* is used then in a dimension of depth; of the ultimate Truth, the *ratio* of God himself; of the words and acts of God in Revelation, the *ratio* proper to the object of faith; and of man's knowledge of the object, the knowing *ratio* which corresponds to the *ratio* of the object.[1] Through the noetic *ratio*, theological inquiry penetrates to the ontic or objective *ratio*, but standing behind all and illuminating all is the *ratio* of God, the *ratio veritatis* identical with God's Being, the divine Word consubstantial with the Father. As the *summa veritas*, God is the *causa veritatis* and so is himself the ground of all knowledge of God.[2] Thus, not only is the truth of our knowing grounded in the object of knowledge but the truth of the object depends not on itself but upon the eternal Word and Being of God, the Truth. Hence the right use of the human *ratio* as determined by its proper object is one in which the Truth that is God himself acts upon it and confers upon it likeness to himself. The human *ratio* is in no sense creative and normative, and even the ontic *ratio* in the object is one conferred upon it with the creation of the object by God. Hence neither as noetic nor as ontic is the *ratio* higher than the Truth but the Truth itself is master of all *rationes*.[3]

This means that theological activity is a rational act answering to the nature and rationality of its object, and when we seek to order and correct our thinking in accordance with the inner form or objective rationality of the object, the divine Truth uses that as the means by which he confers upon our knowing its adequate relation to the object, i.e. its truth. We may express that the other way round by saying that Anselm operated with a dynamic rationality deriving from the active self-communication of the divine Truth, and for that reason refused to abstract man's attempt at penetrating to the objective rationality of the object of his knowledge from the divine activity which both illuminates man's mind in his obedience to the Word and brings him into conformity to it. Man's theological activity derives from and is determined by the activity of God himself in his Word, for it is that Word communicated through Holy Scripture which is the real object of his knowledge. What is of fundamental importance here is the profound sense of the

[1] P. 44f.   [2] P. 45f.   [3] P. 46f.

objective rationality with which theological activity is concerned, for it is only when we are engaged with it that our theological statements can be said to be scientific, that is, engaged in a process of ascent from one *ratio* to an ever higher *ratio*.[1]

As we have seen, all our theological statements are in themselves inadequate to their object. The actual Word of Christ spoken to us, however, is not inadequate, although our attempts to reproduce it in thought and speech fall short. Of course, when our statements are simply and formally identical with statements of the text of Scripture in which Christ speaks his Word to us, they are directly authoritative. But theology is not content with the repetition of biblical texts, for it seeks to make statements about truth revealed in the inner text, and therefore must seek a conformity to the truth at a deeper level beyond formal conformity to the external text. Since the statements we make in this way are not directly covered by formal biblical authority, they are contested statements and require to be tested to find the measure of their adequacy to their proper object. Hence, scientific theological activity begins where straightforward biblical quotations end, precisely because it is the task of theology to penetrate to the solid truth upon which biblical statements rest. That does not mean that scientific theology can leave the ground of the biblical teaching, for the inner text with which it is concerned is only to be discerned in and along with the external text, but it does mean that it must penetrate into the inner *ratio* of the Scriptures and so into the inner logic and form of the Word which it hears, and seek to articulate it in an orderly manner or *ratio* in our understanding.[2]

This is of immense importance for Barth, for it means that genuine theology cannot remain at the level of a biblical theology that is concerned only with the recital of the acts of God as recounted in Holy Scripture, or with a linguistic and phenomenological exegesis of the Scriptures. Certainly theology takes place only within the field of exegetical study and only on the ground of what the apostles and prophets have witnessed, but because it is only in God himself, in whom Truth and Being are one, that the basis of knowledge and speech about him is identical with its proper content, theology must press on to inquire into the relation between biblical thought and speech and their source in the Truth and Being of God. Hence it is the specific task of theology to inquire into what we ourselves have to say on the basis of the biblical revelation, and to articulate its relation to the object in such a way, that

[1] P. 32.   [2] Pp. 30ff.

our knowledge may be established as true. Moreover, unless this theological inquiry is present, if only in an incipient form, in exegetical study of the Scriptures, we are not engaged upon genuine exegesis, for then we are setting aside the all-important relation between the external text and the inner meaning and objective basis upon which it rests. No exegesis that is content only with noetic rationality can be regarded as properly scientific, for scientific activity must penetrate through noetic rationality into the ontic rationality of its basis and so lay bare its inner necessity. While there is undoubtedly a realm of knowledge which the theologian, operating through *fides quaerens intellectum*, shares with the unbeliever who limits himself to the external text (or, in the language of Anselm to the mere *vox* of Scripture), nevertheless because the word of Scripture signifies a reality beyond it (*vox significans rem*), the decisive point in interpretation is not reached until there is inquiry into the reality signified. True interpretation arises where perception of the meaning of the letter of Holy Scripture and understanding of the reality it indicates are one.[1]

(4) In the foregoing discussion it must be clear that for Anselm the rational nature of knowledge involves a relation of likeness or a resemblance between it and the object. That does not mean, however, that we come to acquire knowledge of God on the ground of a likeness to God or a capacity for him latent in our thought and speech, but rather that this relation of likeness arises from the activity of God's self-revealing or self-communicating. Just as Anselm did not reach the notion of God as he than whom no greater can be conceived, from the deficiency of human thought but from the positive revelation of God, so here he reaches an understanding of the resemblance between our knowing of God and God himself, not from an inherent capacity of human thought but from the positive relationship established by God in making himself known to us. Thus along with Anselm's notion of dynamic rationality there goes a notion of dynamic analogy carrying a relationship of adequacy and inadequacy, of partial likeness and partial unlikeness, between the knowledge of faith and its proper object. It is important to see, however, that the partial unlikeness or inadequacy arises precisely out of the correspondence or agreement of our knowledge with the nature of its object, the self-revelation of God as he than whom none greater can be conceived. Hence the inadequacy of theological statements does not mean that they are false, but on the contrary reflects the *truth* of their

[1] Pp. 23f, 163f. Cf. also John McIntyre, *St Anselm and his Critics*, Edinburgh 1954, p. 26f.

relation to their object. Everything depends here upon the activity of God who so reveals himself to us in his Word that the gift of the Word and the effect of it in us go together, for it is in that act of divine grace that the reason is given capacity for God and exercises that capacity rightly, not in mastering the object of knowledge but in being mastered by it, so that all its thoughts and judgments are subject to the creative power of the Word.[1]

Anselm was aware that this resemblance between our knowing of God and God himself as he is known takes place within the realm of creaturely objectivity, and indeed must do so, for it is there that the incomprehensible God reveals himself to us in terms of something other than what he is in himself. This is something we can understand, for even within our ordinary creaturely knowledge we often see a thing not precisely as it is in itself, he says, but through an image and likeness as when we look into a mirror. In this way we express and yet do not express, we see and do not see, one and the same object, for we see and express it through another, and not by its own proper nature. That is the way in which God reveals himself to us, and therefore the way in which we know him. But for this very reason theology is always exposed to misunderstanding. The truth into which it inquires cannot be discerned in the terms we use, for they are drawn from within our experience of created realities and as such indicate to us only created objects, but theology employs them in such a way as to transcend their merely creaturely reference to the ineffable nature of God. This is really possible both because human beings were made for the purpose of loving and knowing the supreme Being, and because God has mediated knowledge of himself in the incarnate Word which is both within the sphere of creaturely objectivity and yet perfectly adequate to God himself, which is both illuminated and illuminating, and which, because it is in the image and likeness of God, assists the inquiring mind in its approach to the supreme Truth of God. Hence it is possible for human terms and expressions which are really appropriate only to creaturely objects that are not identical with God to be true expressions even when these expressions are applied to God who can never be expressed.[2]

But Anselm is also aware that this takes place properly only within the Church, for there is nothing in the world which is *simile* to the human reason as such and *per se*, which is necessary to it and which quite independently of anything outside of itself is also a medium for

---

[1] *FQI*, pp. 33 f, 37 f, 46 f, 54 f, 70 f, etc.
[2] Pp. 29 ff, 39 f. See especially Anselm's *Monologion*, 65 f.

knowledge of God. That there should be such a sphere of media requires the existence of the Church, revelation and faith, for it is there that knowledge of God through resemblance is actualised as a possibility open to mankind.[1] Concretely, that means within the *credo* of the Church where the Word of Christ is proclaimed and heard, and faith arises and seeks understanding of the reality mediated through the Church's proclamation. For Anselm the Church provides the realm within which faith arises and operates and therefore the proper realm within which theological activity is pursued, for there alone can there take place the right relation between the knowing of man and the object known without which inquiry into the understanding of the reality believed would fail.[2]

(5) The rational nature of theological knowledge involves a relation of *necessity* between it and the object given, necessity meaning the impossibility of being otherwise. Corresponding to the distinction between ontic and noetic rationality, Anselm distinguishes a necessity peculiar to the object of faith, its impossibility of being other than it is, or its basis, and a necessity peculiar to knowledge of the object of faith, the impossibility for thought to conceive the object of faith as other than it is. Thus corresponding to the basis in the object of faith there has to be a reason in our knowledge of it; to the ontic necessity there is a corresponding noetic necessity. It is in that correspondence that the rationality of theological knowledge lies, and in that correspondence that theological thinking takes place under the compulsion of God himself.[3]

If this is so, there then can be no exercise of noetic rationality according to a necessity or law of its own, without its being conditioned by an ontic necessity or a basis in the object—for that would be irrational. Hence, in all scientific theological discussion we can only operate with reasons that arise on the ground which we are investigating, i.e., on the same basis in which the question to be answered is raised. We can only make use of criteria arising out of the objective depth of our knowledge, i.e., out of an ontic necessity underlying the noetic necessity. It would be unscientific and false to seek criteria outside this area of correspondence between ontic and noetic necessity, or in some kind of noetic necessity that is not backed up by ontic necessity. Truth is not primarily in knowledge but only secondarily so—it is primarily in objects, primarily Truth in itself. Therefore the truth of thinking or speaking stands or falls with a compulsive relation to independently existing reality.[4]

---

[1] Pp. 29f, 117f.   [2] Pp. 33f, 38f.
[3] Pp. 49ff, 134, 167.   [4] Pp. 123f, 163f.

We may express this otherwise by saying that in scientific theological activity the reason is unconditionally bound to its object and determined by it, and that the nature of the object must prescribe the specific mode of the activity of the reason. Therefore, theology cannot engage in any free or self-willed thinking over against its object or in detachment from it, for that would be the height of irrationality. It belongs to the rationality of theology that the reason should operate only with objects of faith, for faith is the specific mode of rationality which is demanded of the reason when it is directed to the knowledge of God. Thus rational theology involves a way of knowing that answers to the nature of its unique and incomparable object, the living God. In so far as it is rational, therefore, theology will refuse to prescribe arbitrarily to its divine object how it is to be known, or how knowledge of him is to be demonstrated. Rather will it submit humbly to what is prescribed for it from the side of the object, refusing to occupy any other ground for the establishment or verification of its knowledge than that on which the knowledge is actually given. It insists that the way of knowledge which it takes must be in accordance with the way which God himself has taken in revealing himself to man. Its specifically critical and scientific task is to explore and articulate the inner rationality of that way in order to let it speak for itself clearly and directly. When theology is able in this way to show forth the hidden law or objective rationality of its faith, then it attains scientific knowledge of what it believes, and actualises for others the possibility of faith and knowledge.

(6) A final cognate point which we may note from Barth's examination of Anselm's thought is the discovery that he did not set out to establish the reality of God on the basis of a previously posited possibility. That is to say, beginning with the object of thought, it presses on to ask whether and to what extent this object stands over against thought and is not itself to be reduced to something that is merely thought. To be true knowledge, knowledge of the truth, it must press on to the knowledge of the existence of the object thus known in itself, to the knowledge of its objectivity. Not till this is done is knowledge really in earnest.[1] But when the theologian does that, he does not seek to understand or establish the possibility of his object from some place outside its actuality where it can be tested and judged, for he cannot bring to the testing of his object some theory of knowledge he has reached apart

---

[1] Pp. 22 f, 100 ff. Thus the decisive statement that distinguishes genuine theological thinking from all existentialist romancing is: *aliud est rem esse in intellectu, aliud intelligere rem esse.* See pp. 163 ff.

from it altogether and that bears no relation to its nature. Rather must the theologian raise and establish the question as to the possibility of the object on the actual ground on which knowledge of the object arises, and then proceed critically from within its actuality outwards to its possibility. The question as to possibility, therefore, cannot scientifically be posed *a priori*, but only *a posteriori*.[1]

However such a procedure might be regarded in any other science, the attempt to proceed from possibility to actuality is, as far as the knowledge of God is concerned, a contradictory or empty movement of thought, for it would involve the claim that it is possible to think beyond and above God, but such an one would not be God, the *quo maius cogitari nequit*.

*

It was with this fundamental conception of theological activity which he learned from Anselm that Barth turned to write his *Church Dogmatics*, but it was characteristic of Barth that he combined it in the most intensive way with Christology. It is that combination that makes his dogmatics so distinctive in the whole history of Christian thought.

One of the most important consequences of it was his final advance into concrete realism in which he took in utter seriousness the absolute reality of God and yet the downright creaturely reality of man. The reality of God is one which we meet within the concrete actualities of our creaturely existence in space and time, within the mode of creaturely being and activity to which he has given its own distinct structure, and yet it is the reality of the God who remains God transcendent above all creaturely being and operation. Now, however, the dialectical relation between the absolute reality of God and his revelation within the actualities of creaturely objectivity, in Barth's thinking, yields to a Christological relation which both conceives of God as lowering himself to human being to share with us our human and creaturely state, and conceives of a divine assumption of our human and creaturely estate into union with God himself—*in Jesus Christ*. It is the Incarnation, the concrete reality of God in space and time, that enables Barth to think out the ontic as well as the cognitive basis for theological activity.

That is apparent in the way in which Barth links so closely together

---

[1] Hence in his discussion of the objective reality and possibility of Revelation, and its corresponding subjective reality and possibility, Barth reversed in his *CD* I.2, pp. 1 ff. and 203 ff the order he had adopted in his *ChrD*, pp. 214 ff and 284 ff.

the analogical relationship set up between the knowing creature and the God known and the ontological relationship between the creation and God as it is revealed and finally made good in Jesus Christ. It is in Christ that we can really see that the original purpose of the works of God in creation is to reflect and image his glory. Therefore, only as we enter into the relation of resemblance set up between us and God through the Incarnate Word and Work of his Son do we discern the validity of our theological terms and expressions, which we employ on the basis of revelation, to be ontologically as well as soteriologically rooted. Thus for Barth it is the concrete reality of Jesus Christ as very God and very Man in one Person that is the foundation of a true theology in which our human forms of thought and speech are given an adequacy and veracity beyond anything they can have in themselves. In Jesus Christ we human creatures may think and speak of God in such a way that although all our theological formulations fall short of the glory and majesty of the Truth of God they are not for that reason false, for they repose upon a completely adequate foundation—theological activity is itself a participation in the act whereby God in Christ assumes our human nature into union with himself.

Thinking of God outside of the concrete act of God in Christ may be an attempt, in Anselm's language, to think speculatively *per similitudinem* but it is not real thinking *per proprietatem* unless it takes place within the reality of Jesus Christ in whom the creaturely and the divine are united. It is only in Jesus Christ, who is both the image and the reality of God, that we can think and speak of God in such a realist way that our human forms are not an empty shell but are filled from above with the Truth of God.

It is interesting to note, therefore, that as Barth advanced to work out his doctrine of God on the ground of this concrete realism, he found he had to direct critical questions to what now appeared to him to be a latent nominalism in the scholastic doctrine of the attributes of God, and preferred to speak of the Being of God in his Act, and of the divine perfections rather than the divine attributes, in order to avoid a false separation between the Being and action of God which the scholastic doctrine implied. Whether or not this charge against scholastic realism can be justified, it is a startling indication of the measure of the realism that came to characterise Barth's dogmatic thinking, a realism which does not require a measure of dialectical idealism to keep it true, for its acknowledgment of the inadequacy of its thought to its object belongs to its very truth in Christ, in whom God has condescended to our creaturely estate and, without abrogating it, to make it his very own. It is the reality of God's grace that performs positively the function which idealism seeks to perform critically in calling for a profounder relation of adequacy of our thought to its proper object in God. It is, therefore, the concrete reality of the grace of Jesus Christ that relativises and displaces idealism.

The other important consequence of Barth's studies in Anselm's theology which we must note becomes apparent when we relate his conception of dynamic rationality to the critical significance of Christology. It is surely in the depths of Christology that theology must think out the relation between noetic and ontic rationality and the corresponding relation between noetic and ontic necessity. Here in Christology, then, we may penetrate into the inner *ratio* and *necessitas* of the object of our knowledge, and in so far as we can do that we will achieve an immense clarification in the whole field of theological inquiry. It belongs to the urgent task of theology, therefore, to uncover the *basic forms* of theological thought.[1]

Is it not failure to do this, Barth asks, that leads to such lack of agreement and indeed to disunity in theology? Why are theologians, compared to those who pursue other sciences and studies, so divided? Is it not because they operate with too many alien presuppositions and axioms and fail to get down to the basic forms and principles that derive from the proper object of theological thought? Hence Barth's own theology renounces with immense determination every form of arbitrary, undisciplined thinking in its complete devotion to a way of thinking prescribed by the inner rationality and necessity of its object. Theology, as scientific, orderly, human thinking, must keep within the bounds and act within the compulsion imposed upon it from its objective ground. Concretely, that means, *the Man Jesus Christ*, for it is in him that God comes within our realm of knowledge as the object of our thinking, and in him God provides the one object of knowledge which is both creaturely within our creaturely objectivities and divine within the ultimate objectivity of God himself. It is in Jesus Christ that we penetrate into the ontic *ratio* which is both created truth within our world and yet the uncreated truth of God, the *ratio fidei* and the *ratio veritatis* in one. It is when we penetrate in our inquiry into that ontic *ratio* backed up by the very Being of God that we think with scientific compulsion which must then be reflected in all our noetic rationality. That is the

---

[1] See for what follows Barth's essay 'Die Grundformen theologischen Denkens', *Evangelische Theologie*, 1936, pp. 462ff, republished in *FuA*, pp. 282ff.

scientific and disciplined significance of Christology for all Barth's dogmatics.

Under the influence of the Reformation (and here in contrast to Anselm), Barth thinks this out in the modern style, and so will not let us forget for a moment that the object of our thought is Jesus Christ, the objective *historical reality* to whom witness is borne in the biblical revelation. Thinking appropriate to this object does not involve a static relation but a living, dynamic relation to the supreme happening at the heart of all history—the Act and Being of God in the *historical* birth and life and death and resurrection of Jesus Christ. It is by letting his thinking take the way laid down by this activity of God in Jesus Christ that Barth brings to view the basic forms of theological thinking. He expounds that in terms of the Way, the Truth and the Life which Jesus Christ was and is and ever will be.[1]

Because Jesus Christ is the *Way*, as well as the Truth and the Life, theological thought is limited and bounded and directed by this historical reality in whom we meet the Truth of God. That prohibits theological thought from wandering at will across open country, from straying over history in general or from occupying itself with some other history, rather than this concrete history in the centre of all history. Thus theological thought is distinguished from every empty conceptual thought, from every science of pure possibility, and from every kind of merely formal thinking, by being mastered and determined by the special history of Jesus Christ.

Jesus Christ is the *Truth*, as well as the Way and the Life. Theology is therefore a critical kind of thought, one that learns to distinguish truth from falsehood. These are distinctions, however, that derive not from the reason or any *ratio* inherent in it, but from the nature of the object, and which the reason acquires through obedience to its object. This is thinking that acts within the relation between the noetic and the ontic necessity where it is impossible for it to think otherwise under the compulsion of God that is laid upon us from the objective rationality of the Word. Here there can be no neutrality, for the question of truth and falsehood is forced upon us as we penetrate into the inner meaning and basis of the text of Holy Scripture and act in accordance with the way in which the divine object makes himself known to us.

Jesus Christ is also the *Life*, as well as the Way and the Truth—that is to say, he is the actual salvation of the man who believes. Theological thinking is thus a practical type of thinking, for it is related to our being

[1] *FuA*, p. 285f.

and action, not just to our minds or our thought. Theology cannot be pursued, therefore, in abstraction from the concrete acts of God in Jesus Christ for our salvation. It is thinking in responsibility, thinking in which we have to give an account to God for our being and action, for our life within the Church and its mission in the world.

All these forms of theological thinking, basic as they may be, are to some extent at any rate, formal forms. But what of the material forms? These are derived from the very substance and content of our theological knowledge, that is, from the inner nature and rationality of the object. They are Christological forms, Trinitarian forms. They cannot be expounded in abstraction from the material content of theological knowledge but are to be brought to view and elucidated only in the full articulation of our theological understanding and in the continual inquiry of constructive dogmatics. That is the task to which Barth has devoted his life, the working out of a positive account of Christian doctrine through a single-minded concentration upon the concrete act of God in Jesus Christ.

We cannot, of course, follow Barth's thought through in his exposition of the material content of the Christian faith, but let it be said that the constructive thinking of the *Church Dogmatics* has contributed so deeply and widely to the clarification of Christian theology that he has surely justified his claim, that theological disagreement results to a very large extent from an uncritical and unscientific approach to the basic forms of theological thinking. Where we do not allow all our thinking to be disciplined by the inner rationality of its proper object, and do not allow that to call in question the presuppositions and prejudices we all inevitably bring with us to the study of theology, then theological thinking breaks apart as it is drawn this way and that down side-tracks by extraneous ideologies and world-views and false axioms and, not least, by the upsurge of man's natural desire to magnify and justify himself before God and men.

If this were Barth's only contribution to modern theology, and if it resulted in a determined attempt by theologians in all Churches all over the world to let their thinking be governed by the concrete act of God in Jesus Christ, then surely there would result such an immense and powerful clarification of the basic forms of theological thinking that we would be compelled into fundamental agreement that was both strictly theological and strictly scientific. That could never mean uniformity, for the very nature of theology as perpetual inquiry and perpetual prayer, and the very nature of the object of inquiry, the Word of God, which is infinitely full of the riches of God's grace and wisdom, could only call forth from all saints a correspondingly rich and manifold understanding, developing differences which would not be contradictions but rather complementary aspects of the truth ministering to the unity and fulness of the Church's understanding of God.

Part Three

BARTH'S PLACE
IN MODERN THEOLOGY

VI

THE BARTHIAN REVOLUTION

OUR examination of the development of Barth's theology from 1910 to 1931 has brought us to the point where we must look back upon it all and assess its place in modern theology. We will not attempt to deal with his handling of individual doctrines or go over the problems he had to face in developing a proper scientific method, but single out several features which may help to throw into high relief the nature and the extent of the theological revolution that will ever be associated with his name.

1. The New Direction in Protestant Theology

Barth himself has indicated the change that has come over theology since 1910 by pointing to the new relation that has grown up between *theology* and *Church*.[1] As we have seen, when Barth was a student and when he began his ministry theology and Church were widely separated from one another. His theological studies had not really been concerned with the Church and its life and mission but with a world of general conceptions and ideas, but then when, as a minister, he mounted the pulpit steps to preach to his people in the name of the Father, Son and Holy Spirit, he was utterly at a loss and became very disturbed over the fundamental misunderstanding of theology and Church. If theology was concerned only with general truth, the Church appeared to be only an institution for the religious and moral betterment of man, or, at best, the instrument for the setting up of the Kingdom of God and the re-ordering of the life of men through a social Gospel. But when he and several other ministerial friends began to take their ministry seriously, studying the Bible and preaching from it in order to bring home to people in the present its message as witness to the revelation and acts of the living God, they found themselves face to face with questions that shook their foundations, altered their entire outlook on Church and theology, and started

---

[1] See the radio address given by Barth in 1940, 'Die Neuorientierung der protestantischen Theologie in den letzten dreissig Jahren', published in *Kirchenblatt für die reformierte Schweiz*, 96.7, pp. 98-101.

a revolution that has had world-wide repercussions and made a contribution to Protestant theology comparable only to the Reformation itself.

That revolution began, as we have seen, with a fresh discovery of the new world within the Bible, and with a new way of reading the Bible. Barth had his own ideas about what was true and good, and his own ideals for the life of the individual and of the nations, and quite naturally he brought these with him when he came to read the Bible. Consequently he tended to hear in the Bible only what agreed with his own presuppositions or at least to value in the Bible only what he could use to support them. But then when the new world within the Bible broke in upon him and uprooted him, calling in question his prejudgments and presuppositions, he learned to read the Bible in a new way, in such a way that the Bible itself was allowed to have the *primary Word*, and therefore in such a way that his own prior understanding was subjected to disciplined questioning and criticism and indeed all his thoughts were brought into obedient discipleship to that primary Word. This meant for Barth an immense liberation for his thinking, for it broke the shackles of prejudice, detached him from the slavery of unconscious dogmatisms, and revealed the subtle determinisms of involvement in cultural heritage, but it was a freedom that arose out of obedience to the creative and emancipating power of God's Word. The discovery that the freedom of Christian thinking consists in obedience was, as Barth has said, nothing less than a Copernican revolution.[1] And he was not slow to see that this was entirely in line with the strictest procedure of the exact and positive sciences. It is sheer attachment to the object that carries with it detachment from all prior understanding and prejudicial thinking, and it is only in methodological pursuit of this detachment that we can achieve scientific objectivity.

This new way of reading the Bible, by letting it speak to us out of itself and disclose its own message to us undistorted and unhindered as far as possible by our presuppositions, carried with it a re-orientation in the relations of theology and Church.

The Church acquired a new meaning for Barth. It was the place where Jesus Christ, his cross and his resurrection, his humility and his lordship, are and are to be proclaimed. It is the place where God speaks to us as he before whom we are lost men, whatever we have achieved for the betterment of mankind, and before whom we are always sinners, but as he who invites us to cast ourselves in utter reliance upon him who on his part extends to us all, whoever we are, his consolation and admoni-

[1] Op. cit. p. 99.

tion and his promises. It is not we who build his Kingdom or achieve our own salvation. He does both in that he gives us his Word and awakens us to faith, and for us there remains a life of thankfulness and obedience and service. That is what we read in the Bible; that is the message which we preach and that becomes the content of our instruction in the Church.

In this event, theology, as the presupposition of the Church's work, scientific biblical research, the task of understanding the Church's past and the systematic question as to the content of the Christian faith, i.e., dogmatics, now had to acquire, and did in fact acquire for Barth, quite a new meaning. The Church stood in need of theology, for if its mission is that of hearing and proclaiming the Word of God, it cannot take seriously enough the task of self-criticism and self-testing. It is in the service of this Church and there alone that theology is an independent science, that is to say, a science that does not need to draw its strength from extraneous sources, for it has its own proper object and its own procedure corresponding to it.

There is, therefore, a reciprocal relation between theology and Church. Theology requires the Church, for it is through the Church that it gets its object and in the Church that it is given the goal for its instruction. Apart from the Church, theology could not but dissolve at once into philosophy, psychology and historical science. It is as service to the life of the Church that theology is free and independent over against the other sciences, because it participates in the freedom of the Church over against the other realms of life. On the other hand, the Church requires theology, for the reason that it cannot celebrate divine service, it cannot undertake instruction or exercise its pastoral office, without knowing what it is about. It does not have any freedom without having to win it again every day. It cannot confess its faith without knowledge and therefore without inquiry. It cannot engage in instruction without being instructed itself. It requires self-criticism, but that is precisely the function of theology in the Church.

When Barth began his ministry, the Christian religion, at least on the Continent, was regarded as an inner aspect of modern culture and theology was the attempt to give that coherent expression, but it could do that only through thorough-going integration with and accommodation to the other more comprehensive aspects of culture. That meant that theology had its justification only as the servant of the general advance of the human spirit in its triumph over nature and therefore inevitably reflected the prevailing world-view of modern man. Theology was co-ordinated with the self-consciousness of man and operated through self-understanding, but the revolution that derived from a handful of Swiss pastors led by Barth, in a new determination to take their ministry seriously as ministry of the Word of God, has given theology a vastly different orientation. Once again, theology is co-ordinated with the self-revelation of God and operates through repentant rethinking of the preaching and teaching of the Church under the critical and creative impact of the Word of God. Instead of being geared to civilisation, and therefore more and more to its secularisation, theology is geared to the mission of the Church in the proclamation of the Gospel to all mankind. As the servant of the learning and teaching Church its function is to direct it into a disciplined discipleship to Jesus Christ and thereby to equip it for its mission.

But this function theology exercises in a strictly scientific way, that is, one in which from beginning to end it acts in conformity to its own proper object, develops a mode of rationality in accordance with its nature and derives appropriate critical criteria from the objective ground on which its knowledge actually arises. It is thus a free, independent science working out within the limits laid down by its object the same kind of scientific procedure which operates in every other pursuit of exact and positive knowledge, yet differing from them in accordance with scientific requirements, through the unique nature of its object, God in his Word.

2. The Centrality of the Incarnation

For more than a hundred years the New Testament documents had been subjected to the most searching scrutiny any documents have ever known, and out of it came an immense focus of attention upon the historical Jesus Christ. But during this period in which Christianity became assimilated to culture, and theology became subservient to general scientific and philosophical ideas, biblical and theological research took over methods that were developed in the empirical investigation of creaturely objectivity and applied them to its own task, but it also took over even more than the natural sciences the philosophical presuppositions that were still attached to these methods. It was ultimately through relation to these philosophical presuppositions that Protestant theology sought its justification as a respectable academic pursuit. In this development biblical and theological research could only produce 'a historical Jesus' that was basically an expression of the contemporary culture, a 'Jesus' dressed up in the clothes of the nineteenth and twentieth century—that line of development reached its peak and its dénouement round about 1910.

Meantime two immense movements had begun to take place. In the realm of empirical and natural science great forward strides were taken in discoveries that called in question and then shattered the philosophical presuppositions of natural science. The result was a profound crisis for modern philosophy which is still reflected in the break-up of the old metaphysical systems before the analytical and mathematical thinking of our own day and the rising power of a new philosophy of science, but it is also reflected in the reactionary movements of existentialist revolt before the critical advance of exact and positive science. The great scientific achievements of our own day have been made only through an emancipation from the philosophical presuppositions of ancient and modern philosophy, and they have demanded an even stricter conception of scientific method which methodologically renounces all prior understanding and preconceived world-views.

The other movement that has been going on concurrently is that which is bound up with the work of Karl Barth, which is a movement within theological science parallel to that within natural science, and has moved in the same way through the calling in question and then the shattering of the philosophical preconceptions of modern theology. The result was likewise a profound crisis for modern philosophical theology, which is reflected on the one hand in the growing attempts to import into theological discussion the analytical and mathematical thinking of modern critical philosophy, but is also reflected in the reactionary movements of existentialism which, out of deep anxiety in the face of objective and scientific criticism, has taken refuge in 'a creative self-understanding'. But the positive theological achievements of our own day have been made only through an emancipation from the presuppositions of idealistic and romantic philosophy, and they have demanded an even stricter conception of scientific method in biblical and theological inquiry which methodologically renounces all prior self-understanding and preconceived world-views.

The immediate concrete result of this for theology may be stated in this way. The immense research of modern times into the New Testament has concentrated our attention upon the historical Jesus Christ in the most intense way, but it failed to retain the historical Jesus, for, owing to its philosophical presuppositions, it lost him in the depths of its own subjectivity. Now, however, with the re-orientation of Protestant theology, the historical Jesus Christ is being interpreted out of himself, out of the concrete act of God in Jesus Christ, and not out of our own creative spirituality. Hence in our day there has arisen a powerful Christ-ology which interprets the object of its thought in terms of its own objective rationality and, because it is able to give the historical Jesus Christ the saving significance that it finds in him in his objective reality, the historical Jesus is not dissolved away but stands before us as the supreme act of God in the midst of history.

Here we reach the great water-shed of modern theology, in the doctrine of the *Incarnation*. On one side of that water-shed the Incarnation is taken seriously as the coming of the Son of God into human existence and history, as the Being of God in space and time at work for us and our salvation, in the atoning life and death and resurrection of Jesus Christ. Here, where theological language is certainly employed in its analogical character, it is language deriving from and reposing upon objective reality, the concrete act of God in Jesus Christ. That supplies the basic frame of reference for all theological doctrines and gives them their realist character. It is here that Karl Barth, standing in the centre of the whole Christian tradition from the earliest times to the present, has given us massive and formidable articulation of the substance of the Christian faith, and in so doing he has laid it more squarely than ever upon its solid foundation.

On the other side of the water-shed the Incarnation is regarded as a mythological construct designed to express in an objectified manner the creative spirituality of the early Christians. Behind this lies a horror for the notion of the Being of God in space and time and therefore for the concrete act of God in the objective historical reality of Jesus Christ. Hence, everything is given a fundamentally symbolic interpretation, not symbolic of an objective reality, but symbolic of a subjective state or of a basic self-understanding of man over against God. The rejection of the Incarnation as the real advent and presence and activity of God in space and time, supplies the frame of reference for a re-interpretation of all other doctrines and gives them anthropocentric character, for they have to be 'demythologised' of their objective content and transposed into determinants of existentialist self-understanding. It is here that Rudolf Bultmann stands in the centre of an anachronistic reaction that moves away from the centre of the Christian faith out on to the marginal areas of gnostic speculation and self-redemption, and in doing so he has pro-vided modern theology with the same testing-point which the Church had to face in the fourth and in the fifteenth centuries when it was

continuity can have their fulfilment. Hence we are summoned to the praise of the Creator, which we cannot yield without enjoying and taking in earnest creaturely existence within the limits allotted to it by God's grace, and under the final affirmation of it by God's concrete act in Jesus Christ.

And yet, as in his doctrine of creation, Barth does not develop an ontology of creation or an independent cosmology as the prior understanding for theological interpretation of God's special work of redemption, so he refuses to develop a phenomenological understanding of man's creaturely actuality or his historico-existential structures as a general frame of reference for a new assimilation of theology to culture. Because Jesus Christ is the one Truth behind all truth, and the creative source of all culture, that does not allow us to detach theological activity from its proper object, the Being of God in his revelation, and to drag it down within the ideological circle of man's independent interpretations of the cultural patterns in his existence. A genuine theology can never be assimilated to any attempt to give meaning to man's life from some point of view determined by man himself, and therefore partaking of the sin and revolt of man from the source of all creaturely being and meaning in the one Truth of God.

Barth's refusal to take that course is dictated not only by propriety of theological method, but by sheer respect for the purpose of God revealed in creation and redemption, that man shall have completeness, unity and wholeness in his sphere as creature, as God is complete and whole in his own sphere. Respect for the creature and its creaturely activities will not allow its meaning to be distorted by an ideology developed out of man apart from Christ, or by one in which man in his independence seeks to transcend his creatureliness in order to ensure some place for himself in the divine. Therefore the *diastasis* which Barth was concerned for so many years to reveal between theology and culture was not only in the interests of good theology but in the interests of good culture, that is to say, of the proper fulfilment and enjoyment of full creaturely being and activity in its own determinate reality and truth. Far from manifesting any element of Philistinism, Barth's Christological theology carries with it the profoundest sense of God's affirming and supporting and guaranteeing and protecting of all that he has made, of his establishment of the creature in a mode of being and structured life of its own, within the limits allotted to it as a creature, and therefore in dependence upon the grace of God, but therefore also in the freedom of a reality to which God gives independent creaturely being and to which he gives glory—and so constancy and permanence—through sharing with it his own eternal glory.

Where Jesus Christ is really known as God in his turning toward man to be man's God, and as man who is the object of the eternal love of God, and therefore as God's man, there can only be the utmost reverence for human life and respect for human activity. It is the Incarnation, the fact that God has become man, and a man, in Jesus Christ in the midst of creation, that reveals that man is the centre and crowning point of all God's ways and works in creation. There he is constituted by God as his covenant-partner, and called to a life on the boundary between heaven and earth where the meaning and goal of all his activity is found in divine support and affirmation, in divine concurrence and blessing, and where man can fulfil his life by being faithful to the creaturely world of men and nature in which God has placed him as well as by being faithful to be heavenly Father through filial love and obedience. In this way all the ways and works of man in his faithfulness on earth belong to the praise and rejoicing of creation in the Creator. Hence Barth can speak of the fulfilment of man's creaturely life and activity as the external aspect, and of the fulfilment of his redemption in Jesus Christ as the internal aspect, of God's eternal purpose of grace. Why should we not speak in a similar way of the realm of human culture as the theatre and setting for the message of Jesus Christ, and therefore as supplying the secondary or external objectivities through which his Word continues to be heard in the world through the Church, and so speak also of the life and history of the Church as the Body of Christ in the world (i.e., the earthly-historical form of his own existence), as pointing to the internal objectivity of God's redeeming and creative work?

Theology by its very nature speaks of God and man, of Creator and creature, but that means that it speaks of God and human activity, of the special acts of God and of the special acts of humanity, and therefore of the employment by man of his God-given endowments. But what else, asks Barth, is civilisation than the endeavour of man to be man, and therefore to set to work and bring to honour the good gift of his humanity? 'That in this endeavour he again and again goes to pieces, and indeed achieves the opposite, is another matter by itself. But this does not alter the fact that man who takes part in this endeavour in one way or another, as producer or consumer, is the being in whom God is interested, or finally the fact that God as Creator and Lord of man is still at liberty on occasion to make of human activity and its results, in spite of their problematic character, parables of His own eternally good willing and doing, in fact of which there could be no place for any arrogant abstinence, but for reverence, joy and gratitude.'[1]

Thus, while Barth will not allow theology at any point to be co-ordinated with any ideological interpretation of culture but insists in maintaining a *diastasis* or eschatological boundary between Christianity and culture, and therefore also between Revelation and historic Christendom, nevertheless, from the side of the recreative and reconciling work of God in Christ, he insists that there is another and a truer connexion between them, which respects both the Being and Act of God in his revelation and redemption, and the reality of the creature in its own existence and meaning and freedom and basis given it by God over against himself as the Creator. Indeed it is because he takes this so seriously that the volumes on creation were so greatly enlarged and the final volume on reconciliation has had to be extended to spell out in a positive way the relation between the Truth of the Gospel and the creaturely truths reflected in human culture, and therefore the relation between the mission of the people of God and world-happening.

As Barth sees that relation, the proclamation of the Gospel in the world awakens an *echo* in the external voices of the world which seem to take up its message and reflect it in ways and manners of its own. The self-revelation of Christ did not take place in a dark and empty and indefinite sphere, but in one which has real existence, fulness, form and brightness, thanks to the creative will and work of God. In the same way the preaching and teaching of the Church take place not in emptiness and abstraction, but in the midst of creaturely activity and human knowledge and all the cultural pursuits of the world. Why should not the Word of God awaken some response and beget some fruit for itself outside the boundaries of the Church, beyond the frontiers of faith, in the world of secular life and culture? To be sure, it could be only a broken echo, and the phenomena in which it reflected the voice of Christ in the cosmos could not but be equivocal and dubious, so that theology could never derive truth from them. It is the Word of God and not its refraction or distorted echo that is the positive object of its inquiry, but why should not the Church listen to these echoes if only as a mirror of its actual, equivocal life, as a challenge to correct its tradition or an impulse to reform? If the Church believes that Christ is the Light of life, why should it not believe that that Light, as it rises and shines upon men, is reflected in the being and existence of the cosmos which is not created accidentally but for this very purpose, that it might

[1] *GGG*, p. 44.

provide the theatre within which every creaturely truth might be made to point back to the one creative source of all truth, in Jesus Christ, the Word of God and the Light of the world? And why then should the people of God not rejoice more than any others in all creaturely being and activity and in the fulfilment of creaturely existence and meaning?[1]

All this is not to imply that dogmatics can make any positive pronouncements on cultural phenomena, nor does it imply that any positive teaching can be heard in the echoing voices of the cosmos, but it does mean that enjoyment of all that God has made and employment of all his gifts to man are part of man's worship and praise of the Creator. Nothing is so godly in creation as the grateful enjoyment of all that God has made, and nothing is so ungodly in the Church as slander upon the creaturely works of God's hand. It is here that we can understand Barth's love for Mozart as the 'incomparable' musician who does not employ his art in an attempt to instruct us, far less to communicate to us his self-understanding, but solely in angelic enjoyment of God's creaturely gifts and therefore in praise of the Creator.

'Why is it that this man is so incomparable? Why is it that for the receptive he has produced in almost every bar he conceived and composed a music for which "beautiful" is not a fitting epithet; music which for the true Christian is not mere entertainment, enjoyment or edification but food and drink; music full of comfort, and counsel for his needs; music which is never a slave to its technique nor sentimental but always "moving", free, liberating, because wise, strong, and sovereign? Why is it possible to hold that Mozart had a place in theology, especially in the doctrine of creation and also in eschatology, although he was not a father of the Church, does not seem to have been a particularly active Christian, and was a Roman Catholic, apparently leading what might appear to us a rather frivolous existence when not occupied in his work? It is possible to give him this position because he knew something about creation in its total goodness that neither the real fathers of the Church nor our Reformers, neither the orthodox nor the liberals, neither the exponents of natural theology nor those heavily armed with "the Word of God", and certainly not the existentialists, nor indeed any other great musicians before him and after him, either know or can express and maintain as he did. In this respect he was pure in heart, far transcending both optimists and pessimists. . . . He heard and causes those who have ears to hear, even today, what we shall not see until the end of time—the whole context of providence. As though in the light of this end, he heard

---

[1] *CD* IV.3.1, pp. 120ff.

the harmony of creation to which the shadow also belongs but in which the shadow is not darkness, deficiency is not defeat, sadness cannot become despair, trouble cannot degenerate into tragedy and infinite melancholy is not ultimately forced to claim undisputed sway. Thus the cheerfulness in this harmony is not without its limits. But the light shines all the more brightly because it breaks forth from the shadow. The sweetness is also bitter and therefore cannot cloy. Life does not fear death but knows it well. . . .

'Hearing creation unresentfully and impartially, he did not produce merely music of his own but that of creation, its twofold yet harmonious praise of God. He neither needed nor desired to express or represent himself, his vitality, sorrow, piety, or any programme. He was remarkably free from the mania for self-expression. He simply offered himself as the agent by which little bits of horn, metal and catgut could serve as the voices of creation, sometimes leading, sometimes accompanying and sometimes in harmony. He made use of instruments ranging from the piano to the violin, through the horn and the clarinet down to the venerable bassoon, with the human voice somewhere among them, having no special claim to distinction yet distinguished for this very reason. He drew music from them all, expressing even human emotions in the service of this music, and not *vice versa*. He himself was only an ear for this music and its mediator to other ears.'[1]

What could express better Barth's understanding of culture and its relation to the Christian faith than this appreciation of Mozart?

Theology is not music, for in it we are not primarily concerned with the lights and truths of the creaturely world as they reflect and echo the Light and Truth of God, but we are concerned with human knowing and human understanding and human articulating of the one Truth and Light of God in Jesus Christ. It is here, then, in theology, perhaps above all, that we are to see the positive relation between the God of all grace and man as his covenant-partner, between God's sovereign togetherness with man and man's free togetherness with God. Theology is both a worshipping of God with the mind and a free act of the creature in partnership with God. Here there arises, and must arise, a genuine culture alongside the other cultural achievements of man and over against them, the culture through which they can be seen in their true light, for it is here above all that we understand the God who meets man and the man who meets God and therefore understand the inner history and meaning of their partnership. We must not allow ourselves to

[1] *CD* III.3, p. 297f.

forget that like every other culture theological culture as such is the sphere of man's reflections and constructions, it is man's work, and to that extent it is always a dubious and equivocal phenomenon. Therefore theological culture cannot itself become the proper object of theological reflection and construction. Only a false theology could arise that way, and only a grave disservice to culture. By its very nature theology points away from its own works, away from its own reflections and constructions, to be the One Truth of God, so that any self-understanding it attains can only be a by-product of its function to echo and bear obedient witness to that truth. Hence the best contribution theology can make to the whole of culture is simply by being genuine theology, for only then can it sound forth in the world of culture the one Gospel of Truth which has the power to awaken an answer to the voice of God beyond the boundaries of the Church as well as within it. It is surely Barth's own *Church Dogmatics* that is the supreme example in modern times of just such a theology, and indeed of a theological culture out of which it is possible to see something of the meaning of all cultures.

None of Barth's contemporaries discerns or appreciates more the positive relation of his theology to historic culture than Hans Urs von Balthasar. It is therefore fitting to end this study with a fine tribute from him to Barth.

'Barth's theology is beautiful, not merely in the external sense that Barth writes well. He does write well because he combines two things, passion and concrete positivity. It is passion for the subject-matter of theology and concrete positivity appropriate to the exciting nature of that subject-matter. Concrete positivity means to be engrossed in the object—it means objectivity. And Barth's object is God as he has revealed himself to the world in Jesus Christ according to the biblical witness. Because Barth—with Calvin, as against Luther—looks away altogether from the state of faith itself to its material content, because he commits himself to a strict theological objectivism ("faith lives from its object"), and thereby differentiates himself in the sharpest way from the Neo-Protestantism of Schleiermacher, he speaks well and without any suspicion of pietistic edifying. The subject-matter is edifying in itself, for it is so gripping and so demanding upon the whole man that here true objectivity coincides with an emotion that pulses through everything and has no independent expression of its own. Barth's theology is thus given a form and a presentation that mark it off from the all too disinterested objectivism of many a Catholic dogmatics. This combination of passion and objectivity is the reason for the beauty of

Barth's theology. Who else in recent decades has known how to expound the Scriptures without becoming unduly exegetical or biblicist, without lapsing into tendentious constructions or pastoral rhetoric, but has concentrated so entirely upon the Word that it alone shines forth in its fulness and glory? And who is there who with unflagging energy has drawn a longer breath, taken a longer look and sustained it, as the subject-matter developed and presented itself before him in its vast extent? One would have to go back to St Thomas to find again this freedom from tension and narrowness, such unrivalled superiority in comprehension and in generosity—generosity which, with Barth, is not seldom charged with humour, but which acquires, above all, a pronounced taste for the proper tempo and rhythm of thought. Barth knows how to convince us that for him Christianity is an altogether triumphant matter. It is not merely because he has the gift of style that he writes well, but that above all he bears testimony, utterly objective testimony to a matter which, since it is about God, has the best style and the finest manuscript.'[1]

[1] Hans Urs von Balthasar. *Karl Barth, Darstellung und Deutung seiner Theologie*, p. 35 f.

SELECTED BIBLIOGRAPHY

A full list of Barth's writings, reviews, articles, essays, sermons, books, etc. (up to 1956) has been compiled by Charlotte von Kirschbaum, and is published in *Antwort*, 1956. Between 1906 and the end of 1931, 147 items are listed.

Early Period

1909 'Moderne Theologie und Reichgottesarbeit', *ZTK* XIX, pp. 317-21
'Antwort an d. Achelis und D. Drews', *ZTK* XIX, pp. 479-86
1912 'Der christliche Glaube und die Geschichte', *STZ* Heft 1 and 2
1914 'Der Glaube an den persönlichen Gott' *ZTK* XXIV, pp. 21-32, 65-95
1916 'Die Gerechtigkeit Gottes', *Neue Wege, Blätter für religiöse Arbeit* X, No. 47; reprinted in *Das Wort Gottes und die Theologie*, München, 1924
1917 *Suchet Gott, so werdet ihr leben* (Sermons, with E. Thurneysen), Bern, 1917; München, 1928
1919 *Der Römerbrief*, Bern, 1919; München, 1920
1920 *Der Christ in der Gesellschaft*, Patmosverlag; reprinted in *Das Wort Gottes und die Theologie*, 1924
1920 *Biblische Fragen, Einsichten und Ausblicke*, München; reprinted in *Das Wort Gottes und die Theologie*, 1924
1920 *Zur inneren Lage des Christentums*, München; reprinted as 'Unerledigte Anfragen an die heutige Theologie' in *Die Theologie und die Kirche*, München, 1928

Göttingen

1921 *Der Römerbrief*, 2nd edit. München
1922 'Das Wort Gottes als Aufgabe der Theologie', *Christliche Welt* XXXVI, pp. 858-73; reprinted in *Das Wort Gottes und die Theologie*, 1924
1922 'Not und Verheissung der christlichen Verkündigung', *ZdZ* Heft 1, pp. 1-25, München; reprinted in *Das Wort Gottes und die Theologie*, 1924
1923 '16 Antworten an Herrn Professor von Harnack', *Christliche Welt* XXXVII, pp. 89-91; reprinted as 'Ein Briefwechsal ... 15 Antworten ...' in *Theologische Fragen und Antworten*, Zollikon-Zürich, 1957
1923 'Das Problem der Ethik in der Gegenwart', *ZdZ* Heft 2, pp. 30-57; reprinted in *Das Wort Gottes und die Theologie*, 1924
1923 'Antwort auf Herrn Professor von Harnacks offenen Brief', *Christliche Welt* XXXVII, pp. 244-52
1923 'Ansatz und Absicht in Luthers Abendmahlslehre', *ZdZ* Heft 4, pp. 17-51; reprinted in *Die Theologie und die Kirche*, 1928

1923 'Reformierte Lehre ihr Wesen und ihre Aufgabe', *ZdZ* Heft 5, pp. 8-39; reprinted in *Das Wort Gottes und die Theologie*, 1924

1924 *Komm, Schöpfer Geist* (Sermons with E. Thurneysen) München, 1924; ET by G. W. Richards, E. G. Homrighausen, K. J. Ernst, 1934

1924 *Das Wort Gottes und die Theologie*, München; ET by Douglas Horton, London, 1928

1924 *Die Auferstehung der Toten*, München; 4th edit. Zollikon-Zürich, 1953. ET by H. J. Stenning, London, 1933

1924 'Brunners Schleiermacherbuch', *ZdZ* Heft 8, pp. 49-64, 1925

1925 'Schleiermachers Weihnachtsfeier', *ZdZ* III, pp. 38-61; reprinted *Die Theologie und die Kirche*, 1928

1925 'Menschenwort und Gotteswort in der christlichen Predigt', *ZdZ* III, pp. 119-40

1925 'Das Schriftprinzip der reformierten Kirche', *ZdZ* III, pp. 215-45; reproduced in *Christliche Dogmatik im Entwurf*, pp. 346ff.

1925 'Die dogmatischen Principienlehre bei Wilhelm Herrmann', *ZdZ* III, pp. 246-80; reprinted in *Die Theologie und die Kirche*, 1928

1925 'Möglichkeit und Wünschbarkeit eines allgemeinen reformierten Glaubensbekentnisses', *ZdZ* III, pp. 311-33; reprinted in *Die Theologie und die Kirche*, 1928

Münster

1926 'Kirche und Theologie', *ZdZ* IV, pp. 18-40; reprinted in *Die Theologie und die Kirche*, 1928

1926 *Der Römerbrief*, 5th edition, with new foreword, München

1926 'Die Kirche und die Kultur', *ZdZ* IV, pp. 363-84; reprinted in *Die Theologie und die Kirche*, 1928

1926 *Vom christlichen Leben*, München; ET by J. Strathearn McNab, London, 1930

1927 'Ludwig Feuerbach', *ZdZ* V, pp. 10-40; reprinted in *Die Theologie und die Kirche*, 1928

1927 'Das Halten der Gebote', *ZdZ* V, pp. 206-27; reprinted in *Theologische Fragen und Antworten*, 1957

1927 'Rechtfertigung und Heiligung', *ZdZ* V, pp. 281-309

1927 'Der Begriff der Kirche', *ZdZ* V, pp. 365-78; reprinted in *Die Theologie und die Kirche*, 1928

1927 'Schleiermacher', *ZdZ* V, pp. 422-64; reprinted in *Die Theologie und die Kirche*, 1928

1927 *Erklärung des Philipperbriefes*, München, Zollikon-Zürich, 1947. ET by James W. Leitch, London, 1961

1927 *Christliche Dogmatik im Entwurf. I. Die Lehre vom Worte Gottes*, München

1928 'Das Wort in der Theologie von Schleiermacher bis Ritschl', *ZdZ* VI, pp. 92-109; reprinted in *Die Theologie und die Kirche*, 1928

1928 'Der römische Katholicismus als Frage an die protestantische Kirche', *ZdZ* VI, pp. 274-302; reprinted in *Die Theologie und die Kirche*, 1928

1928 *Die Theologie und die Kirche*, München; ET by Louise P. Smith, with an Introduction by T. F. Torrance, London and New York, 1962

1929 'Schicksal und Idee in der Theologie', *ZdZ* VII, pp. 309-48; reprinted in *Theologische Fragen und Antworten*, 1957

1930 'Zur Lehre vom Heiligen Geist' (with Heinrich Barth), *ZdZ* Heft 1; ET *The Holy Ghost and the Christian Life*, by R. Birch Hoyle, London, 1938

1930 'Die Theologie und der heutige Mensch', *ZdZ* VIII, pp. 374-96

1931 *Fides quaerens intellectum, Anselms Beweis der Existenz Gottes*, München; 2nd edit., Zollikon-Zürich, 1958. ET by Ian Robertson, London and Richmond, Virginia, 1960

1931 'Die Not der Evangelischen Kirchen', *ZdZ* IX, pp. 89-122

1931 *Fragen an das Christentum*, Geneva; republished in *Theologische Fragen und Antworten*, 1957; ET by R. Birch Hoyle, London, 1932

1932 'Vorwort zur englischen Ausgabe des *Römerbriefs*', *ZdZ* X, pp. 285-94; ET in *The Epistle to the Romans*, translated by Sir Edwyn C. Hoskyns, London, 1933

1932 *Die Kirchliche Dogmatik*, I.1. *Die Lehre vom Worte Gottes*, München

Principal Works in English

The Word of God and the Word of Man, tr. by D. Horton, London, 1928

The Resurrection of the Dead, tr. by H. J. Stenny, London, 1933

The Epistle to the Romans, tr. by E. C. Hoskyns, London, 1933

Come, Holy Spirit, tr. by G. W. Richards, E. G. Homrighausen, K. J. Ernst, New York and London, 1934

God's Search for Man, tr. by G. W. Richards, E. G. Homrighausen, K. J. Ernst, New York and London, 1935

God in Action, tr. by G. W. Richards, E. G. Homrighausen, K. J. Ernst, New York and Edinburgh, 1936

Credo, tr. by J. Strathearn McNab, London, 1936

Church Dogmatics, I.1, *The Doctrine of the Word of God*, tr. by G. T. Thomson, Edinburgh, 1936

The Holy Ghost and the Christian Life, tr. by R. Birch Hoyle, London, 1938

The Knowledge of God and the Service of God, tr. by J. L. M. Haire and I. Henderson, 1938

Natural Theology (comprising 'Nature and Grace' by Emil Brunner and 'No' by Karl Barth), tr. by P. Fraenkel, London, 1946

The Teaching of the Church regarding Baptism, tr. by E. A. Payne, London, 1948

Dogmatics in Outline, tr. by G. T. Thomson, London, New York, 1949

Against the Stream (Shorter Post-War writings, 1946-52), tr. by E. M. Delacour and S. Godman, edit. by R. G. Smith, London, 1954

From Rousseau to Ritschl, tr. by B. Cozens and H. H. Hartwell, London and New York, 1959 (title of U.S.A. edit. *Protestant Thought: from Rousseau to Ritschl*)

Christ and Adam: Man and Humanity in Romans 5, tr. by T. Smail, edit.
by T. F. Torrance and J. K. S. Reid, *SJT Occasional Papers*
No. 5, Edinburgh, 1957

God, Grace and Gospel, tr. by J. Strathearn McNab, edit. by T. F.
Torrance and J. K. S. Reid, *SJT Occasional Papers* No. 8,
Edinburgh, 1959 (cf. *The Humanity of God*)

*The Faith of the Church (A Commentary on the Apostles' Creed according
to Calvin's Catechism)*, tr. by G. Vahanian, New York, 1958,
London, 1959

A Shorter Commentary on Romans, tr. by D. H. van Daalen, London, 1959

Deliverance to the Captives, tr. by M. Wieser, with a Preface by J. Marsh,
London and New York, 1961

The Humanity of God, tr. by J. N. Thomas and T. Wieser, Richmond,
Virginia, 1960; London, 1961 (2 of the 3 essays having already
been translated in *God, Grace and Gospel*)

Theology and Church, tr. by L. P. Smith, with an Introduction by T. F.
Torrance, London and New York, 1962

Church Dogmatics, edited by G. W. Bromiley and T. F. Torrance,
Edinburgh (1956-1962)

I.1 *The Doctrine of the Word of God.* Prolegomena, Part 1, tr. by
G. T. Thomson, 1936

I.2 *The Doctrine of the Word of God.* Prolegomena, Part 2, tr. by
G. T. Thomson and H. Knight, 1956

II.1 *The Doctrine of God*, Part 1, tr. by T. H. L. Parker, W. B.
Johnston, H. Knight, J. L. M. Haire, 1957

II.2 *The Doctrine of God*, Part 2, tr. by G. W. Bromiley, J. C. Camp-
bell, Iain Wilson, J. Strathearn McNab, H. Knight, R. A.
Stewart, 1957

III.1 *The Doctrine of Creation*, Part 1, tr. by J. W. Edwards, O.
Bussey, H. Knight, 1958

III.2 *The Doctrine of Creation*, Part 2, tr. by H. Knight, G. W.
Bromiley, J. K. S. Reid, R. H. Fuller, 1960

III.3 *The Doctrine of Creation*, Part 3, tr. by G. W. Bromiley and
R. Ehrlich, 1960

III.4 *The Doctrine of Creation*, Part 4, tr. by A. T. Mackay, T. H. L.
Parker, H. Knight, H. A. Kennedy, J. Marks, 1961

IV.1 *The Doctrine of Reconciliation*, Part 1, tr. by G. W. Bromiley,
1956

IV.2 *The Doctrine of Reconciliation*, Part 2, tr. by G. W. Bromiley,
1958

IV.3 *The Doctrine of Reconciliation*, Part 3, vols. i and ii, tr. by G. W.
Bromiley, 1961 and 1962

Church Dogmatics. A Selection with Introduction, by H. Gollwitzer, tr. and
edited by G. W. Bromiley, Edinburgh and New York, 1961

INDEX OF NAMES

INDEX OF SUBJECTS